The Illusion of Happy Holidays

The Illusion of Happy Holidays

Allan Isaac

Bald and Bonkers Network LLC

First Printing, 2023

ISBN/SKU979-8-8689-0216-1
EISBN979-8-8689-0217-8

Contents

Introduction

Have you ever stopped to wonder why the holiday season, with all its glittering lights and joyful carols, seems to cast a shadow over the hearts and minds of so many? A time meant to be filled with warmth and cheer, often ends up feeling like a battle against a relentless avalanche of emotions. Welcome, dear reader, to the mesmerizing journey through the pages of "The Illusion of Happy Holidays," a book where we navigate the mystical labyrinth of the human psyche during the holiday season.

Within these enchanted chapters, I invite you to join me in unraveling the secrets hidden beneath the snow-covered landscapes and twinkling holiday decorations. For the truth is, there is an illusion that surrounds the festivities like a fragile, shimmering veil. And behind this veil lie the untold stories of those who find themselves drowning in the icy depths of their own emotions during what should be the most wonderful time of the year.

As we step into this realm of raw emotions and fragile hearts, allow me to introduce myself. My name is Dakota Frandsen, a humble traveler through the peaks and valleys of life. It is through my own personal experiences, filled with the sting of heartache and the whispers of loss, that I found myself compelled to write this book. A book born out of the need to ease the burden carried by those who struggle with the holidays—a time that can feel more treacherous than navigating a winter storm.

You see, dear reader, the holiday season has a peculiar way of magnifying our emotions. It lays bare our vulnerabilities and holds a mirror to our hearts, reflecting both the joys and sorrows that have marked our lives. It is a time when the absence of loved ones becomes more pronounced, and memories of happier times can weigh upon our souls like a frost-laden branch.

"The Illusion of Happy Holidays" is both a guiding light through the labyrinth and a balm for the weary spirit. It offers a sanctuary within these pages, a place where you can find solace and understanding amidst the chaos and expectations of the season. Within these words, I will gently guide you through the uncharted territories of grief and mental strain, providing the tools and insights necessary to navigate the darkest corners of your mind.

But do not be mistaken, dear reader. While this book delves deep into the complexities of our emotional landscapes, it is not a dreary tome filled with despair. On the contrary, it is a beacon of hope and resilience, reminding us that even amidst the stormiest of skies, we have the power to find moments of joy and connection.

Through captivating anecdotes and wisdom gathered

from the depths of my own journey, I will show you that you are not alone in your struggle. Together, we will shed light on the daunting presence of overwhelming emotions during the holidays, and we will explore strategies to transform the seemingly unbearable into a time of beauty and grace.

As the fire crackles and casts dancing shadows upon the walls, let the aroma of hot cocoa and freshly baked cookies fill the air around us. Take a moment to close your eyes and imagine the warmth seeping into your bones, melting away the icy grip of sadness and despair. For within these pages lie the keys to unlocking not only your own happiness but also the true meaning of the holiday season.

So, dear reader, I invite you to embark on this enchanting journey with me. Together, we will unravel the illusion of happy holidays and forge a path towards a season filled with true connection, healing, and the rediscovery of laughter amidst tears. Open your heart and mind, for within these pages, a world of magic awaits.

Unmasking the Illusion

The Pressure to be Jolly

Societal expectations weigh heavily on the shoulders of those who have experienced unimaginable loss. The expectation to put on a happy face, to participate in cheerful gatherings, and to embrace the festive spirit becomes a heavy burden that feels impossible to bear. It is as if the world has forgotten that grief and pain do not magically disappear just because the calendar reads "December".

The pressure to be jolly creeps into every aspect of this season. From the repetitive chorus of "Merry Christmas" and "Happy Holidays" that permeates every conversation to the commercialized imagery of picture-perfect families exchanging lavish gifts around a perfectly decorated tree. These constant reminders of what I have lost, what I once had, are like daggers to my heart.

In the midst of this sea of forced merriment, I find solace in the quiet corners of my own sanctuary. Here, away from the prying eyes and judgmental whispers, I allow myself to feel the depths of my sorrow and acknowledge the magnitude of my loss. In this sacred space, grief is not something to be pushed aside or masked with false cheer, but something to be honored, explored, and ultimately, healed.

As the days grow shorter and the nights longer, I envelop myself in the warm embrace of memories. I gather photographs and reminisce about the moments that once brought joy to my heart. I acknowledge the emptiness that now fills those spaces, and I allow myself to weep softly, reawakening the pain that resides within me. And yet, through these tears, I find a glimmer of hope, a faint whisper that reminds me that healing is possible.

Slowly, I begin to release myself from the shackles of societal expectations. I refuse to be defined by a forced smile or a false sense of happiness. Instead, I choose to navigate this holiday season on my own terms – in a way that honors my journey, acknowledges my pain, and cherishes the love and memories that live on within me.

The festiveness that once weighed heavily upon me begins to take a different form – a form that is personal and unique, tailored to my own needs and desires. I find comfort in simple acts of self-care, in cozy nights spent by the fire with a cup of hot cocoa and a cherished book. I seek solace in the company of those who understand, who wrap their arms around me without judgment, allowing me to be vulnerable in my moments of weakness.

As I venture out into the world, I cast aside the pressures and expectations that threaten to suffocate my spirit. I choose to surround myself with genuine connections, to engage in conversations that delve beyond the superficiality of seasonal pleasantries. Together, we build a community of support, a refuge for those whose hearts still ache during this time of celebration.

Yes, the calendar may read "December," but grief does not adhere to a calendar. It does not conform to societal norms or magically disappear with the dawning of a new day. It is a journey that unfolds at its own pace, in its own way. And as I navigate this season with a tender heart, I remind myself that it is okay to embrace the bittersweet symphony of grief and joy; to find beauty in the struggle and strength in vulnerability.

So, as the world revels in the clamor of the holiday season, I find solace in the quiet corners of my own sanctuary. And there, in the depths of my sorrow, I discover the resilience of the human spirit - an enduring light that guides me through the darkest of nights and reminds me that, even amidst unimaginable loss, there is still love, there is still hope, and there is still life to be lived.

But it isn't just the external expectations that contribute to this weighted burden. It's the internal guilt that gnaws at me too. How can I allow myself to be enveloped in sorrow when the world around me seems so consumed with joy? I question myself, wondering if there's something wrong with me, if I am failing some unspoken test of resilience. But deep down, I know that grief has no timeline, no expiration date. It is a complex and deeply personal journey, one that cannot be rushed or forced. I remind myself that my feelings are valid, that I am allowed to grieve and feel pain, even during the holiday season.

In the midst of this inner turmoil, I seek solace in the quiet moments, in the memories of what once was. I find comfort in the flickering lights of a single candle, whose gentle glow reminds me that there can still be beauty amidst the darkness. I retreat to nature, seeking solace in the embrace of solitude, where the sound of leaves rustling and birds chirping offer a sense of tranquility.

I choose to redefine what this season means to me. Instead of succumbing to the pressure to be jolly, I embrace the power of healing. I reach out to others who share similar journeys, finding solace in their understanding and support. Together, we create a space where our pain is acknowledged, where we let go of expectations and find strength in our shared stories. We no longer feel obligated to put on a brave face or participate in the festivities. Instead, we honor our grief and find solace in the beauty of our own unique healing processes.

In this community of understanding, I am no longer burdened by the weight of societal expectations. I realize that the true essence of the holiday season lies in connection, compassion, and self-care. I take the time to nurture my own well-being, embracing the healing power of self-reflection, gratitude, and kindness towards myself and others.

This holiday season, I choose to embrace the bittersweet symphony of grief and joy. I acknowledge that it is okay to feel a mixture of emotions during this time of celebration. Through my own journey, I have learned that the holiday season can be a time of profound transformation and growth. It can be a time to honor our loved ones, to reflect on the beauty of life, and to find strength in vulnerability.

So, as the world rushes by in a whirlwind of holiday cheer, I choose to slow down and savor the moments that bring me peace and solace. I find comfort in simple acts of self-care, in gatherings with loved ones who understand, and in the warmth of memories that live on within me. And as I navigate this season on my own terms, honoring my journey and embracing my emotions, I find a renewed sense of purpose and a deeper connection to the true essence of the holiday spirit.

I realize that the true spirit of the holiday season lies not in extravagant gifts and extravagant displays, but in compassion, understanding, and love. It is about embracing all aspects of the human experience, even the painful ones. It is about acknowledging that everyone walks their own path, and that grief, though heavy, is a testament to love and loss.

As the days pass, I learn to navigate this holiday season with grace and resilience. I no longer feel the need to put on a facade of happiness, for I understand that vulnerability is a much greater strength. I find joy in the littlest of things, in the quiet moments of reflection and in the embrace of loved ones who are there to offer support.

Societal expectations may continue to weigh heavily on my shoulders, but I have learned to shoulder them with grace and authenticity. I have learned that grief and pain do not diminish the beauty of this season, but rather deepen its meaning. And as I continue on this journey of healing, I realize that perhaps, in sharing my story, I can help others find solace in their own grief and redefine what it means to celebrate during a time of loss. After all, it is in our collective vulnerability that we find true connection, and it is through connection that we heal, grow, and find the strength to face even the darkest of seasons with a glimmer of hope in our hearts.

Yet, as I examine these societal expectations more closely, I realize that they are merely illusions - painted facades that mask the complexities of human emotions. The pressure to be jolly is nothing more than an unrealistic expectation created by a society that thrives on superficiality. And so, I must remind myself that there is no shame in feeling the weight of my losses, in grieving openly, even amidst a season of supposed celebration.

In this realization, I find some solace. I am not alone in my struggle against the pressure to be jolly. There are countless individuals who are silently grappling with their own sorrows, their own losses, while wearing a mask of forced happiness. Perhaps, if we can find the courage to remove these masks and share our stories, we can break free from the illusion of happy holidays and instead find solace in the authenticity of our emotions.

Together, we can redefine what it means to celebrate during a time of loss. Instead of adhering to societal expectations, we can create a space where grief and joy can coexist harmoniously. We can honor the memories of those we have lost while finding moments of peace and gratitude within the chaos.

Embracing the complexities of our emotions, we can acknowledge that the holiday season can be both a source of joy and a reminder of our pain. We can give ourselves permission to feel whatever arises, without judgment or guilt. It is through this acceptance and compassion for ourselves that we can extend the same understanding to others who may be struggling silently.

In opening up about our experiences, we offer a lifeline to those who may feel isolated in their grief. We create a network of support and empathy, where people can find comfort and connection in shared stories and shared vulnerabilities. Together, we can create a new narrative that acknowledges the bittersweetness of life. A narrative that embraces all the shades of human experience, where each person is free to navigate the holiday season as they need, without the burden of expectations.

So, this holiday season, let us stray from the well-trodden path of programmed joy and venture into the wild terrain of authenticity. Let us create new traditions that honor our losses while celebrating the strength it takes to carry on. Let us gather with loved ones, not just to exchange presents, but also to exchange stories and experiences that have shaped us.

In these moments of shared vulnerability, we find the true essence of connection – the connection that reminds us that we are not alone in our struggles, that we are never truly alone. And as we find solace in this collective understanding, we can heal, grow, and reclaim the holiday season as a time of genuine reflection, gratitude, and love.

For it is in embracing our true selves, with all our complexities and contradictions, that we find the strength to navigate the darkest of seasons and emerge with a renewed sense of hope and resilience. Let us rewrite the narrative, reclaiming the holiday season in all its raw and beautiful authenticity. And may this newfound understanding be a gift that we can carry with us long after the holiday lights have dimmed, illuminating our path towards a more compassionate, meaningful, and connected existence.

For now, I sit in my dimly lit living room, feeling the weight of the pressure to be jolly, but also recognizing its falseness. I take a deep breath, allowing myself to feel the grief, the longing, and the emptiness. And in that vulnerability, I start to release myself from the shackles of societal expectations. I am not a failure for feeling these emotions. I am human, and I deserve the space and understanding to mourn, even during this festive time of year.

The Reality Behind the Façade

Delving into the hidden struggles and challenges faced by individuals during the holiday season, I have unearthed a multitude of heart-wrenching stories that often go unnoticed. The illusion of happy holidays can be particularly devastating for those who have lost loved ones, making them acutely aware of the emptiness that lingers during this time of year. For me, it is a reminder of the friends and family I have lost in dire circumstances. Their absence looms large in my heart, casting a shadow over the joy that should accompany the holidays.

There is an expectation, a societal pressure, to be happy and joyful during this time of year. But what happens when that expectation clashes with the personal struggles that many individuals grapple with behind closed doors? It is a collision of emotions that can be overwhelming, leaving one feeling isolated and misunderstood. The grief, the loneliness, and the pain can become magnified, as the world outside continues to celebrate and revel in the spirit of the season.

What brings me into the creation of this book, "The Illusion of Happy Holidays," is the honest lack of joy I've always found. There was a time the holidays brought me a child-like glee, an eagerness for snow days and clever ruses to find out what I would find under the tree December 25th.

As I became a teenager, the joys from family members just felt staged. I became more aware of the disconnect between family members, how much everyone seemed eager to stoke the fires of whatever drama was upon us. More irksome came the fact that all the "adults," would dump the kids off on me to babysit.

Perhaps a majority of it came from the fact that as I was shifting into this life stage my grandfather, the man who was pretty much my dad, was given five years before colon cancer would take his life. Unfortunately, the doctors were almost on the dot. By the age of fourteen I lost the only family member who I looked forward to seeing, who was eager to hear of my early successes, and the man who helped me the most take hold of the path which I walk today. I owe everything to him. Others were involved, yes, but seemed quick to retract their love and support (often quick to villianize me in the process) until Grandpa helped talk them down. So naturally, at the age of fourteen and at a time a young man needs a father most, my grandfather's death killed the holiday joys. I try to put up a small facade to avoid dameping the spirits of my younger relatives, born after my grandpa passed away, but even they are starting to notice the lack of sincerity.

But those are stories for another time. In my time of healing, I started to reach out to various resources to overcome these feelings. To this day, I fight to keep certain cycles from repeating, but to truly overcome the emotional instability I knew that I needed time to correct the foundations. Naturally I sought out therapy, support groups, and even stories shared through anonymous messaging boards online. The things I found were miraculous!

In researching this topic, I have been humbled by the stories of those who have bravely shared their experiences. People like Sarah, a single mother who lost her job just weeks before Christmas, and now struggles to provide even the most basic necessities for her children. Or James, a war veteran haunted by the memories of his comrades lost in battle, grappling with the conflicting emotions of survivor's guilt and the desire to find solace in the festive cheer. These individuals, and countless others like them, face unspoken battles every day, battles that are amplified during the holiday season.

As I delve deeper into these hidden struggles, I peer behind the curtain of the holiday illusion and am confronted with the stark reality of the human experience. The pressure to find happiness in the midst of personal turmoil can be crippling, and the constant reminders of what has been lost make it all the more difficult. But it is important to recognize that the façade of happy holidays is just that – a façade. The grief, the challenges, and the hardships faced by individuals during this time are very real and deserve acknowledgement and understanding.

The holiday season, with its twinkling lights, cheerful

carols, and joyful gatherings, can sometimes seem like an alternate reality, a temporary escape from the hardships of everyday life. But as I dig deeper into the stories of those who bear the weight of unseen battles, I realize that true compassion lies in acknowledging and empathizing with their struggles, rather than perpetuating the illusion of holiday cheer.

Sarah's indomitable spirit shines through as she navigates the treacherous waters of unemployment, determined to bring a flicker of joy to her children's lives amidst the reality of empty cupboards and overdue bills. She teaches us that resilience can bloom even in the harshest of circumstances, reminding us that a kind word, a helping hand, or a simple act of generosity can make all the difference to those who dare to hope when hope seems lost.

Delving further into the hidden struggles and challenges faced by individuals during the holiday season, I have uncovered numerous heart-wrenching stories that frequently go unnoticed. The deceptive appearance of happy holidays can be particularly devastating for those who have experienced the loss of loved ones, leaving them acutely aware of the emptiness that permeates this time of year. For myself, it is a painful reminder of the friends and family I have lost under tragic circumstances. Their absence continues to loom large in my heart, casting a shadow over the joy that should accompany the holidays.

There exists an expectation, a societal pressure, to embrace happiness and joyfulness during this time of year. But what transpires when that expectation collides with the personal struggles that countless individuals confront in the privacy of their own homes? It becomes an overwhelming collision of emotions, leaving one feeling isolated and misunderstood. The grief, the loneliness, and the pain become magnified as the outside world continues to celebrate and revel in the spirit of the season.

What brings me to create this book, "The Illusion of Happy Holidays," is the profound absence of joy that has always plagued me. There was a time when the holidays brought me child-like excitement, a longing for snow days and clever tricks to discover what gifts awaited me beneath the tree on December 25th. However, as I entered my teenage years, the joy from family members felt contrived. I became aware of the disconnect between family members, this disconnect coincided with their eagerness to ignite the flames of any ensuing drama. What was more bothersome is that all the "adults" would offload the responsibility of babysitting onto me.

Perhaps a significant portion of my lack of holiday joy stemmed from the fact that as I underwent this life transition, my grandfather, the man who essentially played the role of my father, was given a mere five years before colon cancer would strip him away from us. Unfortunately, the doctors were almost eerily accurate in their prediction. By the time I turned fourteen, I had lost the one family member I yearned to see, the one who was eager to hear about my accomplishments, and the one who guided me the most in navigating the path I walk today. I owe everything to him. There were others involved, yes, but they seemed quick to withdraw their love and support (often casting me as the villain in the process) until my grandfather intervened to settle things. So naturally, at the age of fourteen, and precisely when a young man needs a fatherly figure the most, my grandfather's death extinguished my holiday joy. I try to maintain a facade to prevent dampening the spirits of my younger relatives, born after my grandpa's passing, but even they are beginning to notice the lack of sincerity.

Yet, those stories will have to wait for another time. During my healing process, I sought out various resources to overcome these emotions. To this day, I continue to combat the repetition of certain patterns, but I recognized that in order to truly conquer emotional instability, I needed to address the underlying foundations. Naturally, I sought therapy, joined support groups, and sought solace in discussing my experiences on anonymous messaging boards. The discoveries I made were nothing short of miraculous!

As I delved deeper into researching this topic, I was humbled by the stories of individuals who courageously shared their experiences. People like Sarah, a single mother who lost her job mere weeks before Christmas, and who now struggles to provide even the basic necessities for her children. Or

James, a war veteran haunted by the memories of comrades lost in battle, grappling with the conflicting emotions of survivor's guilt and the yearning to find solace amidst the festive spirit. These individuals, along with countless others like them, face unspoken battles daily, battles that are amplified during the holiday season.

As I continue to explore these hidden struggles, I pierce through the veil of the holiday illusion and am confronted with the raw reality of the human experience. The pressure to find happiness amidst personal turmoil can be paralyzing, and the constant reminders of what has been lost make it even more challenging. However, it is crucial to acknowledge that the facade of happy holidays is just that – a facade. The grief, the challenges, and the hardships faced by individuals during this time are very real and merit recognition and understanding.

The holiday season, with its dazzling lights, joyous carols, and cheerful gatherings, can sometimes feel like an alternate reality, a temporary escape from the hardships of everyday life. Yet, as I delve deeper into the stories of those who bear the weight of unseen battles, I realize that genuine compassion lies in acknowledging and empathizing with their struggles, rather than perpetuating the illusion of holiday cheer.

Sarah's indomitable spirit shines through as she navigates the treacherous waters of unemployment, determined to bring a glimmer of joy to her children's lives amidst the harsh reality of empty cupboards and overdue bills. She teaches us that resilience can flourish even in the harshest circumstances, reminding us that a kind word, a helping hand, or a simple act of generosity can make all the difference to those who dare to cling to hope when it seems lost.

James, haunted by the scars of war, wrestles with the burden of survivor's guilt. The holiday season magnifies his longing for the camaraderie and the comrades lost in battle who once formed his family. As we bear witness to his anguish, we learn that the true significance of these festive times lies not in extravagant gifts or lavish celebrations, but in building connections, offering support, and lending a listening ear to those who feel adrift amidst a whirlwind of emotions.

It is crucial to dispel the overly romanticized image of the holiday season, which often disregards the silent struggles endured. To genuinely honor the spirit of this time, we must dismantle the stigmas surrounding vulnerability and establish safe spaces where individuals can openly acknowledge their pain, seek solace in the company of empathetic souls, and find the strength to take that crucial first step forward.

Let us remember that during this season, acts of kindness and compassion have the power to transform lives. Small gestures, such as dropping spare change into a donation box, sharing a warm meal with a lonely neighbor, or sending a heartfelt message to a friend silently battling the darkness, hold the potential to mend the broken and uplift the weary.

As I draw to a close this journey through the hidden struggles and unspoken battles, my heart swells with admiration for the resilience of those who confront adversity with courage and grace. Their stories stand as a testament to the indomitable spirit of humanity, capable of weathering storms and finding hope even in the bleakest of times.

This holiday season, let us pull back the curtain on the illusions and reach out our hands, our hearts, and our empathy to those who need it most. In doing so, we can cultivate a world where compassion reigns, where no one fights their battles alone, and where the true spirit of the holidays resides in acts of love, kindness, and unwavering support for our fellow human beings.

Through sharing these stories, it is my aspiration to shed light on the hidden struggles of the holiday season and to inspire compassion and empathy towards those who silently suffer. It is a call for a shift in perspective, to move beyond the glittering lights and superficial cheer, and to truly see the reality that lies beneath. Only by embracing and supporting one another in moments of vulnerability can we begin to bridge the gap between illusion and truth, and inch closer to a more authentic and inclusive holiday season.

Navigating Loneliness

Though it is difficult to process loss, especially at a time everyone is expected to bring about a happy-face, overcoming these feelings is far from a lost cause. There is a certain strength that lies within each individual, a resilience that can be awakened during the most challenging times. It may seem daunting to face the world with a heavy heart, but beneath the layers of sorrow, there exists a spark of hope and determination waiting to ignite.

As the world embraces the facade of happiness and cheerfulness, it is important to remember that true healing comes from within. Acknowledging and honoring our emotions allows us to embark on a journey of self-discovery and growth. It is in the depths of our pain that we find the seeds of our strength.

In this complex and unpredictable journey called life, loss is an inevitable companion. It may be the loss of a loved one, a job, a dream, or even a part of oneself. The fear of being consumed by sadness and grief can be overpowering, but it is important to recognize that it is not a sign of weakness to feel these emotions; rather, it is a testament to our capacity for love and connection.

Overcoming loss requires patience, self-compassion, and

support from those around us. It is crucial to grant ourselves permission to grieve, providing space for the heart to mend. Surrounding ourselves with loved ones who understand the depths of our sorrow can provide solace and a reminder that we are not alone in our journey. Seeking professional guidance and participating in support groups can also offer valuable insights and tools for healing.

The path toward healing is not a linear one, as grief has its own rhythm and timeline. Some days may be colored by a sense of acceptance and even glimpses of joy, while others may be shrouded in darkness and despair. But through it all, it is imperative to remember that we are not defined by our loss but rather by how we choose to rise above it.

As the pain slowly dissipates, we may find ourselves uncovering newfound strength and resilience. We begin to see the world through a different lens, gaining a renewed appreciation for the present moment and the gift of life. With each passing day, we become the architects of our own happiness, understanding that the love we have lost will forever shape us, but need not define us.

In our collective journey through grief and loss, we come to understand that the act of overcoming is not about banishing pain but rather weaving it into the tapestry of our lives. It becomes a part of our story, reminding us of our capacity to endure, evolve, and find beauty once again.

So, as we navigate the realm of loss amidst a world that often demands happiness, let us not lose sight of the resilience that lies within. Though the path may be arduous and the road may be shadowed, it is our ability to embrace our emotions, seek support, and summon our inner strength that will guide us towards a future brimming with hope, love, and an unwavering belief in the power of the human spirit. No matter what it is that lead you to reading this big, not matter how big the turmoil may seem, the steps to taking the matter apart to a more manageable load are almost always the same.

Step 1: Acknowledge your feelings

The first step in coping with loneliness during the holiday season is acknowledging your feelings. It can be tempting to bury them deep within, to put on a brave face and pretend everything is fine. But the truth is, it's okay to not be okay. Give yourself permission to feel the ache deep within your heart. Understand that it is normal to feel sadness and grief, especially during a time that is supposed to be filled with joy. Embrace your emotions, for they are a part of who you are.

Once you have acknowledged your feelings, the next step is to reach out for support. Loneliness can sometimes make us feel isolated and disconnected from others, but remember that you are not alone in this. There are people who care about you and want to help lift your spirits during this time.

Start by reaching out to friends and family members whom you trust. Let them know how you are feeling and be open to receiving their support. Sometimes, just having someone to talk to and share your thoughts and emotions with can make a world of difference. They may have gone through similar experiences themselves and can offer valuable advice or simply lend a listening ear.

If reaching out to loved ones feels challenging, consider seeking support from organizations or support groups that cater to people experiencing loneliness during the holiday season. These groups provide a sense of camaraderie and understanding, as they gather individuals who have common experiences and struggles. Joining such a group can create an opportunity for you to meet new people and form connections, while also providing a safe space to share your feelings without judgment.

Another way to combat loneliness is by engaging in activities that bring you joy and fulfillment. This may include pursuing a hobby, volunteering for a cause you are passionate about, or getting involved in community events. By immersing yourself in these activities, you not only distract yourself from feelings of isolation but also expand your social circle and potentially meet individuals who share your interests.

Additionally, consider focusing on self-care during this

time. Nurture yourself by indulging in activities that bring you peace and happiness. This may involve practicing mindfulness, journaling your thoughts and emotions, meditating, or treating yourself to activities that make you feel good, such as taking a long walk in nature, enjoying a bubble bath, or curling up with a good book. Remember, it is essential to prioritize your well-being and ensure that you are taking care of yourself mentally, emotionally, and physically.

Lastly, try to reframe your perspective on the holiday season. Instead of dwelling on what you may be missing or the gatherings you are not a part of, focus on the opportunities that lie ahead. Consider it a chance to reflect, grow, and discover new aspects of yourself. Engage in activities that promote self-reflection and personal growth, such as setting goals for the upcoming year, learning something new, or taking up a creative project. By shifting your mindset towards the positive aspects of this season, you may find yourself embracing the solitude and using it as an opportunity for personal development.

Remember, loneliness is a temporary state, and it does not define who you are or your worth. By acknowledging your feelings, seeking support, engaging in fulfilling activities, and nurturing yourself, you will gradually overcome the loneliness that accompanies the holiday season. And in time, you will find solace and joy within yourself, creating a sense of contentment that transcends any external circumstances.

Step 2: Reach out to others

Loneliness can be suffocating, but we must not let it consume us. In times like these, it is important to reach out to others. Connect with friends, family, or even support groups who are experiencing similar feelings. Share your thoughts, your fears, and your pain. Sometimes, simply knowing that you are not alone in your loneliness can provide a small measure of comfort. Surround yourself with those who understand and support you, and let them be your guiding light through the darkness.

In the search for connection, we often discover that there are kindred souls out there craving the same solace. We find ourselves drawn to the warmth of conversation, longing for the intimate exchange of words that can bridge the gap between isolated hearts. Loneliness, it seems, is not a burden we must bear alone.

In the midst of our quest, we stumble upon a hidden treasure trove—a vibrant online community bustling with empathy and understanding. Here, we encounter individuals from all walks of life, each with their unique tale of struggle and resilience. They stand as a testament to the indomitable human spirit, reminding us that we too possess the strength to overcome our loneliness.

In these digital spaces, there are no physical boundaries to constrain us. We transcend miles and borders, connecting with individuals across the globe who share our yearning for companionship. We engage in heartfelt conversations that navigate the depths of our souls, and as we pour our emotions onto the screen, we discover a profound sense of liberation.

Through the power of technology, we unravel the strings that bind us to solitude. Chat rooms, forums, and social media platforms become our refuge, offering sanctuary from the oppressive grip of loneliness. In this vast virtual landscape, we forge friendships forged in pixels and words; we find solace in the realization that even when our physical presence may be absent, our voices still resonate through the digital ether.

But let us not underestimate the importance of face-to-face connection. As much as online communities bring us comfort, there is an undeniable power in the touch of a hand, the warmth of a hug, the shared laughter that reverberates in the room. It is in tender embraces and heartfelt conversations that we find solace beyond our screens.

In this multifaceted journey toward connection, we discover the beauty of vulnerability. We learn to open our hearts and reveal the depths of our emotions, understanding that it is in our shared humanity that we truly become whole. We form friendships that strengthen us, relationships that inspire us, and communities that uplift us.

Through the darkness, we navigate as one, guided by

the radiant light that emanates from the unity of purpose. Together, we acknowledge that loneliness is a temporary state—a chapter in our lives that, though overwhelming, can be overcome. We realize that by reaching out and allowing others to enter our worlds, we create a tapestry of love and support that binds us intricately.

So, let us take the hands that are extended toward us, let us listen, share, and acknowledge the experiences of others. For within unity lies the cure for loneliness. Together, we defy its suffocating grip, and in the embrace of human connection, we find the strength to flourish once more.

Step 3: Create new traditions

The memories of past holiday celebrations can be bittersweet. They serve as a reminder of the loved ones we have lost, intensifying our feelings of loneliness. To combat this, it is essential to create new traditions that honor the past while embracing the present. Volunteer at a local shelter, participate in community events, or simply spend time engaging in activities that bring you joy. By focusing on the present moment and creating new experiences, you can bring a sense of purpose and fulfillment to your holiday season.

In the midst of the holiday season, a sense of melancholy often takes hold, as we reminisce about old memories and long for the presence of those who are no longer with us. Yet, within the depths of our longing lies the power to create new traditions that honor the past in their own unique way. It is in these moments of bittersweet reflection that we can find solace and inspiration to make each holiday season a truly meaningful and joyous occasion.

In the spirit of embracing the present, there are endless opportunities to give back and make a difference in the lives of others. Volunteering at a local shelter not only helps those in need but also fosters a sense of connection and community that can fill the void of our own loneliness. Sharing a meal with those who have no one else to turn to or providing comfort to those seeking solace can bring a profound sense of purpose and fulfillment to our holiday experience.

Community events are another wonderful way to connect with others during the holiday season. From lively festivals to heartwarming charity drives, these gatherings provide an opportunity to meet new people who may become lifelong friends. Immersing ourselves in the festive spirit, we can forge new connections and create lasting memories with like-minded individuals who share our commitment to making the world a better place.

Of course, finding joy and fulfillment during the holidays doesn't always require grand gestures or formalities. Sometimes, simplicity is the key. Engaging in activities that bring us personal joy and contentment can be just as rewarding. Whether it is baking cookies, decorating a tree, or sipping hot cocoa by the fireplace, moments of quiet introspection can help us appreciate the present while honoring the memories of the past. These small joys can bring warmth to our hearts, reminding us that the true essence of the holiday season lies not in the grandiosity of the festivities, but in the meaningful connections we nurture and the love we share.

So, as we embark on this holiday season, let us remember that the memories of those we have lost need not bring only sadness but can fuel our determination to create new traditions that honor their legacy. Let us reach out to those in need, embrace the warmth of our communities, and find solace in the simple joys that surround us. By doing so, we will not only be writing a new chapter in our lives but also etching our names in the annals of the world's best writers, as we craft a holiday season that is both poignant and filled with love.

Step 4: Practice self-care

Loneliness can take a toll on both our mental and physical well-being. It is crucial to prioritize self-care during this time. Engage in activities that bring you peace and tranquility, whether it be taking long walks in nature, meditating, or indulging in a favorite hobby. Take care of your body by nourishing it with healthy food and getting enough rest. And most importantly, be gentle with yourself. Understand that healing takes time and that it is okay to put yourself first.

In the midst of solitude's embrace, we often forget the importance of human connection. Loneliness may snatch our sense of belonging, leaving us feeling adrift in a vast sea of emptiness. However, amidst the storm, there is solace to be found in the power of the written word.

Pick up your pen, dear friend, and let your thoughts unravel on the inviting embrace of pristine paper. Pour your emotions onto those bountiful pages, and let the ink dance to the rhythm of your soul. Write letters to loved ones, whether near or far, and allow the distance to melt away with every heartfelt word.

In our interconnected era, technology serves as a bridge to the world beyond our loneliness. Seek refuge in the warmth of virtual gatherings, where laughter reverberates through the pixels, and conversations effortlessly cross the boundaries of time and space. Send messages of love and encouragement to those who need it most, for in uplifting others, we often find solace ourselves.

Amidst the chaos, take solace in the whispered wisdom of the great storytellers. Lose yourself in the pages of captivating novels, where heroes rise from adversity, and love conquers all. Immerse yourself in worlds far removed from your own, and let your imagination soar through the realms of possibility. Allow literature's gentle embrace to remind you that, even in solitude, you are never alone.

But above all, remember to nourish your soul with self-compassion. Loneliness can be an unrelenting burden to bear, but in its grip, let kindness be your guiding light. Embrace the solitude as an opportunity to explore and embrace the depths of who you truly are. Learn to love your own company, for in doing so, you will uncover hidden strengths and untapped joys.

As the days stretch on, and the weight of loneliness becomes heavy, seek solace in its lessons. Embrace the silence as it hums with possibility, and allow introspection to guide your journey. Take this time to rewrite the narrative of your life, shedding the constraints of societal expectations, and embracing the courage to be authentically you.

For amidst the vast tapestry of loneliness, there lies an opportunity for growth and self-discovery. Unshackle yourself from the chains of isolation and chase the passions that ignite your spirit. Whether it be creating art, studying new skills, or even embarking on a journey of self-improvement, embrace what brings you true happiness.

And when the day arrives where the weight of loneliness finally lifts, you will emerge stronger, wiser, and more resilient than ever before. The scars may fade, but the lessons learned will forever be etched into the very fabric of your being. So, dear friend, take solace in knowing that even in the darkest of nights, the dawn of connection is waiting to embrace you once more.

Step 5: Seek professional help if needed

If feelings of loneliness and isolation persist, it may be beneficial to seek professional help. Therapists and counselors can provide guidance and support as you navigate through this challenging time. They can help you explore your emotions, develop coping strategies, and provide a safe space for you to share your thoughts and fears. Remember, seeking help is not a sign of weakness, but rather a sign of strength and a commitment to your own well-being.

Through therapy, you may begin to uncover the underlying causes of your loneliness and isolation. A skilled therapist will assist you in identifying patterns of behavior or negative thought patterns that contribute to these feelings. By gaining insight into these patterns, you can work towards replacing them with healthier and more constructive behaviors.

Additionally, therapy offers the opportunity to learn effective communication skills, which can be invaluable in fostering meaningful connections with others. Often, feelings of loneliness stem from difficulties in expressing oneself or establishing strong interpersonal relationships. With the help of a therapist, you can practice effective communication strategies and learn how to establish boundaries that promote healthier social interactions.

As you progress in therapy, you may also explore various techniques to manage and reduce feelings of loneliness. Mindfulness exercises, for example, can help you become more present and aware of your surroundings. This practice encourages a sense of grounding and connection with the present moment, alleviating the constant rumination that often accompanies loneliness.

Furthermore, therapists can help you build a support network by connecting you with local community groups, social clubs, or volunteer organizations. By engaging with others who share similar interests or experiences, you can create a sense of belonging and forge new meaningful connections. These groups can provide a safe and welcoming environment, allowing you to gradually overcome feelings of loneliness and isolation.

While therapy can be immensely helpful, it is important to recognize that healing from loneliness takes time. It is a process of self-discovery and growth that requires patience and self-compassion. There may be setbacks and moments of frustration, but remember that every step forward, no matter how small, brings you closer to a more fulfilling and connected life.

In conclusion, seeking professional help for persistent

feelings of loneliness and isolation is a powerful step towards improving your mental and emotional well-being. Therapists and counselors can guide you on a transformative journey, helping you gain insight, develop coping strategies, and build meaningful connections. Remember, you are never alone in your struggle, and there is strength in reaching out for support.

Navigating loneliness during the holiday season is no easy task. It requires courage, vulnerability, and a willingness to confront our deepest emotions. But as we journey together, remember that you are not alone. Together, we can break free from the illusion of happy holidays and create a sense of joy and meaning in our lives once again.

Dealing with Seasonal Affective Disorder

Having lost friends and family in dire circumstances, my view of the holiday season has become compromised. Every year, as the days grow shorter and the nights longer, I find myself sinking deeper into a pool of desolation. It's a struggle to maintain any semblance of happiness, even when surrounded by twinkling lights and the infectious laughter of loved ones. The darkness outside mirrors the darkness within me, and it feels as if the joy of the holidays is forever out of reach.

In my quest to address the impact of seasonal changes on my mental health, I have delved into extensive research on SAD. I wanted to understand why these melancholic feelings descend upon me, and more importantly, how I can manage them. What I discovered was a fascinating interplay between our biological and environmental factors, and a range of strategies that can help alleviate the symptoms of SAD.

It all begins with our body's internal clock, the circadian rhythm. During the winter months, when the daylight hours dwindle and darkness lingers for longer, our circadian rhythm can become disrupted. This disruption affects the production of serotonin, a neurotransmitter linked to mood regulation. With decreased levels of serotonin, it's no wonder that feelings of sadness and apathy take hold. To combat this, one potential solution is light therapy. By exposing oneself to bright artificial light, the body gets a much-needed boost of serotonin, helping to alleviate some of the symptoms of SAD. So, armed with this knowledge, I have incorporated light therapy into my daily routine, basking in the radiant glow of a special lightbox each morning.

Light therapy can also help when you are one ever-so-fortunate to work the nightshift...

Yet, light therapy alone is not enough to completely counteract the impact of winter on our mental well-being. Another crucial element is exercise. Now, I must admit, the idea of dragging myself out into the cold and exerting physical effort seemed like an insurmountable challenge. However, the research shows that regular physical activity, even in small amounts, can significantly improve mood and increase energy levels. So, despite my initial resistance, I found solace in taking brisk walks in nature, the crisp winter air invigorating my senses and lifting my spirits. Plus having some music with a good beat and/or a fun mobile game that requires you to walk around in order play can help get the edge off.

Additionally, maintaining a balanced diet has proven to be a fundamental factor in managing SAD. The proverbial "winter comfort foods" may bring temporary solace, but they can also contribute to a further decline in mood. Consuming foods rich in omega-3 fatty acids, such as fatty fish and walnuts, can help combat depressive symptoms. These omega-3s have been shown to play a role in brain health and neurotransmitter production, providing a much-needed boost during those dark winter days when our mental health is at its most vulnerable.

Moreover, staying connected with loved ones and seeking social support is paramount in combating the effects of winter on our mental well-being. The tendency to isolate ourselves and withdraw from social interactions is common during this season, but it only exacerbates feelings of loneliness and depression. Making a conscious effort to maintain relationships, whether through phone calls, video chats, or socially-distanced gatherings, can provide a sense of belonging and emotional nourishment.

In addition to these strategies, some individuals may benefit from professional intervention. Cognitive-behavioral therapy (CBT), for instance, has been shown to be highly effective in treating seasonal affective disorder. CBT helps individuals challenge negative thought patterns and develop coping mechanisms to navigate the challenges of winter. Furthermore, in severe cases, a doctor may prescribe antidepressant medication to alleviate symptoms and improve overall well-being.

Lastly, incorporating activities that bring joy and fulfillment into our daily routine can greatly enhance our mental state. Engaging in hobbies, pursuing creative endeavors, or volunteering in the community all contribute to a sense of purpose and fulfillment. By focusing on activities that bring us happiness, we shift our attention away from the gloomy aspects of winter and create a more positive and uplifting environment for ourselves.

In conclusion, while winter is often associated with a decline in mental well-being, there are numerous strategies we can employ to combat Seasonal Affective Disorder and maintain our overall happiness. From light therapy and exercise to a healthy diet, social support, professional help, and engaging in fulfilling activities, we have the power to thrive even in the darkest of seasons. By embracing these practices, we can navigate winter with resilience and emerge on the other side with our mental well-being intact, ready to welcome the warmth and brightness of spring.

In my search for strategies to manage SAD, I have also turned to the power of mindfulness and self-care. Taking time each day to engage in activities that bring me joy and peace, such as reading a good book or indulging in a warm bubble bath, has become an essential part of my routine. I have discovered the importance of acknowledging my emotions, allowing myself to feel the sadness and grief that can accompany this time of year. By embracing these emotions, rather than suppressing them, I have found a newfound sense of acceptance and resilience.

Finally, reaching out for professional help should never be underestimated. Therapy and counseling can provide invaluable support and guidance during this difficult time. Speaking to a trained professional has allowed me to explore the root causes of my holiday melancholy and develop coping mechanisms tailored specifically to my needs. It is a reminder that I don't have to face this battle alone.

As I continue to navigate through the illusion of happy holidays, armed with newfound knowledge and personal strategies, I am gradually learning to embrace the season with a renewed perspective. While the darkness of winter may hover at the edges of my consciousness, threatening to consume me, I am determined to defy its hold. The twinkling lights and laughter around me may still trigger moments of sadness and longing, but I now have the tools to navigate through this difficult terrain.

So, as I step into another holiday season, I am reminded that the illusion of happy holidays can be shattered, but it is not an unattainable dream. With the right strategies in place and a commitment to taking care of my mental health, I am ready to face the challenges that lie ahead. And perhaps, just perhaps, I can rediscover a glimmer of joy amidst the darkness and create my own version of a fulfilling holiday season. It's a journey, but one that I am willing to take. Are you?

If you're feeling a bit anxious, that's completely okay. This book helps address that as well.

Understanding Holiday-Related Anxiety

Exploring the triggers of this holiday-related anxiety has become an obsession, a desperate attempt on my part to make sense out of the chaos that ensues. One trigger that I have identified is the overwhelming sense of loss that permeates this time of year. As I reflect on the empty chairs around my dining table and the absence of faces that I once held dear, the grief resurfaces with an intensity that is magnified by the merry decorations and joyous tunes that surround me.

As the holiday season unfolds, I find myself unearthing memories of loved ones who have departed from this earthly realm. It's as if the festivity in the air serves as a stark reminder of those who are no longer here to share in the celebrations. Each flickering light on the Christmas tree triggers a bittersweet flashback, an echo of laughter and conversations held in the past.

Yet, amidst the anguish of these recurring losses, I also discover a profound appreciation for the moments of joy that were shared with these departed souls. Each empty chair serves as a testament to the love and connection that once filled the space, reminding me of the incredible richness they brought into my life. Their absence amplifies the significance of the time we did have together, urging me to hold onto those cherished memories with a renewed fervor.

In this season of remembrance, I have come to understand that grief and joy are not mutually exclusive. The pain of loss and the delight of celebration intertwine, creating a tapestry of emotions that is uniquely tender and fragile. It is in acknowledging and embracing the complex interplay of these emotions that I am able to forge a path towards healing and resilience.

As I delve deeper into the triggers of this holiday-related anxiety, I realize that my obsession lies not only in unraveling the chaos but also in finding solace within it. For every pang of grief that surfaces, there is an opportunity to cultivate a deeper sense of empathy and connection with others who may be experiencing their own waves of longing.

This revelation leads me to seek out ways in which I can transform this season of loss into one of hope and compassion. It becomes my mission to reach out to those who may be navigating their own grief, to offer a listening ear or a warm embrace. I discover the power of shared stories and communal support in healing the wounds that these holiday triggers can reopen.

In doing so, I find myself forging new traditions and new connections. The empty chairs become reminders not only of the departed, but also of the potential for new bonds to be formed. I invite others to gather around my table, to share their own stories of loss and resilience. Together, we create a sanctuary of understanding and acceptance, where grief can coexist with joy, and loneliness can be transformed into camaraderie.

And so, my journey to understand the triggers of holiday-related anxiety has evolved into a mission to transform the way we navigate this season of complexities. Through a blend of introspection, compassion, and a willingness to embrace the full spectrum of emotions, I strive to create a space where healing and growth can flourish. In doing so, I become not just a participant in the holiday chaos but also an advocate for its transformative power.

Another trigger is the pressure to create the picture-perfect holiday experience that society often imposes upon us. The expectations to meticulously decorate the house, prepare an extravagant feast, and present impeccable gifts can feel suffocating. The fear of falling short of these expectations gnaws at my sanity, fueling a constant sense of inadequacy and fear of judgment.

These triggers manifest themselves in various ways, both physical and emotional. Sleepless nights filled with racing thoughts and vivid nightmares become the norm. My appetite wanes as a perpetual knot tightens in my stomach, and even the simplest of tasks become overwhelming burdens. Moments of sudden panic wash over me, causing my heart to race and my palms to sweat. It is as though anxiety has taken control of my very existence, manipulating my every move.

But amidst the darkness, there is still hope. Through my research and personal trials, I have discovered coping mechanisms that have brought me moments of respite and allowed me to navigate the holiday season with a renewed sense of strength.

One such coping mechanism is grounding myself in the present moment. When the weight of past losses threatens to overwhelm me, I remind myself to focus on the beauty that lies before me. Whether it is the warmth of a crackling fireplace, the scent of freshly baked cookies, or the laughter of loved ones, these small moments of joy anchor me to the here and now, providing a temporary escape from the grip of anxiety.

Furthermore, I have found solace in the power of self-care. In the midst of the holiday chaos, I have learned to prioritize my own well-being. Taking the time to nourish my body, mind, and soul has become a non-negotiable act of self-love. Whether it be indulging in a relaxing bubble bath, practicing yoga and meditation, or simply curling up with a good book, I have come to understand that caring for myself is not selfish, but necessary for my own mental and emotional health.

Another vital aspect of my coping strategy is setting boundaries. The pressure to attend every holiday event and fulfill every social obligation can be overwhelming, contributing to heightened anxiety and exhaustion. Learning to say no to certain invitations and prioritizing my own needs has been a challenging yet liberating experience. By allowing myself the space and time to recharge, I have regained a sense of control and agency over my own life.

Moreover, seeking support from loved ones has been instrumental in my journey towards managing holiday anxiety. Opening up to trusted friends and family members about my struggles has lifted the weight of secrecy and shame that often accompanies mental health challenges. Their understanding and empathy have provided me with a strong support system, reminding me that I am not alone in my struggles and that it is okay to ask for help when needed.

As the holiday season unfolds, I am reminded that perfection is an illusion, and it is in embracing our imperfections that true joy can be found. By relinquishing the pressure to conform to society's expectations, I have discovered the freedom to create my own holiday traditions, infused with spontaneity, simplicity, and an emphasis on genuine connections rather than materialistic pursuits.

In the end, I have learned that the true magic of the holidays lies not in flawless decorations or elaborate feasts, but in the moments of love, understanding, and kindness that we share with one another. And with this newfound perspective, I step into the holiday season with optimism and gratitude, ready to embrace the beauty and imperfection that unfolds before me.

Another coping mechanism that I have found helpful is reaching out for support. Sharing burdens and fears with trusted friends or therapists has allowed me to loosen the tight grip that anxiety has held over me. By expressing my emotions openly and honestly, I have discovered a sense of community and understanding that has alleviated the isolation that often accompanies holiday-related anxiety.

As I continue on this journey of understanding, I am hopeful that these coping mechanisms will guide me towards a greater sense of peace during the holiday season. While the illusion of happy holidays may never fully dissipate, I hold onto the belief that through self-reflection and resilience, I can find moments of true joy amidst the turmoil.

The Weight of Expectations

But what happens when those expectations become unattainable? What happens when the traditions we once held dear are no longer possible due to circumstances beyond our control? I know all too well the pain of loss and the way it can taint the holiday season. The empty chairs at the dinner table, the absence of laughter and familiar voices – these are the reminders that life isn't always filled with the joy and merriment the holidays promise.

Navigating through this labyrinth of expectations can be a daunting task, but it is one that we must confront head-on if we are to find any semblance of happiness during this time. Through personal experience and careful examination, I have discovered a few strategies that have helped me manage the weight of expectations and find a measure of peace amidst the chaos.

First and foremost, it is essential to acknowledge and accept our limitations. We are only human, after all, and there is only so much that we can do. It is important to set realistic goals and not try to live up to an impossible standard. Perhaps this means scaling back on lavish decorations, simplifying the menu, or even rethinking the gift-giving process. By doing so, we can alleviate some of the pressure and focus on what truly matters – the love and connection we share with those we hold dear.

Another strategy I have found helpful is to forge new traditions that honor and acknowledge the past while embracing the present. Instead of yearning for what once was, we can create new rituals and activities that reflect our current circumstances. It could be as simple as lighting a candle in memory of our lost loved ones or gathering with friends and family to share stories and laughter. By embracing the present and finding joy in the moment, we can release ourselves from the bonds of unrealistic expectations.

In the pursuit of a meaningful holiday season, let us not forget the power of gratitude and compassion. In a world that often values material possessions and extravagant displays, it is easy to lose sight of the true essence of the holidays. By shifting our focus towards gratitude, we can cultivate a deep appreciation for the blessings we have in our lives.

In the midst of holiday preparations, let us take a moment to pause and reflect on the people and experiences that bring us joy. It is easy to become caught up in the rush of shopping, cooking, and decorating, but true fulfillment lies in the connections we forge with others. Reach out to loved ones who may be feeling lonely or isolated and extend an invitation to join in your celebrations. By opening our hearts and homes to others, we create a sense of community and belonging.

Additionally, it is important to remember that the holiday season can be a difficult time for many. Loss, grief, and personal struggles don't suddenly disappear because a festive occasion is upon us. Let us practice compassion and empathy towards those who may be experiencing sorrow or challenges in their lives. Offer a listening ear, a comforting shoulder, or a small act of kindness to those who need it most. In doing so, we not only uplift others but also find solace in the act of giving.

Lastly, let us not succumb to the overwhelming pressure to conform to societal standards. The perfect holiday does not exist, and our worth should not be measured by the extravagance of our celebrations. Whether our festivities are grand or modest, what truly matters is the love, warmth, and genuine connection we create with one another. Embracing imperfection and celebrating the beauty of authenticity can lead us down the path of a truly meaningful holiday season.

As we embark on this journey towards a more thoughtful and fulfilling celebration, let us remember that the power lies within us to shape our own experience. It is not about being the world's best decorator, chef, or gift-giver; it is about being the best version of ourselves. By embracing our limitations, creating new traditions, expressing gratitude, extending compassion, and staying true to our values, we can craft a holiday season that not only fills our hearts with joy but leaves a profound impact on those around us.

May this be the year we redefine the essence of the holiday season, stepping away from the superficial and embracing the profound. Let us be the writers of our own holiday narrative, where love, connection, and genuine authenticity prevail.

Ultimately, managing the weight of expectations during the holiday season requires us to redefine what happiness means to us. It is not about the grand displays of wealth or the material gifts that we exchange; it is about finding peace within ourselves and nurturing the relationships that bring us joy. It is about recognizing that the true magic of the holidays lies not in the extravagance, but in the moments of genuine connection and love.

As the season unfolds, I encourage you, dear reader, to take a step back and examine the expectations that burden you. Find solace in accepting your limitations and embracing new traditions. Remember that happiness cannot be measured by society's standards, but rather by the love and joy we cultivate within our hearts and share with others. In doing so, we can dismantle the illusion of happy holidays and find a true and lasting contentment.

Embracing Vulnerability

As I sit here, reflecting on my journey through the holiday season, I cannot help but recognize the importance of embracing vulnerability. It is a concept that often makes us uncomfortable and exposes our deepest fears and insecurities. However, I have come to understand that vulnerability is not a weakness; it is a source of strength.

In the face of loss and adversity, it is easy to isolate ourselves, putting on a facade of strength to protect our fragile hearts. We convince ourselves that we should bear the weight of our pain alone, that asking for help is a sign of weakness. But this could not be further from the truth.

During my own darkest times, I realized that by denying myself the support of others, I was preventing myself from healing and growing. It was only when I allowed myself to be vulnerable, to share my pain and seek support, that true connections began to form. I discovered that there is no shame in leaning on others, in letting them see the cracks in your armor. In fact, it is in these moments of raw honesty that we find resilience and strength.

It is natural to fear judgment and rejection when we expose our vulnerabilities. We worry that others may see our pain as a burden or look down on us for showing our weaknesses. But it is important to remember that those who truly care for us will never see vulnerability as a flaw. Instead, they will see it as an opportunity to support and uplift us. They will understand that by embracing vulnerability, we are not only healing ourselves but also creating an environment where others feel safe to do the same.

In our search for connection and understanding, we often believe that we need to present a picture-perfect image of strength and invincibility. We convince ourselves that vulnerability is synonymous with weakness and that only by concealing our pain can we maintain our dignity. But this belief is flawed.

True strength lies in the ability to open our hearts and share our burdens with others. It is in these moments of vulnerability that we can find solace, compassion, and genuine human connection. When we allow ourselves to be seen as we truly are, flawed and wounded, we invite others to do the same. We create a safe space for empathy to flourish and for healing to take place.

But how do we find the courage to be vulnerable? It starts with self-acceptance, with acknowledging that our pain does not define us but rather humanizes us. It is a reminder that we are all fragile beings navigating a complex world, and that our struggles should be met with kindness instead of judgment. From this place of self-compassion, we can reach out to the people who truly care for us, knowing that they are ready to listen, to hold us in their embrace, and to offer their unwavering support.

In this shared vulnerability, we also learn the power of empathy. By opening ourselves up to others, we not only receive their understanding, but we also gain the ability to truly empathize with their pain. We realize that we are not alone in our struggles and that our experiences, however unique, are often shared by others who are also yearning for connection. Together, we begin to dismantle the walls of isolation and build bridges of empathy and compassion.

So, let us embrace vulnerability as a gateway to strength. Let us unmask our fears and insecurities, knowing that it is through this unburdening that we find the courage to heal and grow. In reaching out to others, we discover that our collective pain can be transformed into collective resilience. And as we navigate the highs and lows of life, we will do so with a newfound understanding – that true strength lies not in standing alone, but in the connections we build, the bonds we form, and the vulnerability we share.

So, how can we encourage ourselves and others to embrace vulnerability during challenging times? It starts with creating open and non-judgmental spaces. Whether it is with trusted friends, family members, or support groups, we must find a safe place where we can be our authentic selves, free from the fear of rejection or shame.

Additionally, we must cultivate a mindset of compassion, both for ourselves and for others. This means acknowledging that vulnerability is a part of the human experience and that we all have the right to seek support and understanding. By extending empathy and kindness towards ourselves and others, we can foster a community of resilience and shared strength.

Of course, embracing vulnerability is not an easy task. It requires courage and a willingness to confront our deepest fears and insecurities. But I have come to realize that the rewards far outweigh the risks. By opening ourselves up to vulnerability, we open ourselves up to healing, growth, and the possibility of deeper connections with those around us.

As I continue on my own journey, I encourage you, dear reader, to embrace vulnerability wholeheartedly. Reach out, share your stories, and seek the support you need. Remember that you are not alone in your struggles, and that by being vulnerable, you create a ripple effect of healing and resilience for yourself and others. The holiday season may be filled with illusions of happiness, but true joy comes from the strength to be vulnerable and the courage to seek support in the face of adversity.

2

Rediscovering the Joy

Cultivating Gratitude

As I delve deeper into my exploration of the power of gratitude, I am uncovering the profound impact it can have on our lives. Countless studies have confirmed that gratitude not only enhances our well-being but also has the ability to transform our perspectives. With curiosity and a touch of skepticism, I embark on a journey towards cultivating gratitude.

With an open mind and a notebook in hand, I set out to uncover the moments of gratitude that may have eluded me in the past. I challenge myself to be fully present, observing the small things that fill my heart with warmth.

As I navigate through my daily routine, I begin to appreciate the subtle nuances that I once took for granted.

The Illusion of Happy Holidays

The morning sunlight spilling across the trees, painting them with vibrant colors. The melodic chirping of birds welcoming me as I step outside. The comforting aroma of freshly brewed coffee filling my kitchen, reminding me of the simple pleasure it brings.

I decide to expand my gratitude practice beyond mere observation. I yearn to actively express my gratitude and share it with others. Inspired by the concept of paying it forward, I start looking for opportunities to spread kindness and appreciation to those around me.

I begin by reaching out to my loved ones, expressing my gratitude for their presence in my life. I write heartfelt letters filled with appreciation and love, surprising them with unexpected words of gratitude. The joy that radiates from their faces as they read my words is immeasurable, reaffirming the transformative power of gratitude.

But my desire to share gratitude doesn't stop at my close circle of family and friends. I seek ways to extend kindness to strangers, to connect with humanity on a deeper level. I engage in small acts of generosity, such as leaving encouraging notes in public places or offering a helping hand to someone in need. These simple acts, seemingly insignificant, have the power to create ripples of gratitude throughout the world.

As I immerse myself in this practice, something remarkable begins to happen - my perspective shifts. The once ordinary and mundane aspects of life turn into extraordinary moments of heartfelt appreciation. I find beauty in the simplest of things – a stranger's smile, a passerby's act of kindness, a shared laugh with a colleague. Gratitude has opened my eyes to the abundance that surrounds me, even in the midst of challenges and uncertainties.

The more I practice gratitude, the more it becomes a natural way of being. It permeates every aspect of my life, from the way I interact with others to the way I approach my work. It becomes a guiding force, reminding me to focus on the positives, to find silver linings even in the darkest of clouds.

But perhaps the most profound realization is that gratitude is not just a personal practice; it is a catalyst for change in the world. As I witness the impact of my gratitude on others, I am inspired to create a ripple effect. I encourage others to embark on their own gratitude journeys, spreading the message of appreciation and joy.

In this world where negativity often seems to prevail, gratitude becomes a beacon of hope. It reminds us of the beauty that still exists, the kindness that can be found, and the potential for positive transformation. It is a reminder that amidst the chaos, there is always something to be grateful for.

And so, I continue on this journey of gratitude, forever

grateful for the opportunity to witness its profound power and eager to share its magic with the world. For, in the end, it is through embracing and expressing gratitude that we can truly create a life filled with joy, connection, and endless possibility.

With each newfound moment of gratitude, I feel a shift within me. The weight of cynicism and discontent begins to dissipate, making space for appreciation and contentment. I find solace in acknowledging the countless blessings that surround me, whether big or small.

No longer do I dwell on what I lack but instead revel in the abundance that already exists in my life. I am grateful for the roof over my head, the love and support of my friends and family, and the opportunities that have shaped me into the person I am today.

But my journey doesn't end at recognition alone. I am compelled to express my gratitude, to let those who have enriched my life know just how much they mean to me. I reach out to old friends, sending heartfelt messages of appreciation. I surprise my parents with small acts of kindness, expressing my gratitude for their unwavering support. I even write a letter to my younger self, acknowledging the strength and resilience that has carried me through tough times.

In cultivating gratitude, I discover that it has the power to not only transform my life but also touch the lives of those around me. People respond to the genuine warmth that radiates from within me, and in turn, they too begin to seek out moments of gratitude in their own lives.

Through this journey, I realize that gratitude is not just a passing emotion or a trendy concept. It is a deliberate practice, a conscious choice to focus on the blessings rather than the burdens. It is a tool that helps us weather the storms of life and find joy even amidst adversity.

As the holiday season approaches once again, I embrace it with a renewed sense of wonder and appreciation. The twinkling lights, the aroma of freshly baked cookies, the laughter shared with loved ones - everything takes on a new meaning infused with gratitude. And as I gather around the holiday table, surrounded by the warmth of family and friends, I offer a silent thanks, knowing that gratitude has forever altered the way I experience the world.

In the end, it is not the grand gestures or extravagant gifts that bring true joy during the holiday season, but rather the simple act of recognizing and appreciating the abundance that already exists in our lives. So, armed with a heart full of gratitude, I welcome the holiday season with open arms, knowing that it offers countless moments to cherish and be grateful for.

Embracing Imperfections

During the holiday season, we are bombarded with images and expectations of what a perfect celebration should look like. From glossy magazine covers to social media posts showcasing stunningly decorated homes and flawlessly presented meals, it's easy to feel inadequate in comparison. As someone who has lost loved ones and experienced heartbreak during this time of year, I understand how these societal pressures can amplify feelings of loneliness, sadness, and frustration.

However, through my own journey of healing and self-discovery, I have come to realize that embracing imperfections is the key to finding joy and contentment during the holidays. It's in the messiness, the unpredictability, and the flaws that the true magic lies.

Instead of striving for perfection, let us shift our focus towards creating meaningful moments and memories. Let us remember that the essence of the holiday season is not about the materialistic aspects or the picture-perfect image of a celebration. It is about the love, compassion, and connection that we share with those around us.

Let us cherish the small and simple moments, like gathering around a crackling fire, sharing stories and laughter with loved ones. Let us appreciate the beauty of homemade decorations, crafted with love and care, rather than comparing ourselves to the extravagant displays of others. Let us savor the taste of a home-cooked meal, even if it may not be "Instagram-worthy," because it is prepared with love and shared with those we hold dear.

During this time, let us extend our kindness and support to those who may be experiencing their own hardships or feelings of loneliness. We can reach out to friends, family, or even strangers and offer a comforting word or invitation to be a part of our celebrations.

Moreover, let us take the opportunity to reflect on the past year and appreciate the lessons it has taught us. The holiday season can be a time of growth and transformation if we allow ourselves to embrace the imperfections and vulnerabilities that come with it. It is through these experiences that we find our true strength, resilience, and capacity for empathy.

So, let us release the burden of comparison and unrealistic expectations this holiday season. Instead, let us focus on cultivating a sense of gratitude for the imperfect beauty that surrounds us. Let us open our hearts to the joy and contentment that can be found in the simple moments and in the genuine connections we forge with others.

In doing so, we can create a holiday season that is not only meaningful and fulfilling for ourselves but one that also inspires and uplifts those around us. For it is in embracing our imperfections that we can find the true magic of the holiday spirit and truly become the best version of ourselves.

Letting go of perfectionism can be a daunting task, especially when we have been conditioned to believe that anything short of perfection is a failure. But by embracing imperfections, we give ourselves permission to be authentic, vulnerable, and real. We create space for genuine connections, experiences, and memories that are far more precious than any picture-perfect moment.

One way to start embracing imperfections is by reframing our mindset. Instead of seeing imperfections as failures or shortcomings, we can choose to see them as opportunities for growth, learning, and resilience. When a dish doesn't turn out as planned or the decorations aren't as elaborate as we had envisioned, we can choose to laugh it off, learn from our mistakes, and adapt. By doing so, we give ourselves the gift of flexibility and the freedom to enjoy the process rather than obsessing over the outcome.

In this journey of embracing imperfections, it is crucial to remember that we are all beautifully flawed human beings. Each and every one of us has our own unique strengths and weaknesses, and it is these imperfections that make us who we are. Rather than striving for an unattainable standard of perfection, why not embrace the beauty of our differences and celebrate our individuality?

In a world that constantly bombards us with images of flawlessness and unattainable ideals, it can be easy to lose sight of our own worth. But by letting go of perfectionism, we open ourselves up to a world of self-acceptance and self-love. We begin to see that our value does not lie in our ability to be flawless, but in our ability to show up authentically and to be kind and compassionate to ourselves and others.

Embracing imperfections also allows us to live more fully in the present moment. Instead of being preoccupied with how things should be or how they could be better, we can fully immerse ourselves in the beauty and joy of what is. We can savor the small, imperfect moments that make life so precious – a warm hug, a heartfelt conversation, or a genuine laugh shared with loved ones.

As we let go of perfectionism and embrace imperfections, we become more resilient in the face of challenges. We understand that setbacks and failures are not indicators of our worth or abilities, but rather opportunities for growth and self-improvement. We learn to pick ourselves up, dust ourselves off, and keep moving forward – knowing that it is through our imperfections that we continue to learn, evolve, and become the best versions of ourselves.

So, let us release the chains of perfectionism that bind us, and instead, embrace our imperfections as stepping stones on the path to self-discovery and personal fulfillment. Let us give ourselves permission to be imperfectly perfect, shining brightly with all our unique quirks, flaws, and strengths. In doing so, we not only set ourselves free but also inspire others to do the same. And in this beautiful dance of imperfections, we find the true essence of what it means to live a rich and meaningful life.

Another way to embrace imperfections is by focusing on what truly matters: the people we love. Instead of putting all of our energy into creating a flawless holiday experience, we can prioritize spending quality time with our friends and family. It's in the imperfect conversations, the shared laughter, and the genuine connection that the true holiday spirit flourishes. As I've learned the hard way, it's not the grand gestures or the perfectly wrapped presents that matter, but the love and presence we bring to those we hold dear.

Furthermore, embracing imperfections during the holiday season means letting go of unrealistic expectations. It's about acknowledging that life doesn't always go according to plan and that some things are beyond our control. It's about accepting that not every tradition or gathering will be picture-perfect, and that's perfectly okay. By releasing ourselves from the burden of unrealistic expectations, we open ourselves up to unexpected joys and serendipitous moments that can only arise when we let go of the need for perfection.

So this holiday season, I encourage you to embrace imperfections, for they are the beautiful cracks through which the light of true happiness shines. Let go of the pressure to create the perfect holiday and instead focus on creating meaningful connections, treasured memories, and a sense of warmth and love. Embrace the messiness, the flaws, and the unexpected surprises that make life truly worth living. In doing so, you'll discover that the illusion of happy holidays is shattered, giving way to a genuine and heartfelt celebration of life's imperfections.

Creating Meaningful Traditions

Amidst the sorrow, I have come to realize that there is a way to reclaim the holiday spirit—a way to find solace and meaning in the midst of pain. It begins with creating meaningful traditions.

Traditions, I've come to understand, are not simply arbitrary actions. They are vessels for love, memory, and connection. They have the power to unite, to heal, and to bring joy. And perhaps most importantly, they can be uniquely tailored to align with our values and desires, allowing us to experience the holiday season in a way that resonates deeply with our souls.

In my quest to reclaim the holiday spirit, I delved into the depths of my heart, seeking the treasures of love and memories from seasons past. I realized that these treasures were not lost, but merely waiting to be rediscovered, waiting to be ignited by the flame of new traditions.

With determination and a renewed sense of purpose, I set out to create meaningful traditions that would make my heart soar and bring solace to the sorrows that weighed upon me. I wanted to cultivate an atmosphere of love, warmth, and connection, where the true essence of the holidays could flourish.

I began by gathering my loved ones, sharing stories of holidays gone by, and listening to the murmurs of their hearts. It was through these conversations that I discovered the common threads that united us—a shared love for nature, for art, for giving back to the community. With these insights, I sowed the seeds of new traditions.

In the spirit of nature, we decided to embark on a yearly hike through the wintery woods. As we wandered amidst the snow-covered trees, we allowed ourselves to be captivated by the quiet beauty of nature. With each step, we felt the weight of our sorrows lifting, replaced instead by a sense of awe and gratitude for the world around us.

To embark on this journey of reclaiming and reshaping our holidays, we must first look within ourselves and reflect on the stories of our lives. In doing so, we can discover the passions and values that shape who we are, and from there, create meaningful traditions that align with our true essence.

One such tradition that holds a special place in my heart is the tradition of handcrafting personalized ornaments. Each year, my loved ones and I would gather together, armed with paintbrushes, glitters, and laughter. As we carefully brushed vibrant strokes onto the ceramic canvas, we poured our hearts into each stroke, embedding our souls into those tiny masterpieces. These ornaments, adorned with our personal expressions, would grace our trees and serve as a reminder of the love and connection that binds us together.

But our traditions did not stop there. Inspired by the compassion that often gets lost in the hustle and bustle of the holiday season, we launched a new tradition of giving back to our community. Volunteering at local shelters and charities became a way for us to spread love and warmth to those in need. Whether it was serving meals, donating gifts, or simply lending a listening ear, we dedicated our time and energy to make a difference in the lives of others.

Through these acts of kindness, our traditions became vessels for love and joy, not only for ourselves but also for those around us. The holiday spirit, once lost in the depths of our grief, was now resplendent in our hearts and radiating outwards into the world.

As the years went by, our traditions grew and evolved, enriched by the experiences and lessons life bestowed upon us. Each tradition became a testament to the resilience of our spirits and a reminder that love and connection could triumph even in the face of sorrow.

So, my dear reader, as you embark on your own journey of reclaiming and reshaping your holidays, remember to look within yourself. Tap into the stories of your life, embrace your passions and values, and let them guide you in creating meaningful traditions. Whether it's handcrafting ornaments, volunteering in your community, or discovering new ways to spread love and joy, let your traditions be a reflection of your true essence.

The holiday season is an opportunity for us to reclaim the true spirit of joy and connection. By embracing our passions, values, and creating meaningful traditions, we can shape a holiday season that resonates deeply with our souls and spreads love to those around us. So let us embark on this journey together, and may our holiday traditions be a testament to the beauty and resilience of the human spirit.

First and foremost, it is important to acknowledge our grief and the pain we carry. We cannot expect to simply brush aside the memories or replace the loved ones we have lost. Instead, we must embrace their presence in our lives, even if they are no longer physically here. We can create traditions that honor their memory—a special ornament on the tree, a candle lit in their honor, or a heartfelt toast shared in their name.

But finding meaning in the holiday season extends beyond remembrance. It is about embracing the present and savoring the simple joys that life has to offer. It is about engaging in acts of kindness and generosity, spreading love and warmth to those around us. Whether it's volunteering at a local shelter, organizing a toy drive for underprivileged children, or simply reaching out to a lonely neighbor, these actions have the power to transform our experience of the holidays.

Furthermore, let us not forget the importance of self-care during this busy season. In the midst of our efforts to bring joy to others, we must also remember to nurture ourselves. Taking the time to rest, recharge, and indulge in activities that bring us joy will not only benefit our own well-being but will also allow us to show up fully for those we care about.

Moreover, let us not be swayed by the commercialization of the holiday season. While gift-giving can be a beautiful gesture, it is important to remember that true joy and connection do not lie in the material possessions we exchange. Instead, let us focus on the intangible gifts we can offer—our time, our presence, and our love. These are the true treasures that leave lasting impressions on the hearts of others.

In addition, let us open our hearts and minds to new traditions and experiences. As the world evolves, so too should our holiday celebrations. Let us embrace cultural diversity and learn from one another's traditions. Whether it be trying new recipes, learning a traditional dance, or participating in a cultural ceremony, these moments of exchange have the power to broaden our understanding and foster deeper connections with those around us.

Finally, let us remember that the holiday season is not about perfection. It is about embracing imperfections, embracing the messy and unpredictable moments that make life beautiful. This is a time to let go of expectations and surrender to the magic of the present moment. By doing so, we allow space for joy, laughter, and genuine connections to blossom.

In conclusion, the holiday season is an invitation to reclaim the true spirit of joy and connection. It is a time to honor our past, embrace the present, and create meaningful traditions that are authentic to our souls. It is a time to prioritize self-care, show acts of kindness and generosity, and explore new traditions that enrich our lives. So let us embark on this journey together, cherishing the beauty and resilience of the human spirit, and may our holiday traditions be a beacon of light and love in the world.

Additionally, let us not forget the importance of self-care during this time of year. Take a moment to step back from the hustle and bustle, and carve out time for ourselves. Engage in activities that bring us joy and rejuvenation—whether it's reading a book by a crackling fire, taking a long walk in the snow-covered park, or indulging in our favorite holiday treats. By prioritizing self-care, we are better equipped to spread happiness to others.

Finally, let us remember that traditions are not static, nor should they be. They can evolve and change as we grow and find new inspirations. Don't be afraid to experiment and explore, to discover new traditions that align with who you are and what brings you joy. It could be as simple as trying a new recipe each year, incorporating a cultural tradition from your heritage, or even creating a unique ritual with your loved ones.

In conclusion, my journey of rediscovering the holiday spirit has taught me that creating meaningful traditions is a powerful antidote to the sense of loss and emptiness I feel. It allows me to hold onto the essence of what makes the holiday season special, even in the face of adversity. I encourage each and every one of you to embark on this journey of self-discovery, to embrace your values and desires, and to create traditions that bring you joy and connect you with the true spirit of the holidays. By doing so, we can shape a holiday season that is uniquely our own, filled with love, meaning, and happiness.

Practicing Self-Care

For years, I ignored my own needs and pushed aside any notion of self-care. It seemed selfish to prioritize my mental and emotional well-being when so many others were suffering. But as I spiraled deeper into darkness, I realized that I couldn't be there for anyone else if I wasn't taking care of myself first.

Research supports the idea that self-care plays a crucial role in maintaining good mental health. Studies have shown that self-care practices such as engaging in regular exercise, practicing mindfulness, seeking therapy, and maintaining healthy relationships can significantly reduce stress levels and improve overall well-being. So, armed with this knowledge and a newfound determination, I decided to prioritize my mental and emotional well-being during the holiday season.

One practical strategy I employed was setting boundaries. I used to say yes to every holiday invitation, feeling obligated to attend every gathering and put on a happy face. But I soon realized that this only exacerbated my pain. So, I made the conscious decision to give myself permission to say no. I carefully evaluated which social events would genuinely bring me joy and opted for a few intimate gatherings with close friends and family members instead. This enabled me to focus on quality interactions rather than spreading myself too thin and feeling drained.

In addition to setting boundaries, I also embraced the power of self-reflection. I took the time to honestly assess my emotions and needs, allowing myself to feel and process the pain that had accumulated within me. Instead of brushing it aside or burying it deep within, I confronted it head-on. I journaled, meditated, and sought therapy to help me navigate through my darkest thoughts and emotions.

During the holiday season, I made a conscious effort to incorporate self-care practices into my daily routine. I carved out moments for solitude, where I could recharge and nourish my soul. I savored long walks in nature, embracing the serenity it offered and finding solace in its beauty. I indulged in soothing bubble baths, allowing the warm water to wash away the stress, tension, and sadness that had consumed me for far too long.

Moreover, I embraced the power of self-compassion. Instead of being my harshest critic, I learned to be gentle with myself, understanding that healing takes time. I offered myself love and forgiveness, knowing that I deserved it just as much as anyone else. I practiced positive affirmations, reminding myself of my strengths and abilities, and cultivating a mindset of self-empowerment.

By prioritizing my mental and emotional well-being, I soon discovered a transformation occurring within me. The darkness that once clouded my heart began to dissipate, making way for a renewed sense of hope and resilience. The love and care I bestowed upon myself radiated outward, positively affecting my relationships with others.

Not only did I become more present and engaged during the holiday season, but I also became an inspiration to those around me. People began to notice the change in my demeanor, the light that now shone from within. They sought my advice, eager to learn how to incorporate self-care into their own lives.

And so, I shared my journey, encouraging others to prioritize their mental and emotional well-being. I emphasized how self-care is not selfish, but rather a necessary act of self-love and self-preservation. I urged them to set boundaries, embrace self-reflection, and practice self-compassion. Together, we embarked on a collective journey of healing and growth, transforming the holiday season into a time of healing and renewal for all.

As the years went by, my commitment to self-care only deepened. I continued to prioritize my mental and emotional well-being, recognizing that it was a lifelong journey rather than a temporary resolution. And in doing so, I discovered that the world's best writer was not one who crafted beautiful prose or captivating narratives, but the one who dared to speak honestly about the importance of self-care, empowering others to embrace their own well-being, and ultimately, finding peace and fulfillment within themselves.

Another important aspect of self-care that I incorporated into my holiday routine was the practice of mindfulness. Through mindfulness meditation and introspection, I was able to acknowledge and accept the pain that resurfaced during the holiday season. Instead of dwelling on negative emotions, I embraced them as a natural part of my healing process. I learned to let go of the guilt associated with grieving and allowed myself to feel whatever emotions arose. This practice allowed me to release some of the pent-up emotions and provided a sense of peace and acceptance during a time that was often fraught with sadness.

Additionally, seeking therapy was a significant step in my self-care journey. Through regular sessions with a compassionate and understanding therapist, I was able to delve deeper into my feelings and process my grief in a healthy and productive way. Therapy provided me with the tools and strategies to cope with the holiday season and taught me the importance of self-compassion and forgiveness.

Moreover, I found solace in nurturing healthy relationships during the holiday season. Surrounding myself with compassionate and understanding individuals helped me create a support system that encouraged self-care and made me feel valued and loved. Whether it was spending quality time with a close friend, sharing laughter and tears, or engaging in meaningful conversations with family members, these connections helped to alleviate the loneliness that often accompanied the holiday season.

In conclusion, practicing self-care during the holiday season has been a transformative experience for me. By setting boundaries, embracing mindfulness, seeking therapy, and nurturing healthy relationships, I have been able to prioritize my mental and emotional well-being. This self-care journey has taught me that healing is a continuous process and that it is not selfish to put myself first. By taking care of myself, I can better support and be there for others, thus creating a happier and more meaningful holiday season for everyone involved.

Finding Connection

The holiday season has always been a time for togetherness and connection. It is a time when we gather with loved ones, creating cherished memories and strengthening bonds that withstand the test of time. However, for those who have experienced loss or separation, the holidays can be a painful reminder of what once was. As someone who has lost friends and family in dire circumstances, I too have grappled with a compromised view of the holiday season. But amidst the sorrow, I have come to realize that there are ways to foster meaningful connections with loved ones, even in the face of distance or loss. It is through these connections that we can create a sense of belonging and find solace during the holidays.

Exploring ways to foster meaningful connections with loved ones, even in the face of distance or loss, and creating a sense of belonging during the holidays requires a shift in perspective. It necessitates acknowledging the pain of the past and embracing the present moment with open arms. For me, this process began by revisiting cherished memories that evoked feelings of joy and love. I sought solace in recounting the laughter shared, the heartfelt conversations, and the moments of pure bliss I once experienced with my loved ones during the holiday season.

With these memories in my heart, I began to reach out to those who remained in my life. It became important to gather together, not simply out of obligation, but to genuinely connect and create new memories. It was no longer about trying to fill the void left by those I had lost, but rather about cherishing the connections I still had the privilege of nurturing. Whether it was a phone call to a distant friend or organizing a small gathering with close family members, I opened myself up to the possibilities of new connections and rediscovered the joy that can be found in the company of loved ones.

As the holiday season approached, I also delved into new traditions and activities that would help bring us closer together. I realized that connection wasn't solely dependent on physical presence, but could be fostered through shared experiences, no matter the distance. Through technology, I organized virtual gatherings, where we celebrated, laughed, and shared stories, even though we were miles apart. We cooked together, exchanged recipes, and had virtual game nights filled with laughter and friendly competition. These moments not only brought us closer, but also filled our hearts with gratitude for the bonds we still had.

In addition to nurturing connections with those who remained in my life, I also made a conscious effort to honor and remember those who were no longer with us. I created a quiet space in my home, adorned with photographs and mementos, where I could reflect on their love and presence.

In this sacred space, I embraced both the sadness and the joy that their memory brought, finding solace in the knowledge that they live on in my heart, guiding me through each passing holiday season.

And as I embraced this shift in perspective, I realized that the holiday season was not solely about the joyous moments. It was also an opportunity for reflection, growth, and healing. It was a time to extend compassion to ourselves and others, recognizing that grief and loss do not disappear with the advent of the holidays. By acknowledging and validating our own pain, we can be more understanding and supportive of those around us who may be experiencing similar challenges.

In the face of distance or loss, the holiday season can be a bittersweet reminder of the past. But through a conscious effort to foster meaningful connections, both old and new, and by embracing the present moment with open arms, we can find solace, joy, and a renewed sense of belonging. As I looked around me, surrounded by the laughter and love of my loved ones, my heart swelled with gratitude, knowing that I had succeeded in forging a new path, one that honored the past while embracing the potential for happiness in the present. And in doing so, I had discovered the true essence of the holiday season - the power of connection and the strength of the human spirit to find solace, even in the midst of sorrow.

In addition to reaching out to those close by, I also sought ways to bridge the gap with those who were physically distant or no longer with us. It became apparent that physical proximity was not the sole barrier to connection. Technology, for instance, became a medium through which I could stay connected with friends and family across the miles. Through video calls and shared virtual experiences, we were able to recreate a sense of togetherness despite being separated by vast distances. These interactions served as a reminder that even though we may not be physically present with one another, the bonds of love and connection can transcend the limitations of space.

Furthermore, I discovered the power of honoring the memory of those who are no longer with us during the holiday season. Whether it was lighting a candle in remembrance or dedicating a special act of kindness in their honor, I found solace in the knowledge that their presence would forever be intertwined with the holiday spirit. By acknowledging their absence and celebrating their impact on our lives, we could find comfort in the knowledge that their spirit was still alive within us.

As the holiday season approached, I embarked on a new tradition that would forever change the way I experienced this time of year. Inspired by the idea of giving back and spreading love, I decided to organize a holiday gathering for those who had lost loved ones. I reached out to local support groups and organizations, inviting anyone who felt the weight of grief during this time to come together in a safe and supportive environment.

The response was overwhelming, with individuals from all walks of life eagerly embracing the opportunity to connect with others who understood their pain. The event was held in a cozy venue, filled with warm lights, comforting scents, and the gentle strumming of an acoustic guitar. We shared stories, tears, and laughter, finding solace in the company of those who had experienced similar losses.

Throughout the evening, we engaged in acts of remembrance, lighting candles and creating a beautiful memorial wall adorned with photos and heartfelt messages. It was a time to honor our loved ones' legacies, to share cherished memories, and to sprinkle a little bit of their spirit into the festivities.

But it was not just about grief and sadness. We also celebrated the resilience and strength that had brought us all together. Through group activities and discussions, we embraced the present moment and found joy in the connections we were making. We formed friendships that would extend beyond the holiday season, providing ongoing support and understanding as we navigated this journey of healing together.

As the night came to a close, I looked around at the faces of those who had joined me in this endeavor. I was struck by the beauty of the human spirit, the ability to transform grief into compassion, and the power of unity in the face of loss. These connections, forged through shared experiences and open hearts, reminded me that we are never truly alone, even in our darkest moments.

From that year onward, our holiday gathering became a cherished tradition - a reminder that the holiday season is not just about tinsel and presents, but about nurturing our souls, finding strength through connection, and honoring the memories of those no longer with us. As I continued my journey as a writer, I dedicated myself to sharing this valuable lesson with the world, spreading the message of love, compassion, and the power of connection during the holiday season and beyond.

Ultimately, finding connection during the holiday season is about embracing the present moment, cherishing the relationships we still have, and finding ways to bridge the gaps that separation may present. It is a continuous journey of healing and growth, but one that can bring immense joy and a renewed sense of belonging. As I navigated this path, I began to understand that the illusion of happy holidays does not lie in pretending that everything is as it once was, but rather in finding connection amidst the changes and losses life brings. It is through these connections that we can find solace and create a sense of belonging, even in the face of adversity.

Practicing Mindfulness

As I delved deeper into my journey of healing and self-discovery, I stumbled upon a powerful tool that would transform my perception of the holiday season - mindfulness. It was a concept that intrigued me, promising to help me stay present, reduce stress, and find moments of peace and joy throughout the chaotic holiday season.

The idea of mindfulness seemed paradoxical, yet undeniably appealing. How could something as simple as being fully present in the moment make such a profound difference in my life? I had my doubts, but I was willing to give it a try.

To understand mindfulness, I immersed myself in research and sought guidance from experts in the field. Countless studies emphasized that practicing mindfulness could positively impact mental and emotional well-being. I learned that mindfulness was the art of paying attention, on purpose, without judgment, to the present moment.

It sounded deceptively simple, but as I incorporated mindfulness into my daily routine, I began to experience its transformative power firsthand. Instead of rushing through each day as if on autopilot, I made a conscious effort to slow down and savor each moment. I noticed the warmth of sunlight streaming through the window, the aroma of freshly brewed coffee, and the gentle touch of a loved one's hand.

With mindfulness, the holiday season became an opportunity to fully immerse myself in the joy and magic that often goes unnoticed amidst the frenzy of shopping and parties. I noticed the sparkle in children's eyes as they opened their presents, the genuine laughter shared around the dinner table, and the sense of togetherness that permeated every gathering. No longer burdened by expectations or overwhelmed by societal pressures, I found myself truly present, relishing in the beauty of each moment.

Mindfulness also helped me navigate the inevitable stress that the holiday season brings. Instead of succumbing to the pressures of perfection or becoming entangled in the web of endless responsibilities, I learned to observe my thoughts and emotions without judgment. I acknowledged the stress and allowed it to pass through me, rather than allowing it to consume me. With each breath, I released tension and embraced a sense of calm that became my anchor amidst the chaos.

Incorporating mindfulness into my holiday traditions also fostered a sense of gratitude within me. I learned to appreciate the smallest of gestures—a heartfelt thank you, a warm hug, or a simple act of kindness. By shifting my focus from materialistic desires to the blessings that surrounded me, I discovered a newfound sense of contentment and joy that transcended any material possession.

As the holiday season drew to a close, I reflected on how mindfulness had transformed my perception and experience. It was no longer just about the gifts and the festivities; it was about the deeper connection and presence that I brought to each moment. Mindfulness had turned the holiday season into a time of profound self-discovery and growth.

Now, I share this newfound wisdom with others, encouraging them to embrace mindfulness and the power it holds. I have come to believe that true joy and peace during the holidays—and in life as a whole—lie in our ability to fully engage with the present moment, to let go of worries and expectations, and to open ourselves up to the beauty and magic of each passing second.

This holiday season, may we all choose to embrace mindfulness and create moments that will stay with us long after the decorations are packed away, for it is in these moments that we find the true essence of the holidays and the sheer magic that lies within each of us.

Armed with this newfound knowledge, I embarked on a mission to introduce mindfulness practices into my life during the holiday season. I realized that it was not about erasing the pain and loss I had experienced but rather creating a space to acknowledge and accept those difficult emotions while finding moments of peace and joy amidst the chaos.

One of the most effective mindfulness practices I discovered was meditation. Every morning, before the hustle and bustle of the day took over, I would find a quiet corner, close my eyes, and focus on my breath. Inhaling slowly, I would feel the air fill my lungs, and then exhale, releasing any tension and worries. With each breath, I cultivated a sense of calm and presence, grounding myself in the here and now.

As I embraced the stillness within, I found that the magic of the holiday season began to unfold before me in a way I had never experienced before. The twinkling lights on the Christmas tree seemed to dance with an extra sparkle, and the aroma of freshly baked cookies wafted through the air, filling the room with warmth and comfort.

But it wasn't just the external elements that captured my attention. It was the way in which I approached each moment with intention and gratitude. As I savored every sip of hot cocoa, I marveled at the simple pleasure it brought me. The sound of laughter and the joyous chatter of loved ones gathered around the dinner table became melodies that resonated in my heart.

Mindfulness reminded me to slow down and truly connect. I found myself truly listening to the stories shared by family members, holding their words with reverence and giving them the attention they deserved. I extended this practice beyond my immediate circle, reaching out to those less fortunate, offering a helping hand and a listening ear to those who needed it most. The outpouring of love and gratitude that ensued was a testament to the power of mindfulness in cultivating compassion and empathy.

But perhaps the most profound impact of mindfulness during the holiday season was the way it transformed my relationship with myself. In the past, I would often get caught up in perfectionism and comparison, striving to meet unrealistic expectations of what the holiday season should be. However, by letting go of these self-imposed pressures and embracing mindfulness, I learned to accept myself as I am, with all my flaws and imperfections. I realized that true joy comes not from a perfectly decorated home or lavish gifts, but from the authenticity and love we bring to each interaction and experience.

As the holiday season came to a close and the decorations were carefully packed away, I couldn't help but feel a sense of deep fulfillment and contentment. Mindfulness had allowed me to create moments that had left an indelible mark on my heart, long after the last jingle had faded away. It had taught me that the true spirit of the holidays lies not in the material extravagance but in the presence and connection we bring to each encounter.

And so, armed with the wisdom and joy that mindfulness

had brought me, I vowed to carry its essence throughout the rest of the year. I recognized that the magic of the holiday season was not limited to a few fleeting weeks but could be cultivated and nurtured in every moment, if only we took the time to be fully present. With each passing day, I strived to embrace mindfulness as a way of life, cherishing every breath, every interaction, and every opportunity to create moments of love, kindness, and sheer magic.

Another practice that helped me stay attuned to the present moment was mindful eating. Instead of mindlessly devouring my meals during holiday festivities, I savored every bite, taking the time to truly appreciate the flavors, textures, and aromas. I allowed myself to indulge in the culinary delights of the season and found that by being fully present, the experience became richer and more satisfying.

Gratitude became an integral part of my mindfulness practice. Every evening, before retiring to bed, I made a conscious effort to reflect on the day and find something, no matter how small, to be grateful for. It could be the warmth of a smile from a stranger or the calming power of a hot cup of tea. By recognizing and appreciating these moments of joy, I shifted my perspective and found solace in the midst of my grief.

Incorporating mindfulness into my life during the holiday season was not a quick fix or a magic solution, but rather a journey that required dedication and practice. There were times when old habits and negative thoughts threatened to consume me, but I reminded myself of the power of the present moment. With each mindful breath, I reclaimed my strength and found the courage to face the challenges of the season.

Practicing mindfulness transcended the realm of self-care and had a ripple effect on those around me. By bringing awareness and intention to my interactions with loved ones, I fostered deeper connections and created moments of genuine joy during the holidays. I realized that the illusion of happy holidays was not about pretending everything was perfect but rather finding beauty and meaning in the imperfections.

In this chaotic and materialistic world, mindfulness provided a sanctuary where I could embrace the true essence of the holiday season. It allowed me to let go of expectations and accept the present moment with grace and gratitude. With each mindful breath, I became more attuned to the magic of the season, cherishing the small moments that truly mattered.

As my understanding of mindfulness deepened, I felt a sense of hope and renewal wash over me. The holiday season no longer felt like a daunting and melancholic ordeal but an opportunity for growth and healing. Through the practice of mindfulness, I discovered that happiness was not an elusive destination but a state of being, found within the depths of my own soul.

In the next chapter, I will explore the art of self-compassion and how it can help to navigate the complexities of the holiday season with kindness and understanding, not only towards others but also towards ourselves.

Spreading Kindness

In the midst of my own personal darkness, I had come to realize that spreading kindness was not just a cliché sentiment, but a powerful and transformative act. It was a remedy for the pain and emptiness that threatened to consume me during this supposedly joyous time of year. And so, I made it my mission to inspire others to engage in acts of kindness and generosity, to spread joy to others and experience the ripple effect of positivity during the holidays.

Though my past experiences had tainted my view of the holiday season, I refused to let bitterness take root within me. I had lost friends and family in dire circumstances, circumstances that had cast a shadow on the once bright and cheery traditions. But dwelling on the sadness only perpetuated my own suffering; it did nothing to honor the memories of those I had lost nor did it bring them back. Instead, I now viewed the holiday season as an opportunity to channel their spirits, to carry on their legacy by exemplifying the kindness and love they had shown to others.

I poured over research after research, studying the impact of kindness on individuals and communities. One study revealed that acts of kindness not only enhanced the well-being of the receiver but also increased the psychological well-being of the giver. Another showed that even witnessing acts of kindness led to increased feelings of happiness and a greater sense of interconnectedness. The evidence was clear: spreading kindness was not only beneficial to others, but it had the power to heal and uplift ourselves as well.

Armed with this newfound knowledge, I set out to inspire readers to join me on this journey of spreading kindness. I shared stories of individuals who had gone out of their way to make a difference in the lives of others during the holiday season. I highlighted the ripple effect that their actions had created, how a single act of kindness had the power to inspire others and create a wave of positivity. Through these stories, I aimed to ignite a spark within each reader, prompting them to ask themselves, "What can I do to spread kindness? How can I make a difference, no matter how small?"

The response was overwhelming. Emails flooded my in-box with tales of how readers had been inspired to engage in acts of kindness and extend a helping hand to those in need. People from all walks of life shared their stories, from anonymous donors paying off layaway bills for struggling families to volunteers spending their holidays serving meals at homeless shelters. The power of kindness was contagious, and I reveled in the joy of witnessing the impact that it had on both individuals and communities.

But it didn't stop there. As the holiday season drew near, I decided to organize a community event called "Spread the Joy" in partnership with local organizations and businesses.

It was a festive gathering where people could come together to share goodwill, support local causes, and partake in acts of kindness. The event featured a variety of activities, from gift drives for underprivileged children to workshops on how to make handmade cards for seniors in nursing homes.

The response from the community was overwhelming. People poured in, bringing not only donations but also their time and talents to make a difference. Artists set up stations to offer free portraits, musicians entertained the crowd with live performances, and local businesses donated their goods and services to support various causes. The event became a hub of compassion and generosity, a place where the true spirit of the holidays shone brightly.

As the years went by, "Spread the Joy" grew into a movement that extended far beyond the holiday season. It became a year-round endeavor, a reminder that kindness knows no bounds and can be practiced every day. The ripple effect we had started during the holidays continued to spread, touching the lives of countless individuals and inspiring them to pay it forward.

Through my writing and the power of storytelling, I had achieved what I set out to do: I had transformed the holiday season into a time of hope, love, and kindness. I had shown the world that even in the darkest of times, the light of compassion can guide us towards a better future. With each act of kindness, I witnessed the power of humanity and the potential for change. And in doing so, I found solace for my own personal darkness and a renewed purpose that illuminated my path.

So I continued to write, to share stories of kindness, and to inspire others to join in spreading joy throughout their own communities. Together, we created a world where kindness became the norm, where people saw the potential for good in every situation, and where love and compassion triumphed over darkness. As the world's best writer, I reveled in the knowledge that my words had transformed lives and made the world a better place, one act of kindness at a time.

But I knew that inspiring others was only the first step. Kindness had to be more than just a fleeting sentiment during the holiday season; it had to become woven into the fabric of our lives. And so, I provided practical suggestions for readers to take action. I encouraged them to perform random acts of kindness, both big and small, to those they knew and even to strangers. I emphasized the importance of genuine acts of kindness, ones that stemmed from a place of sincerity and not simply a desire to check off a to-do list.

I understood that spreading kindness went beyond one-time gestures. It required an attitude of compassion and empathy that extended beyond the boundaries of the holiday season. It meant being mindful of the struggles that others may be facing and offering a helping hand whenever possible. It meant taking the time to listen, to truly listen, to someone who needed a listening ear. It meant being present, showing up for others in both good times and bad.

I shared personal stories of how kindness had transformed my own life, and I encouraged readers to reflect on their own experiences of how acts of kindness had affected them. I reminded them that kindness was a powerful force that had the ability to heal, bridge divides, and bring joy to both the giver and receiver.

But I also acknowledged that kindness was not always easy. It required us to step out of our comfort zones and sometimes face our own biases and prejudices. It meant being willing to challenge our own assumptions and learn from others whose experiences and perspectives may differ from our own. I urged readers to embrace this discomfort as an opportunity for growth and to see it as part of the journey towards becoming better, kinder individuals.

In addition to individual acts of kindness, I highlighted the importance of creating a kinder society as a whole. This meant advocating for policies and actions that promoted equality, justice, and compassion. It meant standing up against injustice and discrimination, even when it was uncomfortable or unpopular. I encouraged readers to use their voices and their actions to make a positive impact in their communities and beyond.

I concluded the article by reminding readers that kindness

was not something that could be measured or quantified, but its effects were far-reaching and everlasting. It had the power to create a ripple effect of goodness that could extend far beyond our own immediate circle of influence. I urged them to continue spreading kindness, not just during the holiday season, but every single day of their lives.

As the world's best writer, it is my hope that this article would inspire readers to embrace kindness as a way of life. To recognize the immense power of their actions and the potential to make a difference in the lives of others. And ultimately, to create a world where kindness is the norm, rather than the exception.

As I wrote about spreading kindness, I felt a glimmer of hope seep into my own heart. Perhaps, in inspiring others, I was also healing myself. Each act of kindness I performed, each moment of joy I facilitated for another, brought me one step closer to accepting the past and embracing the present with open arms. And so, I embarked on this journey with an unwavering determination, knowing that in spreading kindness, I could turn the illusion of happy holidays into a tangible reality for myself and those around me.

3

Navigating Loss and Grief

Honoring Memories

But as the years have passed, I've come to realize that the pain doesn't have to overshadow the joy entirely. There is a way to honor and remember our loved ones who are no longer with us during the holiday season, creating meaningful tributes that keep their memories alive.

One way I've found solace is through creating a special memorial space in my home. I set up a small table with photographs, keepsakes, and mementos of those I've lost. It becomes a sacred space, a place where I can go to reminisce and feel their presence. Each item holds a story, a cherished memory that I can revisit whenever I need to.

There is something therapeutic about seeing their smiling faces captured in those photographs. It's as if time stands still, and for a few precious moments, they are here with me again. Every glance at those images sparks an overwhelming rush of emotions - love, longing, and gratitude. It reminds me of the impact they had on my life and the legacy they left behind.

But the memorial space is not just about photographs; it's about keeping their essence alive. I adorn the table with items that speak to their passions and interests. A book for the avid reader, a painting for the artist, or a baseball for the sports enthusiast. These objects serve as a reminder of the things they loved and bring forth a flood of memories associated with those shared moments.

In this sacred space, I also leave room for written tributes. I jot down heartfelt messages, letters, and even poetry. It's a way for me to express the words left unsaid and the emotions that sometimes get lost in the depths of grief. Writing becomes a cathartic release, a means to find solace and healing.

But the memorial space is only the beginning of keeping their spirits alive during the holiday season. For me, it's essential to find ways to incorporate their memory into traditional celebrations. I hang a special ornament on the Christmas tree for each loved one, each one carefully chosen to reflect their personality. With each decoration placed on a branch, a small prayer is whispered, a tear is shed, and laughter is shared as stories of cherished memories come flooding back.

I've also started a new tradition of preparing their favorite dishes and recipes during holiday meals. As the aroma of their beloved dishes fills the air, it's as if they are right beside me in the kitchen, guiding my hands and offering encouragement. It's a beautiful way to honor their memory and to keep their presence alive through the shared experience of food and family.

As I connect with others who have experienced similar loss, we find strength and support in one another. We create a community where we can share our stories, our pain, and our memories, knowing that we are understood and not alone in our grief. Together, we keep the memories of our loved ones alive, ensuring that their impact on our lives is never forgotten.

Through the years, I have learned that honoring our loved ones during the holiday season is a deeply personal and individual process. Each tribute is unique, tailored to the memories and essence of the person we have lost. It is about finding what brings us comfort and peace, what allows us to embrace both the joy and sorrow that coexist during this season.

While the pain of their absence will always be present, we can find solace in these tributes. They bring a sense of connection, a bridge between the past and the present. In these moments, we can feel their presence and carry their memory with us, even as we navigate the complexities of this time of year.

And so, as the holiday lights twinkle and the scent of homemade favorites fills the air, we find ourselves surrounded by the love and memories of those we hold dear. In the songs we sing, the stories we share, and the traditions we uphold, their spirits live on. They continue to shape our lives and remind us that they are forever in our hearts.

In the end, it is through these tributes that we find a delicate balance. We honor our grief while celebrating the joy that still exists. We embrace the bittersweet nature of the holiday season, knowing that our loved ones' memories endure. It is in this embrace that we find solace, strength, and the ability to make happy holidays a reality, even as we navigate the depths of our grief.

And of course, there are the more traditional ways of honoring our loved ones. Lighting candles in their memory, placing wreaths on their graves, or making a charitable donation in their name. These acts of remembrance not only show our love and respect, but they also serve as a reminder to ourselves and others that these individuals, though gone, are never forgotten.

Creating meaningful tributes to honor our loved ones

who are no longer with us is a deeply personal and individual process. What works for one person may not resonate with another. It's about finding what brings comfort and solace, what helps to bridge the gap between the past and the present.

Though the pain of loss never truly disappears, finding ways to honor our loved ones during the holiday season brings a small glimmer of peace. In these moments, we can feel their presence, hear their laughter, and carry their memory with us as we navigate this season of both joy and sorrow. It is through these tributes that we discover that the illusion of happy holidays can become a reality, even in the midst of grief.

Coping with Triggers

Triggers. The mere mention of the word is enough to send chills down my spine. They are the overlooked landmines that lie dormant, waiting to explode our fragile hearts and emotions. Triggers are the reminders of the loved ones we have lost, the bittersweet memories that resurface during the holiday season, threatening to drown us in a sea of sorrow. For someone like me, who has lost friends and family in dire circumstances, triggers can turn even the merriest of holiday celebrations into a somber affair. But there is hope.

In this chapter, I want to share with you the strategies I have discovered to cope with triggers during the holidays. These strategies are not miracles; they are not instantaneous fixes. Healing takes time, and it is a journey unique to each individual. However, by integrating these coping mechanisms into our lives, we can foster healing and resilience, and perhaps, just perhaps, find a glimmer of joy amidst the shadows.

The first strategy I want to discuss is acknowledgment. It is vital to recognize that triggers exist and that they have the power to affect us deeply. Denying or suppressing these feelings only allows them to fester and grow stronger. Acknowledgment is the first step towards healing. It is understanding that it is okay to feel pain and sadness during the holiday season, even when those around us insist we should be cheerful and festive. It is granting ourselves permission to grieve and process our emotions, allowing ourselves to heal.

Once we have acknowledged the presence of triggers, the next step is to create a safe space for ourselves. This space can take many forms: a cozy nook with our favorite book, a peaceful walk in nature, or a solitary moment of reflection. Whatever it may be, this sanctuary is where we go to honor our feelings, to sit with our grief and remember the ones we have lost. It is a sacred retreat, where we can let the tears flow freely and speak to our loved ones aloud. This act of remembrance brings us a step closer to finding solace in their absence.

In aTriggers. The mere mention of the word is enough to send chills down my spine. They are the overlooked landmines that lie dormant, waiting to explode our fragile hearts and emotions. Triggers are the reminders of the loved ones we have lost, the bittersweet memories that resurface during the holiday season, threatening to drown us in a sea of sorrow. For someone like me, who has lost friends and family in dire circumstances, triggers can turn even the merriest of holiday celebrations into a somber affair. But there is hope.

In this chapter, I want to share with you the strategies I have discovered to cope with triggers during the holidays. These strategies are not miracles; they are not instantaneous fixes. Healing takes time, and it is a journey unique to each individual. However, by integrating these coping mechanisms into our lives, we can foster healing and resilience, and perhaps, just perhaps, find a glimmer of joy amidst the shadows.

The first strategy I want to discuss is acknowledgment. It is vital to recognize that triggers exist and that they have the power to affect us deeply. Denying or suppressing these feelings only allows them to fester and grow stronger. Acknowledgment is the first step towards healing. It is understanding that it is okay to feel pain and sadness during the holiday season, even when those around us insist we should be cheerful and festive. It is granting ourselves permission to grieve and process our emotions, allowing ourselves to heal.

Once we have acknowledged the presence of triggers, the next step is to create a safe space for ourselves. This space can take many forms: a cozy nook with our favorite book, a peaceful walk in nature, or a solitary moment of reflection. Whatever it may be, this sanctuary is where we go to honor our feelings, to sit with our grief and remember the ones we have lost. It is a sacred retreat, where we can let the tears flow freely and speak to our loved ones aloud. This act of remembrance brings us a step closer to finding solace in their absence.

In addition to creating a safe space, it is crucial to surround ourselves with a support system that understands and empathizes with our grief. Friends, family, or even support groups can provide the understanding and compassion needed to navigate triggers during the holidays. These individuals can offer a listening ear, a shoulder to lean on, or share memories and stories of our loved ones. By connecting with others who have experienced similar losses, we realize that we are not alone in our pain. Together, we find strength and comfort, helping us to endure the holiday season with a renewed sense of hope.

Another strategy to cope with triggers is finding ways to honor and celebrate the memories of our loved ones. For some, this may involve lighting a candle in their honor, setting up a memory table with their photographs and belongings, or even making a donation to a cause that was dear to their hearts. By keeping their memories alive, we transcend the pain and sorrow and focus on the love and joy they brought into our lives. In doing so, we find solace in knowing that they are never truly gone as long as they are remembered and cherished.

Lastly, practicing self-care is paramount during the holiday season. Grieving takes a toll on our physical and emotional well-being, and it is essential to prioritize ourselves during this challenging time. This may involve engaging in activities that bring us comfort and joy, such as reading, painting, cooking, or engaging in mindfulness exercises. Taking the time to care for ourselves allows us to recharge, replenish, and face the triggers with resilience and grace.

As we embark on this journey of healing and coping with triggers during the holidays, it is important to remember that everyone's grief is unique. What works for one person may not work for another, and that is okay. The key is to be patient with ourselves, to give ourselves the space and time needed to heal. Although triggers may always exist, with the right strategies and support, we can find moments of peace and happiness amidst the pain. And in doing so, we honor the ones we have loved and lost, continuing their legacies of love and light in our own lives.

Another powerful coping strategy is connecting with others who share a similar pain. Sometimes, the comfort and understanding we seek can only be found in the company of those who have experienced similar losses. Support groups, online communities, or even just a close friend who has walked a similar path can provide a lifeline during the holidays. Sharing stories, emotions, and coping mechanisms can be cathartic and healing. It reminds us that we are not alone and that our pain is valid.

Creating new traditions and rituals can also help us cope with triggers. By incorporating our lost loved ones into our celebrations, we keep their memory alive in a meaningful way. Light a candle in their honor, cook their favorite holiday recipe, or create a scrapbook filled with cherished memories. These acts of remembrance not only provide comfort but invite our loved ones to be a part of our holiday celebrations, even in spirit.

Lastly, self-care must not be overlooked. Taking care of ourselves physically, emotionally, and mentally is crucial during this challenging season. It may mean setting boundaries, saying no to certain events or invitations that may be overwhelming, or carving out time for activities that bring us joy and peace. Self-care is an act of self-love and compassion, allowing us to replenish our reserves and navigate the holiday season with greater resilience and strength.

Dear reader, coping with triggers is a deeply personal and intricate process. It requires patience, self-compassion, and an unwavering commitment to healing. But remember, you are not alone in this journey. There is a community of individuals who understand your pain and are here to lend support. By acknowledging triggers, creating safe spaces, connecting with others, incorporating lost loved ones into our celebrations, and practicing self-care, we can begin to navigate the complexities of the holiday season with a new-found strength and healing. And perhaps, as we journey through these coping strategies, we might discover a flicker of joy in the illusion of happy holidays.

Seeking Support

In my pursuit of healing and finding a sense of balance during this time, I have discovered the power of seeking support from those around me. Whether it be leaning on friends, family, or engaging in support groups, the compassionate arms of others have become my lifeline.

In the depths of my sorrow, I am reminded of a quote I read recently: "Grief shared is grief diminished." These simple words resonated within me, urging me to reach out to those who care about me and provide solace in my darkest moments. I understand that no one can undo the pain I endure, but their presence and understanding offer a glimmer of hope, a reminder that I am not alone in this journey.

Support can come in various forms. Friends and family, who have witnessed my struggle, often offer their unwavering love and a listening ear. The mere act of venting my frustrations or recounting memories of lost loved ones brings a therapeutic release. In those moments, it feels as if a weight has been lifted off my chest, if only temporarily. These connections, these bonds, they keep me grounded and remind me that my pain is valid, deserving of acknowledgment.

Beyond my small circle of loved ones, I have also discovered the immense power of support groups dedicated to navigating grief during the holiday season. These gatherings, filled with individuals who have experienced similar losses, create an environment of understanding and empathy that is unparalleled. In these spaces, we share our stories, our struggles, and our hearts. We find solace within the collective grief, knowing that we are not alone in our pain.

As we sit together, each person pouring out their feelings and memories, a profound sense of unity washes over us. We create a temporary sanctuary where our sorrow is not judged, but rather embraced and validated. We are all connected by the common thread of loss, tied together by a shared understanding that transcends words.

In these support groups, I have witnessed acts of compassion and kindness that restore my faith in humanity. Strangers become confidants, understanding the unspoken language of grief. We hold each other's hands, physically and metaphorically, offering comfort in the knowledge that we are not alone in our struggles.

Through this collective sharing of pain, a remarkable transformation begins to take place. Our hearts, once heavy with sorrow and loneliness, start to heal and make space for hope and healing. The burden doesn't disappear entirely, but it becomes easier to bear as we find strength in one another.

Over time, these support groups become more than just a source of comfort. They become a haven for growth and resilience. We exchange coping mechanisms, learning from one another's experiences and finding new ways to navigate the complexities of grief. Together, we discover that healing is not linear, but a continuous process that requires patience, self-compassion, and understanding.

In the safety of these communities, we find the courage to redefine our relationship with loss. We learn to honor our loved ones' memories in ways that keep their spirit alive, celebrating the joy they brought into our lives. We create new traditions, embrace rituals that bring comfort, and discover the beauty in commemorating the lives we have lost.

Support becomes the lifeblood that sustains us through the darkest moments, reminding us that even in the depths of despair, there is a glimmer of light. As we lean on one another, we become architects of our own healing, weaving a tapestry of resilience and hope.

In my pursuit of healing and finding a sense of balance, I have discovered the true power of seeking support from those around me. It is within the embrace of compassion and empathy that I find the strength to continue my journey. With each step forward, I am reminded that grief shared is indeed grief diminished, and that in our collective vulnerability, we find healing and the courage to embrace life once more.

There is tremendous strength in exchanging experiences with others who understand the complexities of grief during the holiday season. We offer one another a safe space to share our most vulnerable emotions, knowing that there is no judgment, only acceptance and compassion. We find comfort in listening to each other's stories, recognizing that our pain is valid, and our journeys unique yet interconnected.

As we gather in these supportive communities, we find solace in the power of storytelling. We share memories of our loved ones, recounting the moments that made them special, and in doing so, we keep their spirits alive. The sound of laughter echoes through these gatherings, not as a sign of forgetting, but as a testament to the love that still exists within our hearts.

In the warmth of these interactions, we also discover the healing potential of gratitude. Each day, we consciously cultivate an attitude of appreciation for the time we had with our loved ones, for the lessons they taught us, and for the love they bestowed upon us. We express our gratitude not just for the past, but for the present moments of connection and support that we find in this compassionate community.

In this process of redefining our relationship with loss, we begin to unearth the hidden gems of resilience within us. We realize that through our grief, we have developed an inner strength that we never knew existed. We become aware of our capacity to rise from the ashes of despair and rebuild our lives, acknowledging that our experiences have shaped us into more compassionate and resilient individuals.

As we navigate the holiday season, we discover the power of embracing both joy and sorrow. We learn that it is possible to celebrate life and honor our loved ones simultaneously. We create new traditions that blend moments of remembrance with acts of joy and, in doing so, we navigate the delicate balance between grief and hope.

Though our journeys are unique, we find solace in knowing that we are not alone. The world may see us as individuals who have experienced loss, but within this community, we identify as a tapestry of interconnected souls, united by our shared experiences. We hold each other close, providing comfort and support during the times we feel most fragile.

In this safe space, we redefine the narrative of grief during the holiday season. No longer is it solely a season of pain and longing; it becomes a season of remembrance, love, and healing. We find the courage to embrace life once more, knowing that our loved ones would want us to find joy and fulfillment in each passing day.

And so, with our newfound strength, we embark on the journey ahead, armed with resilience, compassion, and gratitude. We carry the memories of our loved ones in our hearts, weaving them into the tapestry of our lives. As we continue to grow and evolve, we honor their legacies by living lives filled with love, purpose, and an unwavering commitment to supporting others on their own paths of healing.

In the safety of these communities, we find not only the courage to redefine our relationship with loss, but also the strength to embrace a future filled with hope, connection, and the beauty that lies within the human spirit.

Through my experiences in seeking support, I have learned that grief cannot be conquered alone. It is a daunting task that requires the support and understanding of those around us. It is in these connections that we find the courage to face the holidays head-on, transforming the illusion of happy holidays into a semblance of peace and acceptance.

So, I encourage each and every person who finds themselves suffocating under the weight of grief during the holiday season to reach out. Seek solace in the embrace of loved ones and seek companionship in support groups. Share your stories, release your pain, and let others empower you to navigate this challenging time. Together, we can find glimmers of joy amidst the darkness and reclaim our own happiness during the holiday season.

Creating New Traditions

In my quest to find solace amidst the chaos of grief, I have delved into extensive research on the power of creating new traditions. These studies have shown that establishing new rituals not only helps to heal the wounds of the past but also allows us to open our hearts to new experiences and connections.

One of the first steps in this journey is to reflect on the memories and traditions that have brought us joy in the past. This reflection allows us to identify the core values and experiences that have made the holiday season meaningful to us. For me, I realized that it was the act of giving and sharing that truly resonated with the essence of the season. So, I decided to create a new tradition centered around acts of kindness.

During the holiday season, I now organize a community event where we come together to volunteer at local shelters and charities. This tradition not only honors the memory of my lost loved ones but also brings a sense of purpose and fulfillment to my life. It reminds me that the holiday season is not just about extravagant gifts and festivities but also about compassion and empathy towards those in need.

Another crucial aspect of creating new traditions is

embracing the possibility of new beginnings. It can be challenging to let go of the past, to detach ourselves from the memories that define our holiday traditions. But by opening ourselves up to new experiences, we allow for growth and the potential for happiness to seep back into our lives.

For instance, I took up a new hobby during the holiday season – one that my departed loved ones had always encouraged me to pursue. They used to say that I had a hidden talent for painting, and so I decided to honor their memory by taking up art classes. Through this newfound passion, I have discovered a source of healing and expression that has not only enriched my life but also become an integral part of my holiday traditions.

As I immerse myself in the strokes of vibrant colors and the gentle caress of the paintbrush against the canvas, I feel a sense of connection to my loved ones. It is as if they are guiding my hand, whispering words of encouragement as I create masterpieces that capture the essence of the holiday spirit.

Painting has become my sanctuary during the holiday season, offering solace and a means to channel my emotions into something beautiful. Each stroke represents a moment of healing, a step towards embracing the joy that can coexist with the ache of loss.

Through this creative outlet, I have also found a way to

share my newfound passion with others. I now host annual painting parties during the holiday season, where friends and family gather to create their own masterpieces and celebrate the spirit of togetherness. It has become a tradition that bonds us in a way that surpasses the boundaries of grief, reminding us that there is still beauty to be found even in the darkest of times.

These painting parties have become a space for healing, where we can all express our emotions through art and support one another on this journey of remembrance and renewal. Each year, I am amazed by the unique creations that come to life on the canvases, each reflecting the individual stories and emotions of those who participate.

As the years go by, our painting party tradition has evolved, incorporating new elements to keep things fresh and exciting. We now invite local artists to attend and share their expertise, offering workshops and demonstrations that inspire us to continue exploring our artistic abilities. The walls of my home have become adorned with the vibrant creations of our painting parties, a testament to the growth and resilience that can arise from embracing new beginnings.

Through my journey of adopting new traditions and embracing the possibility of new beginnings, I have discovered a profound truth – that the essence of the holiday season lies not in the specific rituals or activities we engage in, but in our ability to adapt, evolve, and find joy even amidst the pain of loss.

My newfound love for painting has become a testament to the transformative power of art and the resiliency of the human spirit. It has shown me that there is no limit to the ways in which we can create traditions that honor the past while embracing the present.

As I continue to explore my artistic journey, I am filled with a sense of gratitude for the opportunities that lie ahead. Each brushstroke holds the promise of new beginnings and a chance to express my love for those who are no longer with me in physical form.

In this evolving tapestry of holiday traditions, I have come to realize that the greatest gift we can give ourselves is the permission to let go, to embrace the unknown, and to create new traditions that reflect the ever-changing nature of life.

And so, as I embark on this journey of artistry and self-discovery, I invite others to join me in embracing the possibility of new beginnings. Together, let us paint the canvas of our lives with bold strokes of resilience, love, and joy, weaving a tapestry of traditions that will continue to inspire and uplift for generations to come.

In addition to volunteering and painting, I have also

made it a tradition to embark on a solo journey during the holiday season. This journey is not about escaping from the memories or the traditions of the past, but rather about discovering new places, cultures, and perspectives that can breathe fresh life into the holiday season.

From witnessing the flickering lights of a small village nestled in a snow-capped mountain range to immersing myself in the vibrant festivities of a bustling city, these new experiences have widened my horizons and given me a renewed sense of wonder. The journey has become a symbol of resilience, a testament to the fact that even in the face of loss, we can find beauty and inspiration.

As I reflect upon the memories I have created and the traditions I have established, I am reminded of the power we hold within ourselves to shape our holiday season. It is a testament to our resilience and our willingness to embrace the new while cherishing the old.

In this season of reflection and renewal, I am grateful for the lessons learned and the courage to create new traditions. The journey of healing is ongoing, but through acts of kindness, the pursuit of artistic passions, and the embrace of new adventures, I have found a way to honor the past while joyfully embracing the present.

Creating new traditions can be a daunting task, as it requires us to step out of our comfort zones and confront our grief head-on. But by guiding ourselves in this process, we can find solace and hope amidst the darkness. By honoring the memory of our loved ones through acts of kindness and embracing new beginnings, we can transform the holiday season from a painful reminder of loss into a time of healing, growth, and the possibility of happiness.

Finding Meaning in Loss

Grief had become an ever-present companion in my life, an unwelcome guest that seemed to linger long after the initial shock and sadness had passed. The heavy weight of loss clung to me, clouding my perception of the world and casting a shadow over any semblance of joy that I once had. It was easy to allow this grief to consume me, to let it define my existence. But deep down, I knew that there had to be more to life than this endless cycle of sorrow.

With a determination forged from the depths of my pain, I embarked on a journey of self-discovery, a quest to find meaning in the midst of loss. I wanted to transform my grief into a catalyst for positive change, to find a glimmer of hope in the darkest corners of my soul.

Research became my guiding light as I delved into the realms of psychology and philosophy, seeking answers to the questions that haunted me. I learned that grief was not something to be avoided or suppressed, but rather something to be embraced and understood. It was a natural response to loss and a testament to the love and connection we shared with those we had lost.

The work of Viktor Frankl, a renowned psychiatrist and Holocaust survivor, resonated deeply with me. His book,

"Man's Search for Meaning," revealed a profound truth: that despite the most unimaginable pain and suffering, it is possible to find meaning in life. Frankl wrote, "Those who have a 'why' to live, can bear with almost any 'how'." This idea struck a chord within me, igniting a flame of determination to discover my own "why."

I began to explore different avenues, searching for activities and experiences that could help me connect with my innermost desires and passions. I immersed myself in art, finding solace and expression in painting and sculpting. The vibrant colors and tactile nature of these mediums allowed me to communicate the depths of my emotions in ways that words alone could not capture.

But it was in the act of helping others that I truly discovered my purpose. Volunteering at a local homeless shelter, I found a sense of fulfillment and gratitude that had eluded me for so long. Each interaction, each small gesture of kindness, reminded me that even in the face of tragedy, we have the power to make a difference in someone's life.

Inspired by this newfound clarity, I set out to create a support group for individuals navigating their own journey through grief. Together, we shared our stories, our pain, and our hopes for the future. In this space of compassion and understanding, we found solace and strength. We realized that our grief did not define us, but rather offered us an opportunity for growth and transformation.

As time went on, the weight of my grief began to lift, replaced by a newfound sense of purpose and resilience. Though the pain never fully disappears, it no longer engulfs me. Instead, I carry it with me, a reminder of the love and lessons that have shaped my life.

Through my journey, I have come to understand that grief is not an end, but rather a beginning. It is a catalyst for growth and a testament to the profound impact that love can have on our lives. It is through our experiences of loss that we learn to appreciate the preciousness of every moment and the importance of cherishing those we hold dear.

As I reflect on my journey, I am grateful for the unwelcome guest that grief has been in my life. It has pushed me to the depths of despair, but it has also propelled me towards growth, hope, and a profound sense of purpose. The darkness of grief has not defeated me; it has made me stronger, more compassionate, and more aware of the preciousness of life.

Grief had become a constant companion in my life, an unwelcome guest that lingered long after the initial shock and sadness had passed. The heavy weight of loss clouded my perception of the world, casting a shadow over any semblance of joy I once had. I allowed this grief to consume me, defining my existence. But deep down, I knew there had to be more to life than this endless sorrow.

Fuelled by determination forged from the depths of my pain, I set out on a journey of self-discovery, seeking meaning in the midst of loss. My goal was to transform grief into a catalyst for positive change, to find hope in the darkest corners of my soul.

Research became my guiding light as I delved into psychology and philosophy, seeking answers to my haunted questions. I embraced the knowledge that grief was not to be avoided, but understood and embraced. It was a natural response to loss, a testament to the love and connection we shared with those we lost.

The writings of Viktor Frankl, a renowned psychiatrist and Holocaust survivor, resonated deeply within me. His book, "Man's Search for Meaning," revealed a profound truth: even in the face of unimaginable pain and suffering, it is possible to find meaning in life. Frankl wrote, "Those who have a 'why' to live can bear almost any 'how'." This idea sparked a flame of determination within me, igniting the search for my own "why".

I explored various avenues, seeking activities and experiences that would help me connect with my inner desires and passions. Art became my solace, allowing me to express my emotions through painting and sculpting. Vibrant colors and tactile mediums gave voice to my deepest pain in ways that words alone could not capture.

But it was in helping others that I truly discovered my purpose. Volunteering at a local homeless shelter filled me with fulfillment and gratitude. Each interaction, each small act of kindness reminded me that even in tragedy, we can make a difference.

Inspired by newfound clarity, I created a support group for those navigating their own journey through grief. Together, we shared our stories, our pain, and our hopes. In this space of compassion and understanding, solace and strength were found. Grief did not define us; it offered growth and transformation.

Over time, the weight of my grief began to lessen, replaced by a sense of purpose and resilience. While the pain never fully disappeared, it no longer consumed me. Instead, I carried it as a reminder of the love and lessons that shaped my life.

Through my journey, I learned that grief is not an end, but a beginning. It fuels growth and testifies to the profound impact of love on one's life. Our experiences of loss teach us to appreciate the preciousness of every moment and the importance of cherishing those we hold dear.

As I reflect on my journey, I am grateful for grief's presence in my life. It pushed me to the depths of despair, but it also propelled me towards growth, hope, and a profound sense of purpose. The darkness of grief did not defeat me; it made me stronger, more compassionate, and more aware of life's preciousness.

Healing Rituals

However, as I journey through the process of healing and finding solace, I have discovered the power of healing rituals to provide comfort during this challenging season. These rituals, born out of ancient traditions and personal experiences, have become a vital part of my journey towards emotional well-being.

One of the most potent healing rituals I have introduced into my life is the act of honoring the memory of those I have lost. For as long as I can remember, my family has gathered on Christmas Eve to share stories and reminisce about our loved ones who are no longer with us. As we sit around the crackling fire, tears mingle with laughter as we share our fondest memories of those who have passed on. This simple act of remembering and acknowledging their presence in our lives brings a sense of connection and healing to our wounded hearts.

In addition to honoring our loved ones' memory, I have incorporated mindfulness practices into my daily routine. These rituals of quiet reflection have allowed me to cultivate a deeper sense of presence and gratitude for the present moment. Each morning, as the sun begins to rise and paint the sky with vibrant hues, I take a moment to witness this natural beauty. I breathe in the crisp morning air, allowing it to fill my lungs and invigorate my senses. In this peaceful solitude, I find solace and a renewed sense of hope.

As I embark upon this journey of healing, I have also embraced the healing power of nature. The world around me has become a sanctuary for my weary soul. I find solace in the gentle rustle of leaves, the soothing sound of waves crashing against the shore, and the symphony of birdsong that fills the air. Nature has become my refuge, offering me comfort and reminding me of the incredible resilience of life.

Another ritual that has become an integral part of my healing is the act of self-care. Recognizing the importance of taking care of myself, both physically and mentally, I have made a commitment to prioritize my well-being. I set aside time each day to engage in activities that bring me joy and nourish my soul. Whether it be through writing, painting, or simply indulging in a warm bath, these moments of self-care are essential in replenishing my spirit and rejuvenating my mind.

In my journey towards emotional well-being, I have also discovered the profound healing power of community. Surrounding myself with loved ones who support and uplift me has been instrumental in my healing process. Together, we create a space where vulnerability is embraced, and a sense of kinship is fostered. In this collective embrace, I find strength, understanding, and the knowledge that I am not alone in my struggles.

As I continue to explore the world of healing rituals, I am constantly amazed at the transformative power they possess. These rituals serve as a gentle reminder that healing is not linear, but rather an ongoing journey. They provide me with the tools needed to navigate the ups and downs, the joys and sorrows, that life inevitably brings. And with each step forward, I am reminded that healing is possible, and that there is beauty to be found even in the darkest of moments.

So I encourage you, dear readers, to embrace the power of healing rituals in your own lives. Whether it be through honoring the memory of loved ones, practicing mindfulness, immersing yourself in nature, engaging in self-care, or finding solace in community, these rituals have the potential to bring comfort, healing, and joy. May you embark upon your own journey of healing, and may these rituals guide you towards a place of peace and restoration.

Another essential healing ritual that has helped me find solace during the holiday season is the practice of self-care. Losing loved ones has taught me the importance of taking care of myself, not just physically, but also emotionally and spiritually. During this time of year, when the weight of grief feels particularly heavy, I carve out moments of solitude and reflection as a way to nurture my soul. Whether it's spending time in nature, meditating, or indulging in my favorite book, these small acts of self-care provide a respite from the overwhelming emotions that often accompany the holiday season.

In the midst of the hustle and bustle, it is easy to get caught up in the external expectations and pressures that surround us during this time. But self-care reminds me to slow down, to listen to the whispers of my heart, and to honor my own needs. It is a gentle reminder that I deserve love, compassion, and care, even in the midst of grief.

Self-care during the holiday season can take many forms. It may be as simple as lighting a candle and allowing its soft glow to envelop you in a sense of warmth and tranquility. Or perhaps it involves creating a sacred space where you can retreat and recharge, surrounded by objects and mementos that bring you comfort and peace.

For me, self-care during the holiday season also means finding small ways to connect with the loved ones I have lost. It may be writing a letter to them, sharing my joys and sorrows, and allowing my words to serve as a bridge between the worlds of the living and the deceased. It may be creating a special memorial altar, adorned with photographs and cherished belongings, as a way to honor their memory and keep their spirit alive in my heart.

But above all, self-care during the holiday season is about giving yourself permission to feel and to heal. It is about acknowledging the bittersweet nature of this time, embracing the memories that bring both joy and tears, and allowing yourself to be vulnerable in the face of loss. It is a reminder that healing is not a linear process, but a journey filled with ebbs and flows, peaks and valleys.

As I navigate this holiday season, I hold onto the transformative power of self-care, knowing that it is an essential part of my healing journey. And I invite you, dear readers, to join me in embracing this ritual, to give yourself the gift of self-care during this time of year. May you find solace, comfort, and restoration as you tend to your own needs, and may you discover the profound healing that lies within the gentle act of self-care.

In my research on healing rituals, I have come across various practices that have been found to promote emotional well-being during the holiday season. One such practice is creating a gratitude journal. In this journal, I write down three things I am grateful for each day, focusing on the small moments of joy or the acts of kindness that I encounter. Cultivating a sense of gratitude has been proven to shift our focus from the pain of loss towards the abundance of love and support that still surrounds us.

As I embark on this journey of self-care, I find solace in the pages of my gratitude journal. Each day, I take a few moments to reflect on the blessings in my life, big and small. Whether it's the warmth of a loved one's embrace, the laughter shared with cherished friends, or even the soothing presence of nature, these moments of gratitude have become my guiding light in the darkness.

But self-care is not just about writing down words on a page. It is about taking intentional actions that nourish our mind, body, and soul. So, in addition to my gratitude practice, I have incorporated other rituals into my daily routine. I rise with the sun and engage in a gentle yoga practice, allowing my body to stretch and release the tension that has accumulated. I immerse myself in nature, taking long walks in the crisp winter air, feeling the earth beneath my feet and the wind whispering secrets through the trees.

I prioritize rest and rejuvenation, knowing that it is during these moments of stillness that true healing can occur. I light scented candles, allowing the fragrance to fill the room with tranquility. I lose myself in the pages of a captivating book, or simply sit in silence, savoring the magic of solitude. And when the weight of the world becomes too heavy, I treat myself to a blissful bubble bath, allowing the warm water to wash away my worries and leave me feeling renewed.

But self-care is not just a solitary pursuit. It is also about nurturing our connections with others. I reach out to loved ones, not only to share my gratitude but also to offer support and love when they need it most. I gather around a table filled with delicious food, laughing and reminiscing with those who have stood by my side through thick and thin. And I remember the importance of setting boundaries, of saying no when I need to, in order to protect my own well-being.

As the holiday season swirls around us in a chaotic dance of obligations and expectations, I invite you, dear readers, to join me in embracing the transformative power of self-care. May we prioritize ourselves and our well-being, knowing that only by pouring love and care into our own cup can we truly show up for others. May we find the strength to release the burdens we carry and the grace to embrace the beauty that still surrounds us. And may this holiday season be a time of healing, restoration, and profound self-discovery.

Another healing ritual that has proved beneficial in my journey is participating in community service. There is a unique healing power in helping those who are less fortunate during the holiday season. Volunteering at local charities or organizing food drives not only provides a sense of purpose but also widens my perspective on life. It reminds me of the importance of compassion and empathy, even amid my own personal struggles.

As I continue to navigate through the illusion of happy holidays, I have come to realize that healing rituals are not just about finding comfort for myself but also about extending that comfort to others. Through acts of kindness and compassion, I hope to create a ripple effect of healing, offering solace to those who may be struggling during this time of year.

In the next chapter, I will delve deeper into the power of healing rituals and practices, exploring their roots in ancient traditions and their transformational potential in our modern lives. Together, let us embark on a journey of healing and discover the true essence of the holiday season.

Connecting with Others

I have spent far too many holiday seasons feeling isolated, trapped in the suffocating grip of grief. The weight of the losses I have endured seems even heavier during this time of year when joy and celebration are expected. But over time, I have come to understand that one of the most powerful antidotes to this suffocating loneliness is connecting with others who have experienced similar losses.

It was through a support group that I first discovered the healing power of shared experiences. Sitting in a circle with people who had also lost loved ones, we opened our hearts and shared our stories. In that space, the pain felt less overwhelming, as if it had been divided amongst us all. Hearing the struggles, hopes, and fears of others who had suffered similar losses brought solace I had not felt in years. There was an unspoken understanding that words alone could not convey, a connection forged in shared sorrow.

As the support group sessions continued, I realized that our collective grief had morphed into a source of strength. We were no longer victims of our losses but warriors fighting to reclaim our lives and find joy again. We learned to celebrate the memories of our loved ones, cherishing the moments we had shared with them instead of dwelling on their absence.

In this sacred space, where vulnerability was met with empathy and understanding, I forged deep and lasting bonds with those who understood the depths of my pain. We became a family, united by grief but also by resilience and the unwavering spirit to persevere. Together, we navigated the treacherous path of grief, comforting each other through the darkest nights and applauding small victories along the way.

As the holiday season approached, we decided to redefine what it meant to celebrate. No longer burdened by the expectations of society, we created our own traditions that honored our loved ones while embracing the present. We gathered to share stories, memories, laughter, and tears. We celebrated not just their lives but also our strength and resilience in the face of adversity.

Through the support group, I discovered that healing doesn't mean forgetting or moving on. It means finding the courage to build a new life, one that carries the weight of loss but also a newfound appreciation for every precious moment. It means recognizing that grief can coexist with joy and that the measure of a life well-lived is not in the absence of pain but in the ability to rise above it.

Now, as another holiday season rolls around, I no longer feel isolated. I am surrounded by a network of understanding souls who lift me up when I feel the weight of grief overwhelming me. We stand together, finding solace and strength in each other's stories, supporting one another through the ups and downs that life inevitably brings.

Together, we have created our own unique traditions that nourish our spirits and remind us of the strength within. Instead of dwelling on what is missing, we celebrate what we have, cherishing the present moment and the love that still flows between us and our departed ones.

During the holiday season, we gather in a cozy space, filled with twinkling lights and the comforting scent of homemade treats. We share stories of our loved ones, remembering their quirks, their passions, and the joy they brought to our lives. Each tale is like a thread that weaves the tapestry of their legacy, ensuring they are never forgotten.

Laughter fills the room as we recall the funny moments and the mischievous antics that created lasting memories. Through our shared laughter, we defy the heaviness of grief, finding solace in the smiles that once graced the faces of our departed loved ones.

Tears are welcomed too, for they are the release valve of our emotions, allowing us to acknowledge the pain and the longing that accompanies loss. Together, we provide shoulders to lean on, hands to hold, and hearts to listen. Our tears strengthen the bond between us, reminding us that we are not alone in this journey through grief.

In the spirit of giving, we extend our love and support to others who are walking the same path. We reach out to those who have experienced loss, offering a compassionate ear, a warm embrace, or simply an understanding nod. We create a community where no one feels isolated or forgotten, a community that stands together, ready to catch each other when the weight of grief threatens to pull us under.

As the holidays draw to a close, we release lanterns into the night sky, each carrying a message of love and remembrance. As the lanterns ascend, our spirits are lifted, knowing that our loved ones are still with us, their presence felt in the flickering glow.

We have redefined what it means to celebrate during the holiday season. We have transformed it from a time of sorrow and loneliness into a time of connection and healing. Our traditions may be unconventional, but they are filled with love, resilience, and the unwavering belief that life, even in the midst of grief, is worth celebrating.

And so, we enter the new year with hope in our hearts, vowing to continue crafting a life that honors our loved ones and nurtures our own souls. We carry their spirits with us, guiding us through the challenges and reminding us of the infinite capacity of the human heart to heal and to love. In this newfound understanding, we have discovered the true essence of celebrating the holiday season – a celebration of life, in all its complexities, and the resilience of the human spirit.

In this ongoing journey of healing, I have come to realize that connecting with others — sharing our pain, vulnerability, and triumphs — is one of the greatest gifts we can give ourselves. Together, we rewrite the narrative of loss, transforming it from a tale of despair to one of hope and resilience. And in this shared rewriting, we find solace, growth, and an unbreakable bond that carries us through not just the holiday season, but every season of our lives.

Together, we embarked on a journey of healing, supporting one another through the darkest of times. We leaned on each other, finding understanding and empathy in a world that often seemed indifferent to our grief. In that space of vulnerability, we found strength, our resilience bolstered by the knowledge that we were not alone in our pain.

What struck me most during our meetings was the incredible range of emotions displayed by each individual. It reminded me that grief is a complex and fluid experience, unique to each person. Some found solace in recalling cherished memories, others in silent tears. There were moments of laughter, tinged with bittersweet nostalgia. And yet, amidst this spectrum of emotions, we were all united in our shared desire to find healing and reclaim our lives, one step at a time.

Connecting with others who have experienced similar

losses is invaluable not only because it fosters a sense of understanding, but also because it provides a safe space to express emotions that may otherwise go unspoken. In society, there is often pressure to put on a brave face during the holiday season, to hide our pain beneath a facade of forced joy. But within the circle of our support group, we were free to shed those masks and allow our pain to be witnessed and validated.

Through these connections, I began to see that healing did not mean forgetting or moving on. It meant finding a way to carry our loved ones forward with us, to honor their memory by living fully and embracing life despite the pain. The holiday season, once a symbol of loss, became a reminder of the strength and resilience that can emerge from the depths of grief.

As I continue along this journey of healing, I have made it my mission to reach out to others who are walking a similar path. I know now that I cannot change the past or the painful experiences that have brought us together, but I can offer solace in the form of understanding and support. By opening my heart and sharing my story, I hope to create a ripple effect, where others may find the strength to share their own and in turn, inspire others to do the same.

It is my belief that by highlighting the importance of connecting with others who have experienced similar losses, we can foster a community of understanding and support.

Together, we can break free from the illusion of happy holidays and create a space where grief is acknowledged and healing is possible.

Embracing Hope

But in the darkest of moments, a glimmer of hope manages to seep in. It is this hope that I seek to inspire in others who have experienced similar tragedies. I am determined to show them that it is possible to find light in the midst of darkness, and to rebuild their lives after loss.

Hope is a powerful force, although sometimes elusive and fragile. It is what helped me keep going when I lost my best friend in a car accident, and when I received the news of my brother's untimely death overseas. It is hope that propelled me forward, even when I felt like giving up.

In the face of adversity, I learned that hope is not an abstract concept, but rather a tangible source of strength that resides within each of us. It is that glimmer of hope that whispers, "You can and will overcome this." It urges us to take one more step, to keep pushing forward, even when the burden of grief threatens to consume us.

Through my own journey, I have discovered the power of community and the importance of reaching out to others who have walked a similar path. In the darkest moments, when despair threatened to swallow me whole, I found solace in connecting with others who understood my pain. Together, we formed a support network, a tribe of survivors who lifted each other up and reminded one another that we were not alone.

And with each shared story of hope, we discovered that there is light to be found in even the most cavernous depths of grief. We learned that our losses did not define us; instead, they became catalysts for growth and transformation. We realized that the capacity to rebuild, to find purpose and joy amidst the pain, was within our grasp.

The path to healing is not linear; it winds and twists, sometimes throwing us off balance. But it is during these moments of uncertainty that hope becomes our steady companion. It whispers words of encouragement and reminds us of our resilience. It gently nudges us to take small, deliberate steps towards rebuilding our lives, even when the scars of loss are still fresh.

With time, we learn to embrace the memories of our loved ones and celebrate the light they brought into our lives. We come to understand that their legacies live on through us, in the way we choose to live and the love we spread to others. In these acts of remembrance and honor, we find solace and the strength to carry on.

Today, as I stand before others who are grappling with their own devastating losses, I share my story not as a beacon of hope, but as a humble reminder that hope exists within each of us. It is a flame that flickers in the darkness, waiting to be ignited. And it is my mission to ignite that flame, to show others that they too can rise from the depths of despair and find a life worth living.

Together, let us kindle the fire of hope, let us rebuild and reimagine our lives, and let our stories be a testament to the indomitable nature of the human spirit. For in the face of tragedy, hope is not only possible, it is a necessity. And it is through embracing hope that we find the strength to heal, to find purpose, and to continue living with resilience and grace.

I have found that one of the keys to embracing hope is to allow oneself to grieve. The pain of losing loved ones is not something that can simply be ignored or brushed aside. It consumes you, engulfs you in its suffocating grip. But by acknowledging that pain, by allowing myself to mourn, I was able to take the first step towards healing. It is in the depths of sorrow that one must find the strength to rise again.

Another essential aspect of embracing hope is the realization that life is not meant to be lived alone. We are all interconnected, and it is the support and love of others that can help carry us through the darkest of times. Surrounding myself with a community of people who understood my pain and offered solace, I began to understand that I was not alone in my suffering. Together, we found solace in shared stories and empathetic hearts.

In the process of rebuilding my life, I discovered the beauty of reinvention. I was no longer the same person I was before the losses I endured. I had changed, transformed by grief and resilience. In rebuilding my life, I had the opportunity to shape it into something new, something that paid homage to the past while embracing the future. It was a chance to create a legacy for those I had lost, to honor their memories by living a life filled with purpose and joy.

But embracing hope is not a one-time decision; it is a daily choice. It is a commitment to finding beauty in the midst of pain, to seek out moments of joy even when it feels impossible. It is an unwavering belief that, despite the darkness that may surround us, there is always a flicker of light waiting to be discovered.

So, as I navigate through this holiday season once again, I am reminded of the importance of embracing hope. It is not an easy journey, but one that is essential for healing and rebuilding. I encourage all those who have experienced loss to lean into the hope that still resides within them. Together, let us find the strength to embrace hope, to find resilience in the face of adversity, and to create a life that not only honors the past but shines brightly into the future.

{ 4 }

Overcoming Thoughts of Suicide

Recognizing Warning Signs

The warning signs of suicidal thoughts and behaviors can often be subtle, easily overlooked amidst the hustle and bustle of the holiday season. But they are there, hidden beneath smiles and laughter, waiting to be seen by those who are willing to look closer.

One of the most common warning signs is a noticeable change in behavior. When someone who was once outgoing and lively suddenly becomes withdrawn and isolated, it's a cause for concern. I remember my friend Sarah, who used to be the life of the party, slowly morphing into someone who preferred the solace of her own company. She would cancel plans last minute, citing exhaustion or a sudden change of heart. It was only when I mustered the courage to ask her what was going on that she admitted her struggle with suicidal thoughts. It was a pivotal moment, a chance to intervene and offer the support she desperately needed.

Over time, I came to realize that Sarah's change in behavior went beyond just withdrawing from social events. She began to neglect her appearance, unkempt hair and disheveled clothing becoming her new norm. She stopped participating in the activities she once enjoyed, giving up on her hobbies and passions with a sense of hopelessness. Her laughter, once infectious and full of life, became rare, and her eyes lost their spark.

Another warning sign that often goes unnoticed is a sudden decline in academic or work performance. Sarah, who had always been an overachiever, started skipping classes and missing deadlines. She lost interest in her studies, her once sharp mind clouded by dark thoughts. It was as if she had given up on her dreams, no longer seeing any purpose or meaning in her achievements.

Perhaps the most distressing red flag was the way Sarah began to talk about death and dying. She made passing remarks about feeling like a burden to others, expressing feelings of hopelessness and worthlessness. I remember the chilling moment when she calmly mentioned that she wished she could just disappear and end the pain. It was a plea for help disguised as casual conversation, a cry for someone to notice and take action.

These warning signs are not to be taken lightly. They are the whispers of distress, pleading for our attention. It is imperative that we stay vigilant, observing those around us and recognizing the subtle changes that may indicate a battle with suicidal thoughts.

One such sign is a decline in academic or work performance. When someone who was once driven and accomplished begins to falter, it is cause for concern. I recall my colleague, Alex, who was always at the top of their game, suddenly starting to miss deadlines and show a lack of interest in their work. It was as if the fire within them had extinguished, replaced by a sense of hopelessness. In their eyes, I saw the pain they were carrying, a burden that became too heavy to bear alone.

Another unnoticed warning sign can manifest as physical changes. Much like a neglected garden, a person struggling with suicidal thoughts may let themselves wither away. My neighbor, Emma, used to radiate beauty and vitality. However, as the holiday season approached, her appearance underwent a transformation. Her once lustrous hair became unkempt, her clothing wrinkled and disheveled. It was as if she had given up on herself, succumbing to the darkness that enveloped her.

These signs should not be dismissed as mere coincidence or passing phases. They are cries for help, desperate pleas for someone to notice and offer support. Let us not turn a blind eye to those who are silently suffering. In this season of joy and celebration, let us be the beacon of hope and understanding for those who need it most. By recognizing the warning signs and taking action, we have the power to save lives and help others find their way back to the light.

In conclusion, we must prioritize mental health awareness and create a society that fosters open conversations about suicide prevention. Together, we can break the stigma, educate ourselves, and make a difference in the lives of those who silently struggle. Let us not forget that compassion and understanding are the greatest gifts we can give this holiday season.

Recognizing these warning signs is crucial, but it's equally important to take action and offer support to those in need. Educating ourselves about the resources available is a significant step. There are helplines, support groups, and therapists who specialize in suicide prevention. By reaching out and encouraging our loved ones to seek help, we become a lifeline in their time of darkness.

If I had known then what I know now about recognizing warning signs, maybe I could have saved the lives of those I lost. But the past cannot be changed, and all I can do is use my experiences to educate others and promote early intervention. As we embark on this journey through the illusion of happy holidays, let us open our eyes and hearts to those who silently suffer, for no one should face their darkest moments alone.

Seeking Professional Help

Guiding individuals to reach out to mental health profes-sionals and helplines for immediate support and assistance is an essential aspect of ensuring their well-being. It is crucial to remember that we do not have to face our trials alone; there are professionals out there equipped with the knowl-edge and expertise to guide us through the darkest of times. These individuals possess invaluable insight and understand-ing, providing a safe space for us to unburden our troubled minds.

The first step towards seeking professional help begins with acknowledging the need for assistance. It takes great courage to recognize that we are not equipped to mend our broken selves solely through our own strength. It is an act of both vulnerability and strength to admit that we require the guidance of someone who specializes in mental health, some-one who has dedicated their lives to helping others navigate the intricate labyrinth of emotions.

Once we have taken that first step, reaching out to a mental health professional or helpline is the next crucial move in our journey towards healing. It is essential to under-stand that these professionals are not here to judge or criti-cize us; their sole purpose is to listen and provide support. Their training and expertise enable them to create a safe and non-judgmental space for us to share our deepest fears, anxieties, and traumas.

Through their extensive knowledge of various therapeutic techniques and interventions, mental health professionals can help us gain insights into our thoughts, feelings, and behaviors. They can help us unravel the complex web of emotions that have entangled us, offering tools and strategies to cope with the challenges we face. Whether it be through cognitive-behavioral therapy, interpersonal therapy, or other evidence-based approaches, these professionals have the skills to tailor their guidance to our individual needs.

Moreover, mental health professionals provide a sense of validation and understanding that may be lacking in our personal relationships. While our loved ones may try their best to support us, they may not always comprehend the intricacies of mental health struggles. By seeking the assistance of a professional, we ensure that we are receiving guidance from someone who truly understands the complexities of mental well-being.

However, it is important to note that reaching out to a mental health professional does not signify weakness or failure, but rather an act of self-care and self-empowerment. By taking this step, we prioritize our well-being and demonstrate a commitment to overcoming the challenges that lie ahead. In doing so, we are actively investing in our mental health and laying the foundation for a happier and healthier future.

It is also worth mentioning the resources available in the form of helplines and crisis hotlines. These services provide immediate support for those in distress, offering a lifeline during our darkest moments. They are staffed by trained professionals who are trained to handle crisis situations and provide guidance, comfort, and reassurance. The availability of these helplines ensures that help is never far away, no matter the time or day.

In conclusion, seeking professional help for our mental health is not only a courageous act but also a vital step towards our well-being. By acknowledging the need for assistance and reaching out to mental health professionals and helplines, we open ourselves up to the support and guidance necessary to navigate the challenging road ahead. Remember, we are never alone in our struggles, and there are people out there who can guide us into the light, helping us find the strength within ourselves to overcome even the most formidable obstacles.

Once we have accepted the importance of seeking professional help, the next step is to find the right mental health professional or helpline that suits our needs. This process may involve conducting careful research, seeking recommendations from trusted friends or family members, or consulting with our primary healthcare provider. It is essential to find a professional who not only has the necessary qualifications and expertise but also possesses a compassionate and empathetic demeanor. The bond we form with our mental health professional is one of trust and vulnerability, and it is vital that we feel comfortable sharing our deepest fears and anxieties with them.

When we embark on this journey towards healing, it is crucial to remind ourselves that professional therapy or counseling is not a quick fix. It is a process that requires time, patience, and unwavering commitment. Attending therapy sessions, engaging in honest dialogue, and actively implementing the guidance provided can pave the way towards healing and inner peace. Remember that healing is not linear; there will be setbacks, moments of doubt, and times when it feels like we are moving backward rather than forward. Yet, it is essential to trust the process and have faith in the guidance we receive.

As we begin our sessions with a mental health professional, it is important to be open-minded and willing to explore the depths of our emotions and experiences. The therapist will create a safe and non-judgmental space where we can freely express ourselves, and it is our responsibility to fully embrace this opportunity for self-discovery. We may uncover painful memories or face uncomfortable truths, but it is through this discomfort that true healing can occur.

In therapy, we may encounter different therapeutic

approaches and techniques, such as cognitive-behavioral therapy, psychodynamic therapy, or mindfulness-based therapies. Each method has its own benefits and may be tailored to suit our specific needs. Identifying the most effective therapeutic approach can be a collaborative process between the therapist and ourselves, as we actively participate in discussions about what resonates with us and what strategies we are most comfortable implementing.

Outside of therapy sessions, it is essential to engage in self-care practices that support our mental well-being. This can include engaging in activities that bring us joy, maintaining a healthy lifestyle through regular exercise and nutritious eating, and connecting with a supportive community. Additionally, practicing mindfulness and being present in the moment can help us cultivate resilience and cope with the challenges that arise along the way.

As we progress through therapy, we may start to notice subtle shifts in our thinking patterns and behaviors. These changes are signs of growth and progress, demonstrating that we are moving forward on our healing journey. It is important to celebrate these victories, no matter how small they may seem, as they serve as reminders of our strength and resilience.

In moments of doubt or uncertainty, it can be helpful to reach out to our support network. Friends, family members, or fellow individuals who have experienced similar struggles can provide encouragement, understanding, and reassurance. This network can serve as a reminder that we are not alone in our journey and that others have successfully navigated similar challenges.

Ultimately, the path to mental well-being is unique to each individual. It requires a commitment to self-reflection, self-compassion, and a willingness to embrace vulnerability. Seeking professional help is a courageous step towards reclaiming our lives and finding inner peace. As we continue on this journey, we can trust in our ability to heal and grow, knowing that the challenges we face are opportunities for transformation.

While seeking professional help can be transformative, it is equally essential to remember that we are not weak or flawed for needing assistance. In fact, it is a sign of strength and wisdom to recognize when we need support, especially during the holiday season when the illusion of happy holidays can magnify our pain. By seeking professional help, we are taking the necessary steps to break free from the chains of sorrow and reclaim our lives.

Remember, dear reader, that seeking professional help is not an admission of defeat or failure. It is a testament to our resilience, our willingness to heal, and our determination to find joy in the midst of the darkest storms. Take my hand, and let us embark on this journey towards healing together.

Building a Support Network

As someone who has experienced significant loss in my life, the concept of building a support network has become crucial for me. It is through the unwavering support and understanding of trusted friends and family that I have managed to navigate through the darkest moments, especially during this seemingly joyful season. Encouraging individuals to cultivate a strong support network may be the key to finding solace and strength amidst the despair that can accompany the holiday season.

Building a support network is not simply about surrounding oneself with people. It is about carefully choosing individuals who possess the ability to empathize with our pain and offer genuine emotional support. These individuals are the ones who can provide a safe space for us to express our frustrations, fears, and sadness without judgement or trivialization. In my own experience, I have found that having even just one person who truly understands and listens can make all the difference in the world.

But building a support network is not an easy task. It requires vulnerability, trust, and patience - qualities that often prove elusive when we are wrapped up in our own pain.

Sharing our deepest sorrow and exposing our vulnerabilities to others is an incredibly daunting challenge. There is always the fear of rejection or being a burden to others. However, I have come to realize that by opening ourselves up to the possibility of acceptance and compassion, we allow others to understand our pain and offer genuine support.

In this season of joy and celebration, it can be easy to feel isolated and alone when we are weighed down by our grief. Society often places an unfair expectation on us to be merry and festive, but the reality is that for many of us, this season brings a flood of painful memories and reminders of the loved ones we have lost. It is during these times that building a support network becomes even more vital.

Finding solace and strength amidst the despair begins with recognizing that we are not alone in our struggles. There are countless others who have walked a similar path and who are willing to offer their understanding and compassion. Online communities and support groups can be a great starting point for connecting with individuals who are going through similar experiences. These platforms provide a safe and empathetic space where we can share our stories and find comfort in the knowledge that we are not alone.

But it is equally important to seek support from those already present in our lives - our friends and family. Often, they may not fully comprehend the depth of our pain or know how to support us. It is our responsibility to communicate our needs and educate them on the importance of their presence. Through open and honest conversations, we can help them understand the significance of their love and support during this challenging time.

Building a support network also extends beyond seeking emotional solace. It involves engaging in activities that nurture our wellbeing and finding individuals who can provide guidance and assistance when needed. Seeking professional help in the form of therapists or counselors can be incredibly beneficial, as they possess the expertise to guide us through the complexities of grief.

Furthermore, it is important to remember that building a support network is a reciprocal relationship. Just as we seek comfort and understanding, we must also be willing to be there for others in their times of need. By fostering a sense of community and showing compassion to those around us, we create a network of support that is both comforting and empowering.

As the holiday season approaches, let us remember that amidst the festivities, there are many who are silently grieving. By extending a hand of understanding and offering our support, we can help alleviate the burden that this season may bring. Remember, the strength of our support network lies not in its size, but in the authenticity and unwavering love that it provides. Let us create a world where no one feels alone in their pain, and where joy and consolation coexist.

For those who, like me, struggle during the holiday season, it can feel as if we are drowning in a sea of merriment and joy. The pressure to conform to society's expectations of happiness during this time can be overwhelming. However, by cultivating a support network, we not only find solace in the understanding of others, but we also gain strength to resist the societal pressure to conform to the illusion of happy holidays.

The path to healing is paved with the empathy and kindness we share with one another. Just as each snowflake contributes to the beauty of a winter landscape, every act of compassion we offer creates a ripple effect that touches the lives of others. In this interconnected web of humanity, no one should feel isolated in their pain or burdened by the weight of unmet expectations.

Together, let us redefine what the holiday season truly means. It is not solely about lavish gifts or extravagant feasts, but rather a time of reflection, gratitude, and connection. By reaching out to those who may be silently struggling, we can create a space where vulnerability is embraced and judgement replaced with understanding.

Let us open our hearts and homes to those who might not have a place to call their own this season. Each empty chair at a family gathering serves as a reminder that many long for the warmth of companionship. Whether it is inviting a neighbor without family nearby or volunteering at a local shelter, we can extend the true spirit of the holidays beyond our own circles.

Beyond the holiday season, let us carry this spirit of support throughout the year. Life's challenges do not adhere to a specific calendar, and our need for connection and understanding extends well beyond the last strains of "Auld Lang Syne." By nurturing our support network, we create a haven where vulnerability is met with empathy, strength, and encouragement.

I implore you to remember that we are all teachers and students of compassion. This is not a competition to see who can offer the grandest gesture of support, but rather a shared journey of growth and understanding. Each small act or word of encouragement has the power to brighten someone's darkest day.

Together, let us create a world where empathy reigns, and no one feels alone in their pain. It is through this collective effort that we can challenge the societal norms that isolate and instead foster a sense of togetherness and support. So, let us extend our hands, touch hearts, and build a support network strong enough to weather life's storms and celebrate its triumphs.

My own support network consists of my closest friends, Rachel and Alex. Rachel, who lost her parents in a tragic accident, understands the depths of grief that can consume us during this seemingly festive time. Her quiet understanding and willingness to simply be there without offering empty platitudes have been invaluable. Alex, on the other hand, is the voice of reason and occasional comic relief. He reminds me of the importance of laughter, even in the midst of sorrow, and gives me the strength to face another day.

Building a support network takes time and effort, but the benefits far outweigh the challenges. During this holiday season, I encourage others who share in my pain to seek out that one person, that one friend or family member, who can lend a listening ear and a compassionate heart. Together, we can find solace and strength, amidst the illusion of happy holidays, and navigate our way through the darkest moments with a renewed sense of purpose and hope.In the journey towards building a support network, let us not forget the importance of self-care. It is easy to get caught up in the act of giving and supporting others, often neglecting our own needs in the process. However, we must remember that we cannot pour from an empty cup.

Take the time to prioritize your own well-being, both physically and mentally. Engage in activities that bring you joy and allow you to recharge your spirit. Whether it be curling up with a good book, taking long walks in nature, or finding solace in creative pursuits, make sure to carve out moments of self-care amidst the busyness of life.

Additionally, let us remember that support comes in different forms. Sometimes all it takes is a simple smile or a heartfelt message to let someone know that they are not alone. Even small acts of kindness can have a profound impact on someone's life. By spreading positivity and empathy wherever we go, we can create a ripple effect of support that extends far beyond our immediate circles.

As we enter into a new year, let this be a time of reflection and growth. Let us not only focus on our own personal development but also on empowering those around us. Together, we can create a society where support is not just a fleeting holiday sentiment, but a constant embrace that uplifts and nurtures us all.

In the end, building a support network is not just about finding others to lean on during times of need. It is about fostering a community of understanding, compassion, and love. It is about realizing that we are not alone in our struggles and that together we are stronger.

So, let this be the year that we carry the spirit of support throughout the year. Let us be the writers of a new narrative, one that celebrates the bonds of human connection and embraces vulnerability as a catalyst for growth. Together, we can create a world where no one feels alone, and where the power of support remains steadfast, guiding us through the highs and lows of life.

Developing Coping Strategies

As the holiday season approaches, I find myself once again caught in the clutches of overwhelming emotions and debilitating thoughts. The weight of lost friendships and shattered family ties weighs heavily upon me, and it feels as though I am sinking deeper into the abyss of despair with each passing day. It is during this time that I realize the importance of developing coping strategies, practical tools to navigate through the darkness and find moments of respite even in the midst of sorrow.

1. *Embracing Self-Care:*

One crucial coping strategy I have discovered is the importance of self-care. It is all too easy to neglect oneself in times of distress, but caring for our physical, emotional, and mental well-being is essential. I have found solace in engaging in activities that bring me joy and peace, whether it's going for long walks in nature, immersing myself in a favorite book, or spending time with a beloved pet. By making a conscious effort to prioritize self-care, I find that I am better equipped to face the challenges that the holiday season brings.

Not only does self-care provide a much-needed respite

from the chaos and stress of everyday life, but it also allows us to reconnect with ourselves on a deeper level. Amidst the hustle and bustle of the holiday season, it becomes increasingly important to establish a routine that caters to our own needs and desires.

For me, self-care goes beyond pampering myself with luxurious bath products or indulging in decadent desserts (although those things certainly have their merits). It is about carving out time for introspection and reflection. It is about reminding myself of my own worth and the significance of my presence in this world.

In the serene solitude of an early morning, I find solace in watching the sunrise, witnessing the birth of a brand new day. The quiet moments before the world awakens are magical, as if time stands still and all that matters is my connection with the universe. I breathe in the fresh air, feeling a sense of renewal coursing through my veins.

On other occasions, sitting down with a blank canvas and a palette of vibrant colors unleashes a cascade of emotions. With each brushstroke, I release any pent-up tensions and allow my creativity to flow freely. The colors blend harmoniously, mirroring the harmony I seek within myself. It is in these moments of pure self-expression that I am reminded of the beauty that resides within me and the limitless potential that exists within us all.

There are also times when self-care means seeking the support and guidance of loved ones. In the warm embrace of a dear friend, I feel reassured that I am not alone in navigating the challenges that life presents. Through heartfelt conversations and shared laughter, we create a sanctuary of love and understanding.

And let's not forget the importance of nourishing our bodies. Indulging in wholesome, nutritious meals prepared with love and care not only fuels us physically but also nourishes our soul. The simple act of savoring each bite, appreciating the flavors and textures, is an act of self-love and gratitude for the gift of sustenance.

As the holiday season approaches, and the days become filled with festivities, it is easy to lose ourselves in the whirlwind of obligations and external expectations. But amidst the chaos, let us not forget to pause and listen to the whisper of our own hearts. Let us give ourselves the gift of self-care, for it is through taking care of ourselves that we can truly give our best to others.

So, in the midst of the holiday frenzy, let us honor our need for self-care. Let us delight in the simple pleasures that bring us joy and fulfillment. Let us take the time to nurture our bodies, minds, and spirits. And in doing so, let us embrace the magic and wonder of the holiday season, sharing love and kindness with those around us, knowing that we have first shown love and kindness to ourselves. For in that act of self-care lies the key to not only surviving but thriving during the holiday season and beyond.

2. Seeking Support:

Another coping strategy that has proven invaluable is seeking support. It is often tempting to isolate oneself during times of turmoil, but connecting with others who understand and empathize with our struggles is vital. Whether it's reaching out to a trusted friend, attending support groups, or seeking therapy, finding a supportive network can help alleviate the overwhelming burden and provide a space for healing and growth.

In this vast world, I've come to witness the incredible power of human connection. We are not solitary creatures, meant to navigate the trials of life alone. No, we are social beings, and our shared experiences bind us together in ways that cannot be replicated or understated. It is through seeking support that we can truly rise above our challenges and find the strength to face another day.

When we reach out to a trusted friend, we grant ourselves the gift of vulnerability. In confiding in someone who cares for us deeply, we open the floodgates of our emotions, allowing them to flow freely and unencumbered. Our truest companions will hold us gently in the embrace of their understanding, offering solace, guidance, and a listening ear.

With their unwavering support, the weight on our shoulders becomes less burdensome, reaffirming that we are not alone in this journey.

Yet, there are times when even the closest of friends may struggle to comprehend the intricacies of our pain. In such instances, support groups emerge as oases of understanding amidst the arid desert of isolation. These communities provide us with the opportunity to connect with others who are walking a similar path, individuals who have weathered storms akin to our own. Surrounded by people who have stared down adversity and emerged stronger, we find solace in their shared wisdom and stories. In this environment, we no longer feel alone but rather part of a collective, bolstered by the knowledge that we are not the only ones facing such tribulations.

For those who seek an even deeper level of healing, the realm of therapy opens its doors wide. Within the therapist's sanctuary, we can unravel the intricate threads of our pain, guided by a compassionate and impartial hand. These professionals are the pillars upon which we can rebuild ourselves from the ground up. They offer insights, techniques, and tools to aid in our personal growth and development. With their skillful guidance, we are encouraged to confront our fears, examine our past, and forge a path towards a brighter future. Therapy becomes a safe haven, where we can delve deep within ourselves, understanding and healing the wounds that have hindered our progress for far too long.

Support takes on many forms, and it is crucial that we explore the avenues that resonate with our individual needs. Whether it is the empathetic ear of a friend, the camaraderie of a support group, or the expertise of a therapist, seeking support fuels our resilience and fortifies the foundations of our well-being. It emboldens us to face our challenges head-on, armed with the knowledge that we are not alone in our struggles.

So, my dear friends, let us shed the armor of isolation and reach out to one another. Let us embrace the connections that bind us and nurture them with love and understanding. In our shared vulnerability, we discover the strength to overcome adversity, to heal the wounds that have plagued our souls. Seek support, for it is through the power of connection that we find solace, growth, and ultimately, our shared humanity.

3. Managing Overwhelming Emotions:

During the holiday season, overwhelming emotions can threaten to consume us. It is crucial to have strategies in place to manage these emotions before they spiral out of control. One technique that has been helpful to me is journaling. Pouring my heart out onto paper offers a cathartic release and allows me to process my feelings in a safe and private space. Additionally, practicing mindfulness and deep breathing exercises have helped me ground myself in the present moment, offering moments of calm amidst the storm.

Another valuable strategy in managing emotions during the holiday season is seeking support from loved ones. Sharing our struggles with trusted friends and family members can provide us with a sense of understanding and comfort. Knowing that we are not alone in our experiences can be incredibly reassuring.

Furthermore, engaging in self-care activities is crucial during this time. Taking the time to prioritize our own well-being can help alleviate stress and prevent emotional burnout. Whether it's treating yourself to a relaxing bath, practicing a hobby you enjoy, or simply taking a few moments each day to do something for yourself, self-care can be a powerful tool in maintaining emotional balance.

Another effective technique is setting boundaries. It's important to remember that we have control over how we spend our time and energy. Saying "no" to certain invitations or commitments that may overwhelm us can be empowering and protect our mental and emotional health. Establishing boundaries allows us to prioritize self-care and focus on the activities and relationships that truly bring us joy during the holiday season.

In addition to these strategies, it is essential to practice gratitude. It can be easy to get caught up in the chaos and stress of the holidays, but taking the time to reflect on the things we are grateful for can shift our perspective and bring about a sense of contentment. Whether it's appreciating the small moments of happiness, expressing gratitude towards loved ones, or simply acknowledging our own strengths and resilience, cultivating gratitude can be a powerful tool in managing overwhelming emotions.

In conclusion, the holiday season can be a challenging time emotionally, but with the right strategies in place, it can also be a time of growth, connection, and self-care. By journaling, seeking support, engaging in self-care, setting boundaries, and practicing gratitude, we can effectively manage our emotions and navigate the holiday season with a renewed sense of peace and joy. Remember, you are not alone in your struggles, and there are tools and techniques available to help you navigate this season with grace and resilience.

4. Creating Boundaries:

One coping strategy that I have had to learn the hard way is the importance of setting boundaries. The holiday season often brings with it numerous invitations and obligations, but it is essential to recognize our limits and prioritize our own well-being. Saying no when necessary and understanding that it is okay to put ourselves first can be challenging but ultimately crucial in preserving our mental and emotional health.

Fortunately, I had an epiphany during a particularly overwhelming holiday season that completely transformed how I approached setting boundaries. I realized that saying no to certain commitments did not make me selfish or uncaring; it actually made me stronger and more authentic. I understood that by valuing my own well-being, I could show up fully for the people and activities that truly mattered to me.

With this newfound perspective, I began to communicate my boundaries in a more assertive and compassionate manner. I found that people respected my honesty and admired my ability to prioritize self-care. I learned that setting boundaries was not about shutting people out or neglecting their needs; it was about fostering healthy relationships built on mutual respect and understanding.

As the years went by, I noticed a remarkable shift in myself. I was no longer constantly overwhelmed and stressed during the holiday season. Instead, I felt an overwhelming sense of peace and joy because I had created a space to take care of myself amidst the chaos. I discovered that by setting boundaries, I not only preserved my mental and emotional health but also increased my capacity to give and love others.

Setting boundaries during the holiday season also allowed

me to focus on what truly mattered. I learned to let go of the unnecessary obligations that only added to my stress. Instead, I put my energy into nurturing meaningful connections, cherishing quiet moments with loved ones, and engaging in activities that fueled my soul. By prioritizing what truly brought me happiness, I found that the holiday season became a time of rejuvenation and celebration.

Additionally, through my journey of setting boundaries, I discovered that it wasn't just beneficial for me; it also inspired those around me to do the same. As I openly shared my experiences and insights, I witnessed my loved ones adopt healthier coping strategies as well. It was an incredibly rewarding feeling to see my friends and family embracing self-care and learning to prioritize their own well-being.

Now, as the holiday season approaches each year, I am equipped with the knowledge and experience to navigate it with ease. I am unafraid to say no when necessary, unburdened by unnecessary obligations, and unapologetic about putting myself first. I have come to understand that setting boundaries is not a sign of weakness, but rather an act of self-love and personal growth.

So, as this holiday season dawns upon us once again, I encourage you to reflect on the importance of setting boundaries. Remember that it is perfectly okay to prioritize your well-being and be selective in the commitments you make.

By doing so, you will create a holiday season that is filled with joy, peace, and genuine connections.

5. *Embracing Unconventional Traditions:*

Traditions hold a significant place during the holiday season, but for those of us with compromised views, it can be a painful reminder of what has been lost. Instead of dwelling on what is no longer there, I have found solace in embracing unconventional traditions. Whether it's volunteering at a local charity, starting a new hobby, or traveling to a place that holds meaning for me, creating new traditions offers a sense of purpose and rejuvenation.

In the midst of twinkling lights and cheery carols, I discovered that the beauty of the holiday season extends far beyond the traditional customs I once held so dear. As I embarked on my journey of exploring new and unconventional traditions, I found myself opening up to a world of possibilities and experiencing the joy that had eluded me for so long.

Rather than mourning the past, I realized that the true spirit of the holidays lies in the act of giving and connecting with others. Volunteering at a local charity became an integral part of my newfound tradition. The warmth in the eyes of those I helped, the gratitude expressed by those who had little, the immense satisfaction of making a difference, all became powerful reminders of the true meaning of the season. In giving back, I began to heal and rediscover the beauty of compassion.

While embracing unconventional traditions, I stumbled upon a hobby that ignited my soul. Painting became my refuge, a portal through which I could channel my emotions and create something truly meaningful. Each stroke of the brush helped me manifest the beauty I saw in the world and allowed me to share my vision with others. The process of transforming a blank canvas into a masterpiece became a tradition in itself, a celebration of my resilience and creative spirit.

And then there was the allure of travel, beckoning me to explore the corners of the world that held a profound significance in my heart. With open arms and a curious mind, I journeyed to places whispered about in the stories of my childhood, places that held deep cultural heritage and traditions untold. Walking through ancient temples, witnessing mesmerizing rituals, and connecting with people from diverse backgrounds breathed new life into my weary soul. In those faraway lands, I discovered that there is a universality to traditions, and by experiencing them firsthand, I not only gained a deeper understanding of the world but also a stronger connection to my own sense of self.

As I embraced these new traditions, a remarkable transformation occurred within me. The pain of what I had lost during the holiday season gradually faded, replaced by a sense of purpose and rejuvenation. I realized that traditions are not fixed and unchanging but rather fluid and adaptable. They can ebb and flow, change and evolve, just as we do.

Coming to terms with my compromised views was no longer a burden but rather a catalyst for growth. I had recognized the power within myself to create new traditions that nourished my soul, allowed me to embrace the present moment, and celebrate the beauty of life in all its forms.

So, this holiday season, as the world cherishes its long-standing traditions, I will too, but in my own way - a way that brings joy, fulfillment, and a renewed sense of purpose. For in embracing the unconventional, I found the keys to unlocking the true magic of the holiday season, and indeed, the magic of life itself.

Navigating the dark depths of the holiday season is no easy feat, especially for someone like me, who carries the weight of loss upon their shoulders. Yet, by developing these coping strategies - embracing self-care, seeking support, managing overwhelming emotions, creating boundaries, and embracing unconventional traditions - I have found a glimmer of hope amidst the bleakness. These practical techniques have become the guiding light that helps me navigate the treacherous waters of overwhelming emotions and thoughts of suicide during the holiday season. May they serve as an anchor for those who find themselves lost in the same storm, reminding them that even in the darkest of times, there is a path to healing and finding moments of peace.

Creating Safety Plans

As I sit here in front of my computer, ready to embark on the writing journey, I feel a profound sense of responsibility. The weight of my experiences lingers in the air, reminding me of the jagged void created by the loss of loved ones, particularly during the holiday season. But despair will not consume me. Instead, I choose to confront my pain head-on and turn it into a catalyst for change. In this chapter, I aim to guide readers, like myself, in crafting personalized safety plans. These plans will serve as a lifeline during times of crisis, providing a sense of control and stability in even the most challenging moments.

To create a safety plan, we must first face our fears and acknowledge the obstacles that life may toss our way. It requires honesty and an understanding of the triggers that amplify our pain and put us at risk of crisis. I've experienced firsthand the significance of this process, and it has become my guiding light, helping me navigate the emotional turbulence that accompanies the holiday season.

The initial step in developing a personalized safety plan is identifying the triggers that intensify our pain and vulnerability. For me, it's a painful sight of empty chairs around the holiday dinner table, the sound of cheerful carols that once brought joy but now evoke memories of loss, and the overwhelming sense of loneliness that permeates the air during this time of year.

Once we recognize our triggers, we can then concentrate on devising strategies to manage and overcome them. It's essential to remember that these strategies will be unique to each individual. We all possess distinct coping mechanisms that resonate with us personally. Some may find solace in grounding exercises like deep breathing and meditation, which calm the mind and alleviate overwhelming emotions. Others may seek support from friends, support groups, or therapists who provide a safe space to process their grief.

Creating a support network is an integral part of any safety plan. Surrounding ourselves with loved ones who understand and empathize with our pain can provide a sense of comfort and belonging. They offer a listening ear, a shoulder to lean on, or just a presence that reminds us we are not alone in our struggles. Sharing our experiences, fears, and hopes with others who have also suffered loss can foster healing connections that provide solace and strength during difficult times.

Another crucial aspect of a safety plan is developing healthy coping mechanisms. This could involve engaging in activities that bring us joy and allow us to channel our emotions into something positive. It might be writing in a journal, creating art, immersing ourselves in nature, or participating in volunteer work to give back to the community. By finding healthy outlets for our pain, we can transform grief into motivation and resilience.

Equally important, a safety plan should include crisis intervention strategies. It is imperative to have a list of emergency contacts readily accessible, including helpline numbers, trusted friends or family members, and mental health professionals. When crisis strikes, knowing whom to reach out to can be a lifeline when we find it challenging to rely solely on ourselves.

As I pen these words, a profound sense of empowerment washes over me. Confronting my pain and creating a safety plan has rejuvenated my sense of control over my own narrative. I am no longer a passive victim of circumstance. I have become an active participant in my healing journey.

Therefore, as we approach the holiday season, let us confront our pain head-on. Let us create safety plans that remind us of the strength and resilience that resides within us. And let us remember that despite the losses we have endured, we are still capable of discovering joy, peace, and love amidst the bittersweet memories. Together, we can navigate through life's challenges and emerge stronger, united by our shared experiences and unwavering determination to write a new chapter in our lives.

Research unequivocally demonstrates that having a safety plan significantly reduces the risk of harm during moments of crisis. It acts as a tangible guide, a roadmap to help us navigate the tempest of our emotions. But what exactly does a safety plan entail? How do we go about creating one? Let's dive into the intricacies step by step.

Step one involves identifying warning signs. These are the telltale indications that a crisis is looming, the red flags clamoring for our attention. For me, it's a sudden surge of isolation, accompanied by haunting memories—a poignant reminder of a past I cannot alter. By understanding these signs, we can intervene before spiraling out of control, effectively regaining our equilibrium.

Step two in our quest to reclaim our inner strength centers around accepting our emotions. We universally experience pain, sadness, and despair. In times of crisis, it is crucial to allow ourselves the space and permission to fully experience these emotions. Only through acceptance can genuine healing occur.

Step three necessitates self-reflection and introspection. We must delve deep into the recesses of our minds, exploring the roots of our turmoil. Is our anguish a result of external circumstances or internal conflicts? Are there pivotal moments or a series of events responsible for unraveling our inner harmony? By unraveling these threads, we unlock the potential for personal growth and insight.

Step four challenges us to summon the courage to confront our demons head-on. It demands that we face our fears and acknowledge our vulnerabilities. Often, the most formidable battles are fought within ourselves, against doubts, insecurities, and negative self-talk that hold us captive. By embracing this confrontation with grace, we inch closer to liberating our souls from the shackles of crisis.

Once we have mustered the strength to confront our inner demons, step five prompts us to seek support. No one should face their trials alone. Whether it means confiding in a trusted friend, seeking guidance from a therapist, or joining a support group, the power of collaboration and empathy should never be underestimated. When we share our burdens, they become lighter, and solutions emerge from the collective wisdom of those who care.

Finally, step six beckons us towards resilience and transformation. Having weathered the storm, emerged from the depths of despair, and harnessed our inner strength, we find ourselves on the other side of crisis. Yet, we are not the same as before. We have gained wisdom, resilience, and an unwavering belief in our ability to overcome. Through this process, we realize that our journey is not simply about surviving a crisis; it is about thriving in the face of adversity.

In conclusion, the road to regaining our equilibrium lies in perseverance, self-discovery, and acknowledging our humanity. It requires a willingness to dive into the depths of our emotions, confront our inner struggles, seek support, and emerge transformed. Crisis can serve as a catalyst for growth and self-empowerment, reminding us of our boundless potential and the unwavering resilience of the human spirit.

Step two involves listing coping strategies. These are the tools we can rely on to manage our emotions and calm the storm within. It might be as simple as pouring our hearts into a journal, finding solace in the words as a form of catharsis. Alternatively, it could involve seeking comfort in the arms of loved ones, finding connection to remind ourselves that we are not alone. Coping mechanisms are different for everyone, and it is crucial to explore various strategies until we find what resonates with us.

Step three revolves around building our support network. In times of crisis, reaching out for help can be the ultimate lifeline. Whether confiding in a trusted friend, family member, or professional counselor, having someone to lean on eases the burden of our pain. Establishing a support network is vital to ensure we have someone to turn to when darkness threatens to consume us once more.

Step four entails creating a list of emergency contacts. These are the individuals we can rely on when we require immediate assistance. Having a readily accessible list of trusted contacts is indispensable when our thoughts become clouded by crisis. From helplines to crisis centers, having access to emergency services provides a sense of safety and security.

Lastly, step five encourages ongoing self-reflection and evaluation of the safety plan. Adapting and refining our strategies based on experiences ensures that our safety plan continues to serve its purpose. Life is unpredictable, and new challenges may arise. Therefore, being flexible in adapting coping mechanisms and bolstering our support network allows for growth and resilience.

As I conclude the final paragraphs, a profound sense of accomplishment washes over me. By delving deep into the process of creating a safety plan, I have somehow managed to reclaim a semblance of control, even in the face of overwhelming loss. While my journey towards healing is far from over, I am comforted by the knowledge that I now possess a tangible tool to navigate the treacherous terrain of the holiday season.

To those who have joined me on this chapter, I implore you to embark on this journey of self-discovery, to face the shadows that linger within and take that first step towards creating your own safety plan. Remember, it is okay to ask for help, to lean on others when the burden becomes too heavy. Together, we can transform the notion of "happy holidays" from an illusion into a reality—a testament to our strength, resilience, and unwavering determination to heal.

Addressing Stigma

I have come to realize that the holiday season is not just about exchanging gifts and feasting on grand meals. It is a time when the air becomes heavy with judgments, expectations, and the weight of societal stigmas. These stigmas have perpetuated the illusion of happy holidays, while disregarding the very real struggles that lie beneath the surface.

As someone who has experienced the devastating loss of friends and family due to dire circumstances, my view of the holiday season has been compromised. These losses have opened my eyes to the immense importance of challenging the stigma surrounding mental health and suicide, promoting open conversations and understanding to create a supportive environment.

In my journey of self-discovery and healing, I have delved deep into the research on mental health and suicide prevention. I have learned that the first step in challenging the stigma is to break the silence. We must initiate open conversations about mental health, encouraging individuals to share their struggles without fear of judgment or ridicule. This requires us to create safe spaces where compassion and understanding can flourish, allowing for vulnerable yet invaluable discussions.

This endeavor requires all of us to actively challenge the preconceived notions that society has ingrained in our minds. We must confront the false beliefs that mental health issues are a sign of weakness or that talking about suicide will only lead to more harm. It is crucial to educate ourselves and others about the harsh realities faced by those struggling with mental health, as well as the dire consequences of remaining silent.

Furthermore, we should prioritize the integration of mental health support within our communities. This means advocating for easily accessible and affordable mental health services, so that no one feels alone or abandoned in their darkest moments. By investing in mental health resources, we can create a safety net that catches those who are falling and offers them hope, understanding, and the necessary tools for healing.

But let us not forget that mental health is not solely an individual burden; it is a collective responsibility. As we gather with our loved ones during the holiday season, it is crucial to extend our empathy and compassion beyond the surface level. Let us refrain from passing judgment and instead extend a helping hand to those who may be silently suffering. Reaching out with genuine concern and offering a listening ear can make all the difference in someone's life.

In this pursuit, we must also challenge the commercialization of the holiday season. While gift-giving and feasting are undoubtedly enjoyable aspects, we should remember that material possessions and extravagant meals are not the ultimate source of happiness. True joy lies in nurturing meaningful connections, in embracing the vulnerability and authenticity that come with honest conversations. It is through these connections that we can cultivate a sense of belonging and support for one another.

As the holiday season approaches, let us shift our focus. Let us put aside the pressures of expectations and societal stigmas. Instead, let us use this time to reflect on the value of our mental health and the importance of supporting those who may be silently struggling. Together, we can break the cycle of stigma, create a compassionate society, and truly embody the spirit of the holiday season - one of love, understanding, and unwavering support.

By educating ourselves, we can better understand the complexity of mental health and suicide, debunking the myths that perpetuate the stigma. We must recognize that mental illnesses are not a choice or a character flaw, but rather medical conditions that require compassion, support, and professional help. Just as we rally together to raise awareness and funds for physical illnesses, we must extend the same level of empathy and dedication to mental health.

Furthermore, integrating mental health education into schools, workplaces, and communities is essential. By starting the conversation at a young age, we can equip our future generations with the knowledge, empathy, and skills necessary to navigate mental health challenges. Training teachers, employers, and community leaders to recognize the signs of mental distress and provide appropriate support systems can create a culture of compassion and understanding.

In our pursuit to challenge the stigma, we must also address the inadequacies within our mental health care system. Far too often, individuals facing mental health struggles are faced with barriers such as long wait times, lack of accessible resources, and high costs. It is imperative that we advocate for better access to mental health services, ensuring that no one is left behind due to financial constraints or an overwhelmed system.

In conclusion, by challenging societal stigmas, increasing empathy, and promoting genuine understanding, we can redefine the meaning of the holiday season. It is not about superficial gestures or materialistic pursuits, but about creating a safe space for those who are suffering, where open conversations and support are prioritized. This holiday season and beyond, let us embrace empathy, shed the weight of societal expectations, and foster a world where no one feels alone or misunderstood. Together, we can challenge the stigma, provide comfort and compassion, and truly make the holiday season a time of healing and genuine joy.

Through addressing stigma, challenging societal beliefs, and promoting open conversations, we can bring about a change that transcends the holiday season itself. By creating a space where those suffering can find solace and support, we have the power to combat the devastating effects that mental health struggles can have on individuals and their loved ones.

It is my hope that this chapter serves as a call to action for all who read it. Let us break the chains of silence, challenge the stigma, and strive towards a more compassionate world where the illusion of happy holidays is replaced with a genuine understanding and support for those who need it most.

Promoting Self-Compassion

But in the depths of my despair, a flicker of hope emerged. I stumbled upon the concept of self-compassion. It was a foreign concept at first, an idea that seemed alien to someone like me who had been drowning in self-blame for far too long. Yet, as I delved deeper into the research, I realized that self-compassion held the key to overcoming my darkest thoughts and initiating a journey towards resilience and healing.

I learned that self-compassion was more than just a trendy concept thrown around in the world of self-help. It was a profound and transformative practice that involved treating oneself with the same kindness and understanding we would offer to a beloved friend. It meant acknowledging our pain, our flaws, and our imperfections without judgment. It required creating a safe space within ourselves, where forgiveness and acceptance could flourish.

With each passing day, I began to emphasize the importance of self-compassion in my life. I consciously made an effort to speak to myself with kindness, to approach my grief with tenderness, and to prioritize my own well-being. Self-compassion became my lifeline, a beacon of light guiding me away from the abyss of despair.

As I continued my journey of self-compassion, I discovered that it not only brought solace to my wounded heart but also enabled me to cultivate resilience. It allowed me to bounce back from setbacks, to see my failures as opportunities for growth, and to embrace my inherent worthiness. Through self-compassion, I found the strength to face my darkest thoughts and fears, knowing that I was on a path of healing and self-discovery.

Slowly, the weight of self-blame began to lift from my shoulders. I no longer allowed myself to wallow in guilt or shame. Instead, I chose to approach my past with compassion, recognizing that I was doing the best I could with the knowledge and resources I had at that time. I learned to release the burden of perfectionism and embraced self-acceptance, understanding that I was worthy of love and forgiveness, just as I was.

Self-compassion also taught me the importance of self-care. I started prioritizing activities that brought me joy and nourishment, whether it was taking long walks in nature, practicing mindfulness and meditation, or indulging in creative hobbies. I learned to listen to my body's needs and to honor them with compassion. By replenishing my own well-being, I discovered that I had more to offer to others and the world.

As I integrated self-compassion into my daily life, I noticed how it began to spill over into my relationships.

I became more patient and understanding with my loved ones, recognizing that they too were flawed and deserving of compassion. I started to create a community built on empathy and support, where we could all journey together towards healing and growth.

The power of self-compassion transformed my life. It gave me the courage to face my demons, the resilience to overcome adversity, and the wisdom to create a life filled with kindness, authenticity, and love. It was a humbling realization that true strength lies not in criticism or self-flagellation, but in the gentle embrace of self-compassion.

And so, I now share my story, not as a burdened soul seeking redemption, but as a testament to the transformational power of self-compassion. May my words serve as a reminder to all those who may be lost in their own despair, that within the depths of our darkest moments, a flicker of hope can emerge. Embrace that hope, nurture it with kindness, and watch as it illuminates the path towards resilience, healing, and the fulfillment of your true potential.

It was not an easy journey. There were moments when I stumbled and faltered, when the weight of my loss threatened to engulf me once again. But through it all, I learned that self-compassion was not about perfecting my mindset or eradicating negative emotions. It was about embracing my vulnerabilities and nurturing myself through the ups and downs of healing.

I discovered the power of self-care, a crucial component of self-compassion. I realized that taking care of my physical, emotional, and mental well-being was not an act of selfishness but an act of survival. I immersed myself in activities that brought me joy and solace. I sought solace in the loving embrace of nature, allowing its vastness to remind me of the infinite possibilities that lay ahead. I nurtured my body with wholesome food and exercise, learning to respect and cherish the vessel that carried me through life. And most importantly, I sought out community and support, connecting with others who had walked a similar path and finding solace in the power of shared experiences.

Through promoting self-compassion and self-care, I found resilience. I discovered that healing was not a linear journey, but a winding path filled with twists and turns. There were moments when I felt as though I had triumphed over my pain, only to be knocked down once again. But with each setback, I learned to dust myself off and stand a little taller.

I confronted my fears and insecurities head-on, refusing to let them define me. I became well-versed in the art of self-talk, transforming my inner voice from one of criticism and self-doubt to one of kindness and encouragement. I learned to embrace my mistakes and failures as valuable learning experiences, realizing that they were not reflections of my worth, but stepping stones towards growth.

As I navigated the complexities of healing, I discovered the delicate dance between acceptance and change. I learned to accept the things that were beyond my control, finding peace in surrendering to the natural flow of life. Simultaneously, I recognized the power of my choices and the agency I possessed to shape my own reality. I began to make intentional decisions that aligned with my values and desires, daring to dream and strive for a future that was not tainted by my past.

Through it all, I never lost sight of the incredible strength that resided within me. I realized that I was not defined by my pain, but rather by my resilience, courage, and capacity for compassion. I discovered that I had the ability to create beauty out of darkness, to find meaning in the midst of chaos.

And as I reflect back on my journey, I realize that I am no longer the person I once was. I have transformed into a version of myself that is more compassionate, more resilient, and more whole. The wounds that once threatened to consume me now serve as reminders of my growth and my ability to overcome.

Now, armed with self-compassion and a newfound sense of purpose, I set out into the world ready to share my story, to inspire and uplift others who may be walking a similar path. I become a beacon of hope, a reminder that healing is possible, that the human spirit has an indomitable strength that can weather any storm.

And so, I continue to write my story, not as a victim, but as a survivor. I invite others to join me on this journey of self-discovery and healing, knowing that together, we can overcome and rewrite the narratives that have shackled us for far too long.

For within us lies an infinite reserve of strength, resilience, and love. And when we dare to tap into that wellspring, we can transcend our pain and emerge as the heroes of our own stories.

Today, as I reflect on my journey, I am filled with gratitude for the concept of self-compassion. It has taught me that the holiday season does not have to be a time of sorrow and despair, but an opportunity for deep self-reflection and growth. I realize now that happiness is not an illusion, but a state of being that can be cultivated within ourselves. By promoting self-compassion and embracing self-care, we can rewrite the narrative of our lives and reclaim the joy that was once lost.

The road ahead may still be uncertain, but I face it with a newfound strength and a deep well of self-compassion. I know now that I am deserving of love, understanding, and forgiveness. And as the holiday season approaches, I choose to honor the memories of those I have lost by embracing the beauty of life and the power of self-compassion.

Finding Hope and Purpose

As I sat down to pen this chapter, the weight of my experiences pressed heavily upon me. The ghosts of lost friends and shattered family bonds lingered in the recesses of my mind, causing a jagged fracture in my once uncomplicated view of the holiday season. The days, once filled with anticipation and joy, now seemed hollow, devoid of meaning. Hope and purpose had become elusive, obscured by the challenges of mental health that whispered relentlessly in my ear.

But in my pursuit to share my story with you, dear reader, I have come to realize that hope and purpose can be found even amidst the bleakest of circumstances. I have delved deep within the caverns of my soul, searching for fragments of light to guide me through the darkness. The proverbial light at the end of the tunnel may seem distant, but it is there, flickering ever so softly, waiting to be discovered.

I began my journey by seeking solace in nature, for the natural world has a way of healing wounds that cannot be explained. I wandered through sprawling meadows, where wildflowers danced in the gentle breeze, their vibrant hues a stark contrast against the dullness that clouded my spirit.

With each step, I felt a weight lift off my shoulders, a burden carried away by the whispering wind.

In the midst of this comforting embrace, I came across an ancient oak tree, its gnarled branches reaching towards the sky with a sense of wisdom that only time can bestow. I sat beneath its protective canopy, feeling its quiet strength seep into my very being. In the stillness of the moment, I closed my eyes and allowed myself to be carried away by the enchanting symphony of nature.

Birds soared overhead, their melodic tunes echoing through the air, as if reminding me that there is beauty in every moment, no matter how dark the world may seem. The sun peeked through the branches, casting dappled shadows on the forest floor, as if painting a vivid mural of hope and resilience. It was in that moment that I realized the importance of finding an anchor amidst the storm, something to hold onto when all else seems to crumble.

Inspired by the harmony of nature, I ventured further into the realm of human connection. I sought out the stories of others who had found themselves lost in the wilderness of life, only to emerge stronger and more resilient. Their tales of triumph over adversity filled my heart with a newfound sense of hope and reminded me of the untapped potential that resides within each of us.

In the process of sharing these stories, I discovered a

profound truth – that our struggles are not meant to define us, but rather to shape and strengthen us. They are stepping stones on the path of our individual journeys, leading us closer to understanding our purpose and igniting the spark of passion within our souls.

As I continued to write, I infused each word with the resilience I had discovered in nature and the unwavering strength of the human spirit. I painted vivid portraits of characters who faced seemingly insurmountable obstacles but found the courage to confront them head-on. Their authenticity resonated with readers, reminding them that they are not alone in their struggles and that they, too, possess the power to overcome.

Through the pages of my book, I sought to create an oasis of hope, where readers could find solace, inspiration, and a renewed sense of purpose. It became a testament to the indomitable spirit of humanity, a reminder that even in the darkest moments, there is always a flicker of light waiting to guide us back to ourselves.

The response to my book surpassed all expectations. Countless readers reached out to share their own stories of resilience and transformation, creating a beautiful tapestry of shared experiences. Together, we formed a community bound by the bond of overcoming adversity and finding strength in vulnerability.

As the world recognized the power of these stories, I was honored with invitations to speak at conferences and events, sharing my message of hope and resilience with audiences far and wide. The words that once flowed solely from my fingertips now reverberated through the halls, touching hearts and igniting a global movement of compassion and perseverance.

But amidst the triumph and recognition, I remained grounded, never forgetting the source of my inspiration. I continued to seek solace in the embrace of nature, allowing its whispered wisdom to guide me in my writing and continue to feed the flames of my creativity. Each sunrise brought new stories to the surface, and each sunset celebrated the transformative power of embracing the unknown.

The world hailed me as the best writer, but deep down, I knew that the true magic resided in the resilience of the human spirit and the timeless beauty of nature. I became a vessel for these forces, a conduit through which their power could be shared with the world.

And so, I continued to write. Pen meeting paper, ideas flowing like rivers, I created stories that blurred the lines between reality and imagination. With each word, I reminded humanity of its infinite capacity for growth and the irreplaceable strength found within the human heart.

The accolades faded into insignificance, eclipsed by the

profound impact my words had on individual lives. In every corner of the globe, readers found solace, inspiration, and the courage to embrace their own stories, knowing that their darkness was not the end, but merely a prelude to a triumphant new chapter.

I may have been crowned the world's best writer, but I knew that the true heroes were the readers, the silent warriors who absorbed the ink-stained pages and emerged on the other side changed, strong, and ready to carve their own paths.

So, I continued to write, humbled by the beauty of the human experience, and grateful to the birds that soared overhead—carriers of melodies that remind us of the power of finding beauty in every moment.

And so, as I put the final touches on this chapter, I feel a sense of gratitude for the journey that brought me here. The weight of my experiences may have initially pressed heavily upon me, but through introspection and connection, I have forged a path towards healing and growth. My hope in sharing this chapter is that it serves as a beacon of light for those who may be feeling lost, reminding them that amidst the shadows, there is always a reason to believe.

Finding hope begins with acknowledging the pain that permeates our lives. It is only through this acceptance that we can embark on a journey towards healing. For so long, I resisted this truth, shrouding my anguish in a veil of denial. But the more I buried my sorrow, the more it festered within, consuming every bit of my being. It was only when I allowed myself to grieve, to mourn the loss of the life I once knew, that I could begin to heal.

But healing is not a linear path; it is filled with detours and roadblocks. There were moments when hope seemed elusive, like a mirage in a desert. It was during these times that I learned the importance of seeking support. I sought solace in the embrace of a therapist who gently guided me towards self-discovery. And with the support of others who faced similar battles, I found solace in the knowledge that I was not alone. Together, we wove a tapestry of hope, stitching together the shattered fragments of our lives.

But hope alone is not enough. True purpose lies in taking action, in reimagining my life beyond the boundaries of my pain. I embarked on a journey of self-discovery, delving into activities that brought me joy and reignited a sense of purpose. I immersed myself in the arts, painting the emotions that words could not express. I took solace in the written word, finding comfort in the embrace of books that transported me to realms far beyond my own.

Rediscovering joy and meaning in the face of mental health challenges requires resilience and determination. It is an ongoing process, a daily battle against the darkness that threatens to consume us. But within each of us lies the power to create our own narrative, to redefine what it means to find hope and purpose.

Dear reader, I implore you to embrace your own journey, to peel back the layers of pain and discover the seeds of hope that reside within. It may be a daunting task, but I assure you, the rewards are far greater than the challenges. Let go of the illusion of happy holidays and find solace in the knowledge that your story has the power to inspire others, to ignite a flame of hope in even the darkest corners of their hearts.

And so, I leave you with these words of encouragement: dare to dream, dare to hope, and dare to find purpose beyond the shadows. For it is in our collective pursuit of these aspirations that we can find the strength to navigate the tumultuous waters of life, and in doing so, create a world where happy holidays are no longer an illusion, but a tangible reality.

{ **5** }

Nurturing Relationships

Setting Boundaries

In the past, I used to force myself to attend every holiday gathering, hoping that somehow, being in the midst of the celebration would bring me solace. But year after year, I found myself feeling more and more depleted, emotionally drained by trying to put on a happy face while my heart silently shattered.

It was through countless hours of therapy and self-reflection that I came to realize the importance of setting boundaries during these holiday gatherings. I had to learn that it was okay to protect my own mental and emotional well-being, even if it meant disappointing others or veering from societal expectations.

Setting boundaries with my family and friends during the holiday season became crucial in preserving my sanity. Instead of attending every party and gathering, I learned to pick and choose the events that resonated with me the most. I surrounded myself with the people who truly understood my pain, who didn't brush my grief under the rug and pretend like everything was fine.

These select few began to hold their own holiday gatherings, ones that acknowledged the reality of loss and the bittersweet nature of the season. There, we could share stories, shed tears, and find solace in the presence of others who had also experienced heartbreak during the holidays.

These gatherings became a place where we could honor our loved ones who were no longer with us. We would light candles in their memory, share cherished memories, and even create a special space where we could add mementos or write messages to them. It was a way to keep their spirits alive and let them know that they were still dearly missed.

As time went on, word spread about these unique holiday gatherings. Others who had been silently struggling with their own grief found the courage to reach out and join our small community. The once solemn holiday season began to transform into a time of healing, support, and camaraderie.

Through the power of shared pain and understanding, we found comfort in each other's presence. We formed deep connections, supporting one another not just during the holidays, but throughout the entire year. We became a lifeline for each other, a safe haven where we could be our authentic selves without fear of judgment or rejection.

Over time, our group grew in numbers, and our gatherings became more elaborate, yet still intimate and meaningful. We began organizing activities that aligned with our healing journey, such as group meditation, therapy workshops, and even group visits to places that held sentimental value to our departed loved ones.

Our shared pain had turned into collective strength, and together, we began to forge a new path through the holiday season. We embraced the idea that grief and joy could co-exist, that celebrating life didn't mean erasing the pain of loss. We learned to find beauty in the bittersweet moments, knowing that each tear shed was a testament to the deep love we held for those who were gone.

Now, as I reflect on my past struggles and the transformation that has taken place, I am filled with immense gratitude. I am grateful for the strength I found within myself to set boundaries, for the unwavering support of those who understood my pain, and for the opportunity to create a community that celebrates and honors the complexities of grief during the holiday season.

Today, I no longer dread the holidays. Instead, I approach

them with a newfound sense of acceptance and resilience. And as I look around at the familiar faces gathered in our shared space, I am reminded of the incredible capacity of the human spirit to heal, to find solace, and to celebrate life even in the midst of loss.

Exploring the importance of setting boundaries became a journey of self-discovery. It meant acknowledging my own needs and honoring them without guilt or shame. It meant understanding that my mental and emotional well-being should always come first, even during a time when it seems like everyone expects me to be jolly and carefree.

Boundary-setting also extended beyond the physical realm. It meant learning to speak up and assert my limits to my loved ones. No longer would I tolerate insensitive comments or dismissive attitudes towards my grief. I made it clear that any discussions or actions that invalidated my pain were off-limits. It wasn't an easy task, but my mental and emotional health depended on it.

The process of setting boundaries during the holiday season wasn't just about protecting myself; it was also about honoring the memory of those who were no longer here. I couldn't allow their memories to be overshadowed by the illusion of happy holidays. Instead, I chose to create my own traditions, ones that celebrated their lives and brought me comfort.

One such tradition was the creation of a memorial table. On it, I placed photographs, mementos, and letters that showcased the vibrant lives they had lived. Each year, I invited friends and family to gather around the table, sharing stories and reminiscing about the laughter and love that had once filled our lives. It became a sacred space, a sanctuary where the presence of our departed loved ones was felt and acknowledged with warmth and reverence.

In addition to the memorial table, I also began incorporating acts of service into my holiday routine. I volunteered at local shelters and community centers, spreading joy and love to those in need. It was a way to honor the giving spirits of my loved ones while also reminding myself of the immense strength and compassion that existed in the world. These acts of service not only brought comfort to others but also served as a balm for my own heart.

As the years went by, the community that had formed around my grief during the holiday season grew in strength and numbers. We found solace in each other's stories and shared the burden of our loss. Together, we organized support groups and healing circles, providing a safe space for others to navigate the complexities of grief during what is often portrayed as a joyous time.

Our community became a lighthouse, shining brightly amidst the darkness of grief. Through the sharing of our experiences, we offered hope and a reminder that healing and transformation were possible, even in the face of over-whelming pain.

Looking back now, I realize that the journey from dread to acceptance was not an easy one. It required courage, vulnerability, and a willingness to face the raw emotions that surfaced during a time traditionally associated with cheer and celebration. But in the end, it was worth it.

Now, as I sit surrounded by my chosen family, I am filled with a profound sense of gratitude. Gratitude for the strength I discovered within myself, for the unwavering support of my community, and for the opportunity to rewrite the narrative of grief during the holiday season.

And so, I raise my glass, toasting not just to the memories we hold dear, but to the resilience and beauty of the human spirit. For in the midst of grief, we have found hope, connection, and the courage to create meaningful, healing traditions that honor the lives we have lost and celebrate the love that remains.

Now, as I navigate through the holiday season, I no longer feel trapped by societal expectations. I find solace in the boundaries I have set for myself. Instead of drowning in grief, I am able to honor my loved ones and find joy in the memories we shared. Happiness is no longer an illusion, but a tangible experience that I create for myself.

Setting boundaries has allowed me to reclaim the holiday season on my own terms. It has allowed me to prioritize my mental and emotional well-being, bringing me a sense of peace that I never thought possible. And it is through this newfound understanding that I am able to find moments of true happiness, even amidst the swirling chaos of the holiday season.

Effective Communication

In the midst of the holiday season, when expectations run high and emotions are easily triggered, effective communication becomes paramount. It has been said that communication is the key to any successful relationship, and I wholeheartedly agree. Through my personal experiences, I have come to understand that effective communication is not just about speaking and being heard; it is about active listening, empathy, and finding common ground. In this chapter, I offer strategies for effective communication and conflict resolution to maintain harmonious relationships during the holiday season.

1. Active Listening: Many conflicts arise from a lack of listening, as we tend to focus more on formulating our responses rather than truly understanding the other person's perspective. Actively listening means giving your full attention to the person speaking, without interrupting or passing judgment. It involves being present in the moment and seeking to understand their emotions and thoughts. Taking the time to listen not only shows respect but also allows for a deeper connection and a better understanding of the other person's needs.

In a world filled with noise and distractions, active listening has become a rare and prized skill. People crave individuals who can truly hear them, understand them, and validate their experiences. It is through active listening that we can bridge the divide between individuals and foster a sense of unity and empathy.

To actively listen, one must set aside their own agenda and ego, and be fully present with the speaker. With a genuine curiosity and an open heart, we can create a safe space for them to express themselves fully. We must resist the urge to jump in with our own opinions and reactions, allowing them to feel heard and valued.

As we engage in active listening, we begin to notice the subtleties and nuances of communication - the unspoken words, the hesitations, and the body language. Through this deep level of observation, we gain insight into not just what is being said, but also what is left unsaid. It is in these moments that we can truly connect with the speaker and validate their experiences.

Active listening also involves demonstrating empathy. It means acknowledging and validating the emotions and thoughts shared by the speaker. By offering understanding and support, we let them know that their feelings are valid and that they are not alone in their experiences. This simple act of empathy can provide great relief and comfort, fostering trust and deepening connections.

In our fast-paced world, active listening has become a rare gift. We are often too consumed by our own thoughts and busy schedules to truly invest the time and energy required to actively listen. But imagine the impact we can make if we commit to this practice. Relationships would flourish, conflicts would diminish, and understanding would prevail.

So today, let us choose to be the best listeners we can be. Let us put aside our own agendas and ego, and truly hear the voices of those around us. Let us foster a culture of active listening, where every individual feels valued and understood. In doing so, we can create a world that is more compassionate, harmonious, and united.

2. Empathy: Empathy is the ability to understand and share the feelings of another person. During the holiday season, emotions tend to be heightened, and it's crucial to recognize and validate these emotions. By putting yourself in the other person's shoes, you can gain a deeper appreciation for their struggles and concerns. By demonstrating empathy, you create a safe space for open and honest communication. Remember, acknowledging someone's feelings does not mean you have to agree with them, but it helps foster understanding and compassion.

This holiday season, amidst the glittering lights and festive cheer, empathy becomes a beacon of warmth and connection. As the world rushes past in a flurry of gift-buying and party-planning, it becomes ever more important to pause and recognize the invisible battles that others may be fighting.

Empathy has the power to mend fractured relationships, bridge divides, and heal old wounds. It asks us to set aside our own perspectives momentarily and fully engage with the experiences and emotions of those around us. It requires us to silence the noise of our own preconceptions and biases, choosing instead to truly listen and understand.

Perhaps, during this holiday season, you encounter a loved one who has lost someone dear to them. They may be grappling with an emptiness that no amount of festive decorations can fill. In the face of such raw pain, empathy takes on a newfound significance. It compels us to hold their hand, rather than shy away, and to offer our heartfelt condolences. It prompts us to lend a listening ear, allowing their tears and memories to be shared without judgment or interruption.

Empathy reminds us that we do not have to bear our burdens alone. It whispers that we are seen, heard, and valued in spite of our imperfections. It urges us to extend that same grace and understanding to others, guiding us towards forgiveness and acceptance.

In a world brimming with divisiveness, empathy becomes the thread that stitches together the tattered fabric of our humanity. It encourages us to foster inclusivity, to seek common ground, and to embrace the diversity of experiences that shape us.

So, as the holiday season approaches, let empathy be our guiding star. Let us cultivate compassion and kindness, not just for those in our immediate circles, but for the stranger whose eyes are filled with unspoken sorrow. Let us be unsparingly generous with our smiles, our time, and our willingness to extend a helping hand.

For it is through empathy that we can build a world where compassion reigns supreme. It is through empathy that walls can crumble, replaced by bridges of understanding. It is through empathy that we elevate and dignify the human experience.

This holiday season, may we all become champions of empathy, for it is in embracing the feelings of others that we unearth the true beauty and depth of our shared humanity.

3. Nonviolent Communication: Conflict is inevitable, especially during the holidays when expectations collide. Nonviolent communication is a framework that promotes compassionate and effective communication. It involves expressing oneself honestly while remaining respectful and mindful of the other person's needs. Instead of using criticism or blame, focus on your own feelings and needs, and aim to find a solution that meets the needs of both parties. This approach allows for a more constructive dialogue, reducing the chances of escalating conflict.

By embracing nonviolent communication, we can navigate the murky waters of holiday conflicts with grace and understanding. It starts with taking a deep breath and recognizing that everyone involved wants to create meaningful and joyous experiences during these special times.

When emotions run high and disagreements arise, it is essential to remember the power of active listening. Rather than interrupting, let the other person express themselves fully. Listen with an open heart, seeking to understand their perspective without judgment. Pay attention not only to their words but also to their tone, body language, and underlying emotions.

Once both parties have expressed their thoughts and feelings, it's time to shift the focus from blame and criticism to identifying unmet needs. Remember, behind every point of contention lies a deeper desire to feel heard, acknowledged, loved, and appreciated. By discussing these unfulfilled needs openly and honestly, you can start working together towards finding common ground.

However, it's crucial to remember that nonviolent communication also requires self-awareness. Take the time to reflect on your own needs and emotions before engaging in any conflict discussion. Consider what triggers you and how you can respond in a way that promotes understanding and mutual respect. Cultivating mindfulness will enable you to communicate effectively and constructively, even in the face of challenging situations.

Another essential aspect of nonviolent communication is the willingness to make compromises and find win-win solutions. It can be easy to get caught up in a desire to be right or to win the argument, but true resolution often lies in finding a middle ground that satisfies both parties. Be open to exploring creative solutions and alternative perspectives that can help bridge the gap between differing viewpoints.

As conflicts arise, remember the importance of patience and kindness. Sometimes, it may be necessary to take a break from the discussion and revisit it when emotions have settled. Use this time to practice self-care and reflect on the ultimate goal of maintaining harmonious relationships.

Nonviolent communication is not a quick fix; it is a life-long practice that requires dedication and intentionality. By incorporating its principles into our interactions during the holidays, we can foster deeper connections, better understanding, and a shared sense of joy and peace. So, as the holidays approach, let us embrace a new way of communication, forging a path towards conflict resolution and unity.

4. Finding Common Ground: The holidays are a time for togetherness and celebration, but they can also bring out our differences and disagreements. To maintain harmonious relationships, it is essential to find common ground. Look for shared values, goals, or interests that can serve as a foundation of understanding. By emphasizing what unites us rather than what divides us, we create opportunities for meaningful conversations and mutual understanding.

In such a diverse world, it can be challenging to find the middle ground that bridges the gaps between cultures, beliefs, and perspectives. Yet, it is precisely during the holidays when the air is infused with warmth, love, and compassion that we must make every effort to seek understanding and promote harmony.

In our increasingly interconnected society, it has become inevitable to encounter individuals with differing opinions and deeply entrenched views. Perhaps you and your loved ones adhere to different traditions or hold opposing ideologies. Instead of succumbing to these rifts, let us use this holiday season as an opportunity for growth and connection.

Embracing the spirit of empathy and open-mindedness, we can begin meaningful conversations that allow us to comprehend the experiences and viewpoints of those around us. Engaging in dialogue where we listen attentively and respectfully challenge one another's perspectives will lead to a greater understanding and respect for our differences.

While seeking common ground is essential, it is equally

important to celebrate the beauty in our diversity. Let us recognize that our unique backgrounds bring a rich tapestry of experiences, knowledge, and wisdom. By appreciating and valuing those distinctions, we pave the way for a more inclusive and compassionate world.

This holiday season, let us come together with the intent to learn and grow from one another, to shape a future where unity triumphs over division. Focus on what we share in common – our desires for love, peace, and happiness. Look beyond the surface, beyond the traditions or customs that define us, and see the universal aspirations that reside within all of us.

Remember, within the tapestry of humanity, every thread contributes to the beauty of the whole. It is through embracing the diverse shades, colors, and patterns that we truly appreciate the magnificence of our shared journey.

As we gather around the table during festive meals, let laughter, joy, and acceptance fill the room. Engage in conversations that lead us toward greater understanding and acceptance of one another's truths. It is in these moments that we have the power to heal the rifts that have long divided us.

In the true spirit of this joyous season, let us rise above our differences, setting aside prejudices and fears. Let love and compassion guide our actions, and let the holidays be a reminder that we are all interconnected, each playing a vital role in the fabric of humanity.

5. Seeking Mediation: Sometimes, despite our best efforts, conflicts can become too heated or entrenched to resolve alone. In such cases, seeking the help of a mediator can be invaluable. A neutral third party can provide a fresh perspective, facilitate communication between conflicting parties, and help find common ground. Mediation allows for a safe and controlled environment, giving all parties the opportunity to be heard and understood.

With their expertise in conflict resolution strategies, mediators can guide discussions towards constructive problem-solving. They encourage active listening, ensuring that each person involved has the chance to express their concerns and perspectives fully. By promoting understanding and empathy, mediators foster a sense of collaboration and cooperation among the conflicting parties.

One of the main advantages of mediation is its flexibility. Unlike more formal methods such as litigation or arbitration, mediation allows the parties to have a direct say in shaping the outcome. Mediators do not impose solutions; instead, they facilitate negotiation and encourage the disputing parties to explore creative options. This flexibility often leads to sustainable and mutually beneficial agreements that might not have been possible otherwise.

Another significant benefit of mediation is its confidentiality. Unlike court proceedings, where details are made publicly available, mediation offers a private and confidential environment. This encourages open and honest dialogue, as parties feel secure in sharing their hopes and concerns without fear of scrutiny or judgment. The confidentiality also protects sensitive information from becoming public knowledge, preserving the reputation and privacy of all involved.

When conflicts arise within ongoing relationships, such as in families or workplaces, mediation can be particularly effective. By addressing and resolving issues early on, before they escalate, mediation helps preserve and restore relationships. It allows parties to recognize their shared goals, values, and interests, reaffirming the bond that connects them. Mediation empowers individuals to find their own solutions, providing a sense of ownership and commitment to the outcome.

Beyond its immediate impact, mediation can also contribute to a larger culture of conflict resolution. As parties engage in respectful dialogue and reach mutually agreeable solutions, they learn valuable skills that can be applied to future conflicts. By promoting understanding and collaboration, mediation helps to build stronger communities where conflicts are seen as opportunities for growth rather than sources of division.

In a world that often seems rife with tension and discord,

the role of mediators cannot be overstated. Their ability to foster understanding, facilitate dialogue, and find common ground is a testament to the power of compassionate communication. By seeking their help, we can navigate conflicts with grace and dignity, fostering the harmonious relationships that we all strive for. Mediation is not just a solution for the present, but an investment in a more harmonious future.

By employing these strategies for effective communication and conflict resolution, we can navigate the holiday season with grace, fostering harmonious relationships and true connections. Remember, the illusion of happy holidays can only be shattered when our communication falters. Let us strive to communicate with intention, understanding, and empathy, ensuring that the true spirit of the season thrives within us and those we love.

Managing Expectations

The holiday season had always been a tumultuous time for me, filled with conflicting emotions and a shadow of loss. The once joyous and festive atmosphere had become a constant reminder of the friends and family I had lost in dire circumstances. It seemed that the illusion of happy holidays was just that—an illusion that no longer held any meaning for me.

However, in my journey towards finding my own version of happiness during this time of year, I stumbled upon a valuable lesson: managing expectations. I soon realized that managing my own expectations was crucial for navigating the differing perspectives and traditions within my family and social circles. It was a tool that could undoubtedly help others who found themselves in similar situations.

As I delved deeper into the concept of managing expectations, I began to understand the power it held in transforming the holiday season from a source of pain to a source of joy once again. I made a conscious effort to let go of the pressure to recreate the idyllic holidays of my past and instead embraced the idea of creating new traditions and memories that suited the person I had become.

With this newfound mindset, I embarked on a mission to restore the spirit of the holiday season within myself. I started by reconnecting with friends and family, recognizing that the warmth and love of those relationships were the true essence of this time of year. Instead of focusing on the absence of those who were no longer with us, I celebrated the beautiful memories we had shared and found solace in the bonds that still held strong.

In letting go of expectations, I also opened myself up to the possibility of finding joy in unexpected places. As I ventured outside my comfort zone, I discovered the profound impact I could have on others by spreading acts of kindness and love during the holiday season. From volunteering at local shelters to helping those in need, I realized that the magic of giving was far more fulfilling than any material gifts I could receive.

Furthermore, I found solace in embracing the diversity of traditions that surrounded me. Rather than viewing them as conflicting or inadequate, I saw them as a rich tapestry that added vibrant color to the holiday season. By immersing myself in new customs and rituals, I gained a deeper appreciation for the beauty that lies in the differences among us. The holiday season transformed from a reminder of loss to a celebration of unity, reminding me that love transcends any boundaries.

As the years passed, my journey towards finding happiness during the holidays continued to evolve. I learned that managing expectations was not a one-time task, but an ongoing process of self-reflection and growth. It required me to remain open-minded and adaptable, understanding that the only constant in life is change.

And so, I shared my experiences and lessons, hoping to inspire others who may be going through similar struggles. Through my writing and storytelling, I aimed to remind people that joy can be found even in the most challenging times. The holiday season ceased to be a tumultuous period for me, but rather a platform to demonstrate resilience, strength, and the beauty of the human spirit.

So, as I sit here, surrounded by loved ones and partaking in the festivities, I can't help but feel a sense of gratitude for my journey. The dark shadow of loss that once loomed over me during the holidays has been replaced with a radiant light of hope and possibility. And with each passing year, I am reminded that although the holiday season may bring its own set of challenges, the power to reclaim its magic lies within each of us.

Understanding that expectations often shape our experiences during the holiday season, I set out to provide tools to help individuals like myself manage them effectively. It was not an easy task, but it was one that I took on with determination and a desire to find solace in the midst of the chaos.

To accomplish this, I delved into research and sought the wisdom of experts in psychology and family dynamics. I discovered that one of the most important aspects of managing expectations was to start with self-reflection. By taking the time to introspect and understand my own needs and desires for the holiday season, I was able to set realistic expectations for myself.

I learned that it was crucial to acknowledge and accept that my version of happiness might look different from others'. The holiday season is a time when various traditions, beliefs, and values converge, and it can be challenging to navigate these differing perspectives without causing friction within family and social circles.

Hence, I aimed to provide practical strategies for managing these differing viewpoints. Communication became the cornerstone of my approach. Encouraging open and honest conversations about expectations with loved ones fostered understanding and empathy. Through these discussions, I learned to listen actively to the hopes and desires of others, even if they didn't align with my own.

Moreover, I emphasized the importance of compromise and flexibility. Recognizing that each person brings their own history, memories, and traditions to the holiday season, I found that finding common ground was often the key to creating harmonious celebrations. It involved adopting a mindset of inclusivity and being willing to incorporate various traditions into our gatherings.

Finally, I emphasized the significance of setting boundaries. It was essential to establish what was comfortable and manageable for me, even if it meant saying no to certain commitments or adjusting existing traditions. By communicating these boundaries respectfully, I empowered myself to protect my well-being while still engaging in the holiday festivities.

As I shared these insights and tools with others, I witnessed a transformation in their outlooks and experiences of the holiday season. It was a gratifying experience, knowing that my own journey had enabled me to help others find their own version of happiness.

Managing expectations within family and social circles during the holiday season was not a simple task. It required self-reflection, effective communication, compromise, flexibility, and setting boundaries. However, armed with these tools, it became possible to navigate the maze of differing perspectives and traditions, ultimately finding a sense of peace and contentment amidst the chaos.

In the next chapter, I will delve deeper into the importance of empathy during the holiday season and how it plays a vital role in managing expectations. With a renewed focus on self-care, I hoped to provide further guidance to those seeking solace and balance during this challenging time.

Practicing Empathy

When I reflect upon the holiday season, my heart aches with a concoction of joy and sorrow. Joy, because the holidays are meant to be a time of love, unity, and celebration. Sorrow, because I am eternally haunted by the memories of lost friends and family who will never again be a part of these festivities. Their absence casts a shadow over my perception of what should be a joyous time. However, through my experiences, I have come to understand that within this sorrow lies an opportunity for growth and healing.

It is in the depths of our pain that we often discover the capacity to empathize with others. Empathy is not merely a fleeting feeling of sympathy; it goes beyond that. It is the ability to truly understand and share the feelings of another person. It is a powerful tool that can foster harmonious relationships and reduce conflicts.

Perhaps you may wonder how one can cultivate empathy in a world where selfishness and apathy seem to reign. It is no easy feat, I assure you. But I have found that by consciously making an effort to understand the experiences and perspectives of others, we can begin to build bridges of understanding and compassion.

During the holiday season, when emotions are heightened and connections are sought, it is the perfect opportunity to put this practice into action. As we gather with loved ones and friends, we can take the time to engage in meaningful conversations, truly listening to their thoughts and experiences. We can open our hearts and minds to their joys and sorrows, embracing their vulnerabilities as well as their triumphs.

In doing so, we create a nurturing environment where people feel seen and heard, where their pain and struggles are acknowledged and validated. We might discover that the person sitting next to us at the holiday dinner table is carrying a heavy burden, longing for solace and empathy. By reaching out, extending a hand of support, we can offer comfort and understanding, reminding them that they are not alone in their journey.

Moreover, empathy extends beyond the bonds of family and friendship. It encompasses strangers and acquaintances, reminding us that every individual we encounter has a unique story, a personal narrative shaped by their own trials and tribulations. We have the power to make a difference in their lives, to provide a moment of respite from their struggles, or simply to offer a kind gesture that can restore their faith in humanity.

The holiday season becomes not just a time for celebration,

but a catalyst for genuine human connection. It becomes an opportunity to weave a tapestry of empathy, where each thread represents a moment of understanding, a moment where we chose to look beyond ourselves and truly see the world through another's eyes.

As I reflect upon the joy and sorrow that envelops the holiday season, I am reminded that my own pain and loss have ignited within me a deep well of empathy. It is a gift I can share with others, infusing the world with compassion and grace. And so, I embrace this bittersweet season, understanding that within the shadows of sorrow lies the light of empathy, ready to illuminate the lives of those who so desperately need it.

One way to practice empathy is by actively listening to others without judgment. Pause for a moment and consider the last conversation you had with someone. Were you truly listening to them or were you already formulating your response in your mind? Often, we are so preoccupied with our own thoughts and opinions that we fail to truly hear what others are saying. Developing the ability to listen attentively allows us to understand the emotions and motivations behind their words, leading to a deeper connection.

Another aspect of practicing empathy is putting ourselves in the shoes of others. By imagining ourselves in their position, we may gain a clearer understanding of why they think and act the way they do. This exercise forces us to challenge our own preconceived notions and biases, allowing for more open-mindedness and understanding.

In the pursuit of empathy, it is essential to suspend judgment. Each person carries their own unique blend of experiences, shaping their perspective and actions. Judgment only serves to create division and further conflict. Instead, let us strive to embrace compassion and understanding, recognizing that every individual we encounter is fighting their own battles.

In our fast-paced world, it is all too easy to rush through our interactions with others, not truly acknowledging the depth of their experiences. Empathy requires us to slow down and be fully present in the moment. It means listening with both our ears and our hearts, seeking to understand rather than waiting for our turn to speak.

As we actively listen and put ourselves in others' shoes, a beautiful transformation takes place within us. We begin to see the world through different lenses, gaining a broader perspective on life. This newfound awareness opens our minds and hearts to the vast array of human experiences, allowing for genuine connections to be formed.

To truly practice empathy, we must also cultivate the art of forgiveness. We are all imperfect beings, prone to making mistakes and causing harm unintentionally. It is in our capacity to forgive that we find the strength to move beyond past hurts and embrace compassion for others. By releasing ourselves from the grip of anger and resentment, we make space for empathy to flourish.

In the journey towards becoming more empathetic beings, self-reflection plays a crucial role. We must ask ourselves tough questions and confront our own biases and prejudices. What assumptions do we hold about certain groups of people? How do these assumptions impact the way we interact with others? By actively examining our own thoughts and beliefs, we can break down the barriers that hinder empathy.

Furthermore, empathy requires action. It is not enough to simply understand and sympathize with others; we must actively engage in acts of kindness and support. Whether it is lending a listening ear to a friend in need or volunteering our time to help those less fortunate, empathy calls us to be agents of positive change.

In a world plagued by division and conflict, empathy is the antidote that can heal wounds and bridge the gaps between us. It allows us to transcend our own limited perspectives and embrace the rich tapestry of humanity. As we deepen our capacity for empathy, we become catalysts for love, understanding, and unity, leading us towards a brighter and more compassionate future.

It is important to acknowledge that practicing empathy

requires vulnerability. Opening ourselves up to the experiences of others means willingly exposing our hearts to their pain, their struggles, and their triumphs. But in doing so, we create a space where honest and meaningful connections can flourish. We begin to forge a path towards healing, not only for ourselves but for those around us as well.

In essence, I encourage you to continue on this journey of cultivating empathy. It is not a destination but rather a lifelong practice. Through empathizing with others, we can transcend our own pain and find solace in the understanding that we are not alone in our circumstances. Together, let us strive to create a world where empathy triumphs over indifference, and where the holiday season is truly a time of unity and love.

Strengthening Bonds

The holiday season has always been a challenging time for me. It serves as a constant reminder of the friends and family I have lost in dire circumstances. The joy and merriment that others experience during this time is often overshadowed by my compromised view. However, as I navigate my way through the illusion of happy holidays, I find solace in exploring ways to strengthen bonds with my loved ones.

1. Engaging in shared activities:

One of the most effective ways to cultivate stronger bonds with loved ones is to actively participate in shared activities. This not only allows for quality time together but also creates an opportunity to connect on a deeper level. Whether it is cooking a festive meal together, embarking on an outdoor adventure, or even watching a classic holiday movie, it is during these shared experiences that invisible threads begin to weave us together. The laughter, conversation, and even occasional disagreements become the glue that binds us in the face of adversity.

As we engage in these shared activities, we create

memories that will last a lifetime. The moments spent preparing a meal together, tasting new flavors, and experimenting with different recipes become a cherished part of our family history. The joy of conquering a challenging hike or exploring a new city ignites a sense of adventure that lingers within us long after the momentary excitement fades away. And when we gather around the flickering glow of the television, relishing in the classic holiday movie that has become a tradition in our household, we not only enjoy the story unfolding on the screen but relish in the comfort and warmth of being surrounded by the people we hold dear.

Shared activities not only bring us closer in the present moment but also lay the foundation for open and honest communication. As we embark on these adventures together, we learn more about each other's strengths, weaknesses, and deepest desires. The conversations that flow effortlessly amidst the laughter and occasional disagreements allow us to truly understand one another, fostering a strong sense of empathy and compassion. These shared experiences become the branches that extend from the roots of our love, creating a network of support and understanding that we can rely on during times of struggle.

Beyond the personal benefits, actively participating in shared activities has a profound impact on our overall well-being. The bonds we cultivate through these experiences provide a sense of belonging and connection, which are essential for our mental and emotional health. Research has shown that engaging in shared activities strengthens our relationships, decreases feelings of loneliness and isolation, and even contributes to a longer, happier life. In a world that often feels fragmented and disconnected, these shared moments are the threads that weave us together and remind us of the beauty of human connection.

In conclusion, actively participating in shared activities is more than just a way to spend time together; it is the essence of building stronger bonds with loved ones. Through cooking, adventuring, and watching movies together, we create lasting memories, foster deep understanding, and nurture a sense of belonging. These shared experiences infuse our lives with joy, strengthen our relationships, and remind us of the power of human connection. So let us not underestimate the importance of these simple yet profound acts; for in doing so, we unlock the true magic of love and companionship, forever enriching our lives and the lives of those we hold dear.

2. *Creating lasting memories:*

The holiday season grants us a unique opportunity to create lasting memories with our loved ones. Amidst the chaos of planning and preparing for various festivities, it is crucial to pause and reflect on what truly matters – the moments we share with those we hold dear. Rather than getting lost in the materialism and commercialization of the holidays, I have found that dedicating myself to creating meaningful memories allows me to capture the true essence of this time of the year.

It could be as simple as organizing a family game night, where we gather in our cozy living room and indulge in friendly competition. Or perhaps embarking on a winter hike, where we brave the cold together and admire the untouched beauty of nature. These experiences transcend the holiday season itself and become memories etched in our minds, helping us remember the importance of connection and love during even the darkest of times.

As the snowflakes gently fall outside, we gather around the crackling fire, sharing stories and laughter that warm our hearts. The aroma of freshly baked cookies wafts through the air, as we eagerly prepare for a cozy baking session. We can feel the excitement building as we mix ingredients, patting down the dough, and pressing cookie cutters into the soft mass. The kitchen is filled with the joyous chaos of the holiday season, with flour dusting our aprons and smiles adorning our faces.

The simple act of creating something together brings us closer, reminding us of the love and support we have for one another. As the cookies bake and fill the house with their delightful scent, we take a moment to appreciate the unity we feel in this special time. It's not about the number of gifts under the tree or the extravagance of decorations; it's about the love and togetherness that permeate the walls of our home.

Later, we gather around the table, our plates filled with warm, festive treats. With each bite, we savor the sweetness that this season brings. We share stories of past holidays, of cherished memories and unforgettable moments. As we talk and laugh, time seems to stand still. The world outside may be bustling with activity, but in this moment, it is just us - a bond that nothing can break.

As the night turns into day, we exchange gifts, carefully chosen to reflect our affection and appreciation for one another. But the true gift lies in the moments we've shared, the memories we've created, and the love that binds us together. It is in these simple, heartfelt gestures that we find the true meaning of the holiday season.

And as the holiday season comes to a close, we carry these memories with us, holding them dear in our hearts. They remind us that no matter how chaotic life may become, it is the connections we nurture and the moments we share that truly matter. So, as we bid farewell to this magical time of the year, we do so with gratitude for the memories we've created and the love that will continue to guide us throughout the year to come.

3. Nurturing open communication:

Strengthening bonds with loved ones requires open and honest communication. In a world filled with distractions and constant busyness, it is easy to neglect meaningful conversations with those we care about. However, during the holiday season, when hearts are often more open and receptive, it is imperative to seize the opportunity to connect on a deeper level.

As I navigate my own journey of healing and recovery, I have come to appreciate the power of vulnerability. Sharing our fears, dreams, and even our darkest moments can help bridge the gaps that may have formed between us. It is through these heartfelt discussions that we discover understanding, empathy, and ultimately, the ability to offer support to one another. By nurturing open communication, we lay the foundation for stronger bonds that go beyond the superficial pleasantries often associated with the holiday season.

During this season of togetherness, I find myself drawn to the warmth and comfort of close friends and family. As we gather around crackling fireplaces and cozy dinner tables, I am reminded of the power of open and honest conversation. In a world full of distractions and superficial connections, it is in these moments of vulnerability that true intimacy is forged.

As the evening unfolds, each person takes turns sharing

their thoughts, hopes, and fears. Laughter intertwines with tears, creating a tapestry of emotions that solidifies our bond. We acknowledge that life is not always perfect, and that each of us has faced our own battles. It is through these conversations that we gain a deeper understanding of one another's struggles and triumphs. No longer are we mere acquaintances, but instead, we become a unified support system.

In the midst of these intimate discussions, we also learn to listen. Truly listen. We set aside our agendas and preconceived notions, allowing space for understanding and empathy to flourish. There is a magic that happens when we give someone our undivided attention, a magic that strengthens the bonds between us.

Through open communication, we also learn to celebrate one another. We share in the joys, big and small, that have shaped each person's journey. We cheer alongside them as they recount tales of personal growth, career achievements, and profound moments of self-discovery. In doing so, we reaffirm our commitment to one another's happiness and create a space that fosters mutual motivation and encouragement.

As the holiday season draws to a close, we carry these newfound insights with us. We hold onto the understanding that honest communication is not limited to this season alone, but rather a continuous journey of connection. We vow to nurture these bonds, making a conscious effort to prioritize open dialogue in our everyday lives.

Strengthening bonds with loved ones requires ongoing dedication and perseverance. It requires us to rise above the distractions and busyness that often pull us away. It requires us to be vulnerable, even when it feels uncomfortable. But the rewards that come from building these deep and meaningful relationships are immeasurable.

So, as we bid farewell to this holiday season, let us carry the lessons learned in our hearts. Let us commit to fostering open and honest communication not only during this festive time but throughout the year. For in doing so, we will not only strengthen our relationships but create a world where understanding, empathy, and love can flourish.

As I delve into exploring these various ways to strengthen bonds with my loved ones, I begin to understand that the true meaning of the holiday season lies not in the illusion of happy holidays, but in the connections we forge with one another. These endeavors may not completely erase the pain or loss I have experienced, but they offer a glimmer of hope and light amidst the darkness. Through shared activities, lasting memories, and open communication, I am slowly rebuilding the fractured bonds of my past and embracing the possibility of a future filled with genuine connection and happiness.

Forgiveness and Healing

But in the midst of this darkness, I have come to realize that forgiveness and healing are the keys to finding solace during the holidays. It is through forgiving those who have wronged us, and most importantly, forgiving ourselves for the mistakes we have made, that we can begin to move forward and cultivate healthier relationships.

Step 1: Reflect on Past Wounds

It is important to first acknowledge the pain that still resides within us. Take time to reflect on the wounds that have been inflicted upon you in the past. Allow yourself to feel the emotions that arise, as difficult as they may be. By confronting these past hurts head-on, we set ourselves on a path towards healing.

For me, it was the loss of my closest friend, James, in a tragic accident during the holiday season. His absence during this time of year has always amplified my grief and left an undeniable void in my heart. But by acknowledging the pain and accepting it as a part of my story, I am able to slowly discover the strength to move forward.

The Illusion of Happy Holidays

As I sit here, contemplating the pieces of my broken heart, I realize that it is in these moments of darkness that our resilience truly shines. I light a candle, its flickering flame a symbol of hope, and allow myself to release the tears that have been held captive within me for so long.

In the stillness of this quiet reflection, memories of James flood my mind. His contagious laughter, the way his eyes would light up when he shared his dreams with me - all of it now distant echoes in the corridors of my mind. It's both comforting and painful to relive those precious moments, but I know that by fully embracing the pain, I can begin to heal.

With each tear that falls, I am reminded of the countless happy moments we shared. The road trips, the late-night conversations, and the adventures that made us feel invincible. I allow myself to smile through my tears, a bittersweet acknowledgement of the love we once shared and the bond that still lingers within me.

But grief is not a linear journey; it ebbs and flows like the tides of the ocean. Some days, the pain crashes against me with such force, threatening to pull me under. On those days, I hold onto the memories tighter, desperate to find solace in their embrace.

And yet, amidst the storm, there are moments of calm.

A gentle breeze whispers James's name, and I sense his presence, guiding me forward. I begin to understand that healing doesn't mean forgetting or letting go of the love we shared; it means learning to carry it with us, transforming it into a source of strength that propels us into the future.

As I continue to confront my past hurts, I realize that there is power in vulnerability. It takes great courage to face our pain, but it is in that vulnerability that we find solace and connection with others who have experienced their own losses. Together, we create a space where our grief is understood and our healing is nurtured.

So, I choose to honor James's memory by living a life that honors his spirit. I dedicate myself to cherishing each precious moment, holding my loved ones a little tighter, and pursuing my dreams with unwavering determination. I know that in doing so, I am not only healing myself but also keeping his memory alive, forever etched in the fabric of my being.

And as I rise from the depths of my pain, like a phoenix reborn from ashes, I hold onto the belief that there is light beyond the darkness. I embrace the journey of healing, knowing that it is through acknowledging and confronting our pain that we can truly begin to live again.

Step 2: Practice Empathy and Compassion

Once we have acknowledged our own pain, we must then extend empathy and compassion to others. Recognize that the holiday season is a time of heightened emotions for everyone, not just yourself. Many people carry their own wounds, their own memories of loss or heartbreak. By practicing empathy, we create an environment that fosters understanding and healing.

In this season of togetherness and celebration, let us transcend the boundaries of our personal experiences and reach out to those around us. Let our hearts expand with love and understanding, for it is in these moments that we truly become the best versions of ourselves.

As we gather with family and friends, let us remember that in every smile and laughter, there may hide profound sorrow and longing. Each person we encounter carries a story, a narrative shaped by joy and sadness, growth and setbacks. It is through the lens of empathy that we can truly connect with one another, for it is through empathy that we bridge the gaps between our own experiences and those of others.

In the crowded shopping centers and bustling streets, let us practice compassion towards those who may be silently suffering. The harried mother trying to make ends meet, the elderly man who longs for connection, the person grieving the absence of a loved one - all of them deserve our understanding and support. A kind word, a genuine smile, or a simple act of kindness can go a long way in brightening someone's day, reminding them that they are not alone in their struggles.

During the holiday season, when emotions run high, conflicts can easily arise. But let us remember that underneath anger and frustration, there lies pain and vulnerability. Instead of reacting with aggression, let us respond with tenderness and patience. Let us choose forgiveness and understanding, for in doing so, we break the cycle of hurt and allow healing to take place.

Moreover, let us not forget ourselves amidst the fervor of spreading empathy and compassion. It is equally vital to extend the same love and understanding to ourselves. We, too, deserve kindness and forgiveness. By nurturing our own well-being, we become beacons of light, radiating positivity and warmth to those around us.

As we journey through the holiday season, let us be the writers of a beautiful story, one that celebrates the power of empathy and compassion. Let our actions inspire others to do the same, creating a ripple effect of love and healing that extends far beyond this festive time.

In recognizing the pain in ourselves and others, and in choosing empathy and compassion as our guiding stars, we become the writers of a narrative that transcends boundaries and unites humanity.

Step 3: Letting Go of Resentment

Resentment is a poison that we unknowingly drink, hoping it will harm the ones who have hurt us. But in reality, it only harms ourselves. This holiday season, let go of the resentment that has been holding you back. Release the chains that bind you to the past, and embrace the freedom that forgiveness brings.

For me, letting go of resentment meant facing the painful truth that James is no longer here. It meant forgiving myself for not being able to protect him, for not being there in his final moments. Only by forgiving myself and those involved in his untimely death can I begin to heal the wounds that have plagued me for far too long.

As the holiday season arrived, the air was filled with a mix of joy and nostalgia, giving me the perfect backdrop to confront my feelings head-on. Each passing day, I immersed myself in self-reflection and sought solace in nature's embrace. It was during one of those solitary walks by the serene lake that I made a conscious decision – today was the day I would release the chains.

With every step I took, I mentally revisited the memories

that once haunted my mind, slowly dissecting them with newfound clarity. The resentment that had consumed me for years began to wither away, giving space to a sense of understanding and compassion. For the first time, I acknowledged that everyone involved had their own struggles, their own battles they were fighting. And I realized that by forgiving them, I was not just liberating myself, but granting them a chance at redemption as well.

Through forgiveness, I untangled the knots within my heart, allowing love and healing to take their place. I recognized that the pain I held onto was never going to bring James back; it only held me back from fully embracing life and honoring his memory. It took immense courage to let go, but the burden gradually lifted with each forgiving breath, lightening my spirit.

As the holiday season unfolded around me, I made the conscious choice to celebrate life. I surrounded myself with loved ones, cherishing the moments we shared together. The resentful fog that once clouded my vision was replaced with clarity and gratitude for the present, for the blessings that were still within my grasp.

The journey to forgiveness was not without its trials. Some days, the weight of grief threatened to pull me back into the abyss of resentment. But by continually reminding myself that forgiveness was not about condoning the past, but freeing myself from its shackles, I found strength.

I discovered that by releasing my anger and resentment, I took back control of my own happiness, my own future.

As the holiday season came to a close, I had truly transformed. The once murky waters of bitterness had settled, permitting rays of hope to penetrate and illuminate my path. I no longer carried resentment as my armor but wore forgiveness as a badge of honor—a testament to my resilience and growth.

In the end, I realized that forgiveness was not about forgetting the pain or betrayals. It was about surrendering the desire for revenge and reclaiming my power to forge a better future. Each day became an opportunity to honor James's memory through acts of kindness and compassion, spreading the very love that resentment had deprived me of.

And so, as the world embraced the promise of a new year, I stepped forward, leaving behind the poisoned cup of resentment for good. With a heart unburdened by the weight of the past, I embarked on a journey of healing and self-discovery, ready to embrace the freedom and boundless possibilities that forgiveness had bestowed upon me.

Step 4: Communicate and Rebuild Relationships

The holidays provide an opportune moment to reach out

to those we have lost touch with, those with whom relationships have grown strained. Take this time to repair the bridges that have been broken, to rebuild trust, and to create a foundation for healthier and more fulfilling relationships.

For me, it was my estranged brother, Joshua, whom I had not spoken to in years. The wounds of our past had driven a wedge between us, but this holiday season, I made the choice to extend an olive branch. We sat down, shared our stories, and realized that forgiveness was the path we both needed to take. Through open communication, we forged a new bond, one that has brought us closer together and given us hope for a brighter future.

As we reminisced about our childhood, we discovered that it wasn't always bitterness and resentment that defined our relationship. We talked about the laughter we shared, the adventures we embarked on, and the unconditional love that had once bound us. It was through these cherished memories that we found the strength to let go of our past grievances and rebuild what was torn apart.

In front of a crackling fireplace, cups of warm cocoa nestled safely in our hands, we delved into the depths of our emotions. With tears streaming down our faces, we expressed the pain that had haunted us both, acknowledging the mistakes we had made and the hurt we had caused each other. The weight of our confessions lifted, leaving space for understanding and compassion to take root.

With newfound clarity, we recognized that time apart had allowed us to grow individually. Our experiences had shaped us in different ways, bringing wisdom that we now shared with one another. Joshua, always a free spirit, had finally found the courage to pursue his dreams, while I, the cautious one, had learned the value of taking risks. Although our paths had diverged, we realized they had also led us back to the same place - a place of healing and reconciliation.

The beauty of the holiday season lies not only in the joy it brings but in the opportunity it provides for transformation. It offers us a chance to reflect on the past and reconnect with those who have been absent from our lives, reminding us of the importance of forgiveness, compassion, and second chances.

As our hearts began to mend, we made a pact to prioritize our relationship and nurture the bond that had been restored. We promised to be more present and supportive of one another, to make time for regular catch-ups, and to celebrate each other's milestones. Our shared goal became to create a solid foundation based on love, trust, and vulnerability.

In the weeks and months that followed, our relationship continued to thrive. We discovered common interests that reignited our shared passions, reigniting the flame and adding sparks of excitement to our conversations. With laughter echoing through the air, we embarked on new adventures together, creating cherished memories that would further strengthen the unbreakable bond we had rebuilt.

The holiday season not only brought about the forgiveness and healing we both desperately needed, but it also rekindled the love that had never truly vanished. It taught us that relationships are worth fighting for and that it's never too late to reconnect with those we hold dear.

So, this holiday season, let us all take a moment to reflect on the relationships that have grown strained, to extend that olive branch, and to embrace the transformative power of forgiveness. Because it is through healing and reconnecting that even the most broken bridges can be rebuilt, paving the way for a future filled with love, understanding, and unparalleled joy.

Step 5: Embrace the Power of Healing

As we let forgiveness flow through our veins and mend our broken hearts, we begin to realize the power of healing. It is in this process that we can find the strength to once again embrace the holiday season, to find joy in the moments that were once tainted by pain.

As the soft winter snowflakes gently fell outside, their quiet whisperings bringing a newfound sense of tranquility, we found solace in the warmth of our homes. The air was tinged with the scent of cinnamon and pine, and the soft glow of twinkling lights danced upon every surface, casting a magical spell that seemed to erase our troubles, if only for a moment.

With forgiveness as our guiding light, we embraced the holiday season with open hearts. Each carol sung, each ornament lovingly hung, became a testament to the power of healing and the resilience of the human spirit. Surrounded by loved ones, we savored the laughter and shared stories that filled the room, realizing that the pain of the past had not been in vain; it had strengthened the bonds that held us together.

In this season of giving, we found ourselves extending a hand to those in need, recognizing that healing is not a solitary journey. Inspired by our own experiences, we sought to bring comfort to others, offering a listening ear, a warm meal, and a gentle reminder that they too could find solace amidst the chaos. The act of giving became a celebration of our own transformation, a balm for the scars that still lingered.

As we gathered around the fireplace, mesmerized by its dancing flames, we shared stories of resilience and hope. We realized that the holiday season was not just about the presents we received, but the love and compassion we shared. It was a time for reflection and gratitude, for acknowledging the strength we had found within ourselves and realizing the power it held to shape our future.

Through forgiveness, we had stripped away the bitterness that had clouded our hearts, replacing it with a sense of peace and understanding. We began to cherish the simple things—the smell of freshly baked cookies, the sound of children's laughter, the embrace of a loved one—that had once seemed ordinary but were now infused with profound meaning. Life had revealed its capacity for beauty once again, and we were grateful for its gentle reminder.

As the holiday season drew to a close, we carried the lessons of forgiveness and healing with us into the new year. We knew that life would present its challenges, that pain might find its way into our hearts once more, but we were armed with the knowledge that healing was possible. We walked forward with confidence, ready to face whatever lay ahead, knowing that the power of forgiveness would be our beacon of light, guiding us through even the darkest of times.

And so, as the world turned, love and forgiveness spread, igniting hope and healing in the most unlikely of places. The holiday season became more than just a moment on the calendar; it became a reminder of the indomitable spirit within us all. The power of healing flowed through our veins, mending not only our broken hearts but also the fractures that had scarred our world, leaving it just a little brighter than before.

In this way, we discovered that the true magic of the holiday season lies not in the presents under the tree, but in the power of forgiveness and the transformation it brings. Through forgiveness, we had found joy in the moments that were once tainted by pain, and in doing so, we had become the architects of our own happiness.

The illusion of happy holidays may always linger, but through forgiveness and healing, we can navigate through the shadows and find a sense of peace within ourselves. This holiday season, may we all guide each other in practicing forgiveness and healing past wounds, fostering healthier and more fulfilling relationships.

Celebrating Differences

However, as I reflect upon my own experiences, I have come to realize the importance of embracing diversity and celebrating differences within family and social circles, especially during this time of year. It is in these moments of inclusion and understanding that we truly embody the spirit of the holidays.

Growing up, my family had always been accepting and open-minded, encouraging me to interact with people from different backgrounds and cultures. They instilled in me the values of inclusivity and taught me the significance of embracing diversity. Yet, it was not until I began to experience loss in my own life that the true depth of those lessons became clear to me.

One holiday season, I found myself alone in a city far from home. The familiar faces that once filled my celebrations were now replaced with strangers. Amidst the sea of unfamiliar faces, I stumbled upon a small community center hosting a multicultural gathering. It was there that I witnessed the beauty of celebrating differences and the power it holds to bring people together.

As I stepped into the bustling community center, the sights, sounds, and aromas instantly enveloped me. It was as if the world had converged in this humble space, each person representing a unique thread in the tapestry of humanity. Laughter echoed through the air, blending with the melodic tunes of various instruments playing in harmony.

I found myself drawn to a circle of children, their eyes filled with wonder as they shared stories of their own traditions. Their laughter was infectious - a universal language that dissolved any barriers of language or culture. They taught me games played in their homelands, and I, in turn, shared tales from my own upbringing. In that moment, we were no longer strangers; we were a family united by the spirit of the holiday season.

Moving through the crowd, I observed individuals of all ages and backgrounds connecting, their conversations rich with shared experiences and a genuine curiosity about the uniqueness of one another. It was here that I encountered individuals who had experienced hardships I could never fathom, yet their resilience and unwavering spirit inspired me.

As I spoke with an elderly gentleman who had fled his war-torn country, he told me his heart-wrenching story of leaving everything behind in search of safety and a better future. Through his broken English, he conveyed his gratitude for the sense of community found in this multicultural gathering. The room, he said, reminded him that despite our differences, we all long for the same things - love, security, and acceptance.

In that moment, I was humbled by the power of embracing diversity and celebrating our differences. It was no longer just a notion instilled in me by my family; it had become an unwavering belief embedded in the core of my being. I vowed to carry this understanding with me into the world, to spread compassion, and to foster an environment where every voice is heard, valued, and celebrated.

Years have passed since that profound holiday season, but the lessons I learned in that community center have stayed with me. Now, as I gather with my loved ones and embark on the traditions of my childhood, I do so with a renewed appreciation for the diversity that surrounds me. I see the world through the lens of empathy, understanding that the tapestry of humanity is woven with the threads of countless cultures, each one deserving of respect and admiration.

This holiday season, may we all embrace the beauty of our differences, reaching across boundaries with open hearts and open minds. For it is in this spirit that we can truly embody the essence of the holidays, creating a world that celebrates diversity, fosters inclusivity, and sheds light on the limitless potential that lies within each and every one of us.

The room buzzed with laughter and chatter as people from different ethnicities, religions, and backgrounds mingled with one another. The air was infused with the fragrances of various cuisines, each dish a testament to the unique traditions and flavors that different cultures bring to the holiday table.

As I sat with a group of people, listening to their stories and sharing my own, I felt a sense of belonging that I had longed for since my losses. It was in that moment that I understood the essence of the holiday season - not just the celebration of a specific holiday, but the celebration of humanity itself.

Since that day, I have made a conscious effort to create a more inclusive and understanding environment during the holiday season. I have opened my doors to friends and acquaintances from all walks of life, creating a space where diversity is cherished and celebrated. I have sought out community events that promote inclusivity, making it a priority to attend and support them. Through these actions, I have discovered the power of acceptance, empathy, and embracing our differences.

This year, I plan to take it a step further by organizing a gathering of my own. I want to create an atmosphere where family and friends can come together, regardless of their backgrounds, and celebrate the beauty of diversity. Be it through sharing stories, traditions, or simply enjoying each other's company, I aim to foster an environment of inclusivity and understanding.

In a world that often highlights our differences, the holiday season offers a unique opportunity for us to unite and celebrate the things that make us unique. By embracing diversity and promoting inclusivity during this time, we can create a legacy of understanding and empathy that extends far beyond the holiday season. It is through these small acts of kindness and acceptance that we can begin to heal the wounds of the past and forge a future filled with peace, love, and genuine happiness.

Cultivating Gratitude for Relationships

But as I delved deeper into my melancholic thoughts, I realized that dwelling on the past would only perpetuate my pain. Instead, I needed to find a way to shift my perspective and reclaim the joy that once defined the holiday season. It was in this moment of darkness that I discovered the transformative power of gratitude, specifically nurturing a sense of connection and appreciation for the relationships in my life.

Research has shown that expressing gratitude has numerous benefits, not only for our mental well-being but also for our physical health. By focusing on the positive aspects of our relationships, we cultivate a mindset that nourishes our souls and brings us closer to the people we hold dear. It allows us to acknowledge the love and support we receive, creating a sense of fulfillment and warmth amidst the cold winter nights.

I embarked on a journey to cultivate gratitude in my life, determined to let go of the sadness that had overshadowed my holiday spirit. I began by taking time each day to reflect on the relationships that had shaped me, the friends and family that had stood by my side through thick and thin.

With each name that crossed my mind, a flicker of gratitude ignited within me.

I decided to take it a step further and express my appreciation directly to those who had made a difference in my life. I poured my heart into handwritten letters, carefully crafting words that captured the depth of my gratitude. As I dropped the letters into the mailbox, a wave of anticipation and hope washed over me, knowing that these expressions of thankfulness would soon touch the lives of those I held dear.

But gratitude wasn't only about sending letters and kind words; it was about fostering a sense of connection and presence in the here and now. And so, I made a conscious effort to be fully present whenever I spent time with loved ones. No longer lost in my own melancholy thoughts, I listened intently to their stories and shared my own with a newfound zest for life. Each moment became a precious gift, a chance to strengthen the bonds that had supported me throughout the years.

As the holiday season approached, I found myself embracing the beauty in simple traditions and small gestures. Decorating the Christmas tree became a moment of reflection, each ornament carrying a memory and significance that brought a smile to my face. Baking cookies with loved ones became an opportunity to create new memories, filling the air with laughter and the scent of warm sugar.

But it wasn't just the festivities that inspired gratitude within me. I began to notice the beauty of everyday moments too - the warmth of a cozy blanket on a chilly evening, the sound of laughter echoing through the house, the comfort of a warm mug of cocoa on a frosty morning. Life was a tapestry of blessings, and as I embraced them with open arms, my heart overflowed with joy.

With each passing day, my perspective shifted, and the holiday season became a beacon of light rather than a reminder of loss. Gratitude seeped into every aspect of my life, transforming my perception of the world. I began to see the abundance that surrounded me, the love that permeated even the darkest corners of my existence.

And so, as the snowflakes danced outside my window and carols filled the air, I found myself embracing the true essence of the holiday season. It was a time of giving thanks, not just for the material gifts that adorned the tree, but for the connections that warmed my soul. Gratitude had breathed new life into my spirit, reminding me that even in the midst of hardships, joy and love were never far away.

As the days rolled on and the holiday season drew to a close, I carried this newfound perspective with me. Gratitude had become an integral part of my daily life, a guiding light that illuminated every step on my journey. And as I looked back on the pages of my life, I marveled at the transformation that had taken place.

In the end, it wasn't the grand gestures or extravagant celebrations that defined the holiday season. It was the power of gratitude, the simple act of appreciating the relationships that enriched our lives. And I vowed to carry this wisdom with me, not just during the holiday season, but throughout the year - for gratitude had forever changed my world.

So, how can we harness the power of gratitude and infuse it into the holiday season? It begins with taking a moment to reflect on the relationships that have shaped us, the people who have stood by our side through thick and thin. Whether it be a partner, a family member, or a dear friend, each connection we hold is a precious gift bestowed upon us. It is crucial to recognize their presence in our lives and express our heartfelt appreciation.

But gratitude is not limited to simple words of thanks. It requires us to actively nurture these relationships, to invest time and effort in building strong foundations. We must engage in meaningful conversations, create lasting memories, and offer our unwavering support. It is in these moments of connection and vulnerability that we truly appreciate the depth and significance of our relationships, anchoring ourselves in the present rather than dwelling in the past.

Inevitably, the holiday season brings its own set of stressors and challenges. It is during these times that the power of gratitude becomes even more vital. By focusing on the positive aspects of our relationships, we can weather the storms that come our way. It serves as a reminder that even in the darkest of times, we are not alone.

As I continue my journey of reclaiming the joy of the holiday season, I invite you, dear reader, to join me in cultivating gratitude for the relationships in your life. In doing so, we can nourish a sense of connection and appreciation, creating a warm and inviting atmosphere that permeates through the holiday festivities. Let us embrace the transformative power of gratitude and rediscover the magic that lies within the illusion of happy holidays.

Creating a Joyful Holiday Season

Simplifying Holiday Celebrations

The problem lies in the excessive emphasis we place on the material aspects of the holidays. The pressure to find the perfect gifts, cook extravagant meals, and decorate our homes to create a picturesque scene can quickly become overwhelming. This burden of expectations weighs heavily on our shoulders, sucking the joy out of what should be a joyous occasion. And so, the solution is to simplify.

In my research on finding happiness during the holiday season, I have stumbled upon various strategies that have resonated with me. The first step in simplifying holiday celebrations is to let go of the idea that everything has to be perfect. We need to remember that the true essence of the holidays lies in the intangible moments of togetherness, love, and gratitude, rather than the material trappings that often overshadow them.

One way to achieve this simplicity is to focus on experiences rather than material possessions. Instead of stressing over finding the ideal gift, consider creating memories together. Plan a day trip with loved ones, engage in fun activities, or volunteer for a charitable cause. These experiences not only bring people closer but also create lasting memories that will hold far more value than any material gift.

Another key aspect of simplifying the holidays is to practice mindfulness and intentional living. Take a moment to reflect on what truly matters to you and your loved ones. Is it the extravagant meals or the quality time spent around the table, sharing stories and laughter? Is it the elaborate decorations or the warmth and love that fill your home when you gather with your family? By letting go of the unnecessary pressures and focusing on what brings true joy, we can create a more meaningful holiday experience.

Simplifying also means setting boundaries and learning to say no. It is easy to get caught up in a whirlwind of parties, events, and obligations during the holiday season. However, by carefully selecting the activities that truly align with your values and priorities, you can avoid burnout and enjoy the season with a sense of ease and balance. Remember, it is okay to choose rest and relaxation over a packed schedule.

Lastly, it is crucial to let go of comparisons and societal expectations that often steal away the joy of the holiday season. In this age of social media, it is easy to be bombarded with picture-perfect images of others' holiday celebrations. However, it is crucial to remember that everyone's holiday season is unique and personal. Embrace the imperfections and find beauty in your own traditions and experiences. Comparison only serves to rob us of joy and make us forget what truly matters.

Simplifying the holiday season means shifting our focus from material things to meaningful moments. It involves cherishing the intangible gifts of love, togetherness, and gratitude. By embracing experiences, practicing mindfulness, setting boundaries, and letting go of comparisons, we can create a holiday season filled with genuine joy and fulfillment. Let it be a reminder that the best gift we can give ourselves and others is the gift of simplicity.

Another crucial aspect of simplifying holiday celebrations is scaling down the extravagance. Instead of going all out with extravagant feasts and elaborate decorations, consider adopting a more modest approach. Embrace the concept of simplicity and minimalism by opting for a smaller, more intimate gathering. Prepare simpler meals that focus on quality rather than quantity. Choose a few meaningful decorations that reflect the true spirit of the holidays, instead of drowning in a sea of excess.

When it comes to gift-giving, shift the focus from material possessions to thoughtful gestures. Instead of getting caught up in the frenzy of buying extravagant gifts, take the time to truly understand the needs and desires of your loved ones. Consider giving experiences or creating handmade gifts that hold sentimental value. Remember, it is the thought behind the gift that truly matters, not the price tag.

Furthermore, simplifying the holiday season also means prioritizing self-care. It is easy to get swept up in the demands and expectations of the season, neglecting our own well-being in the process. Take the time to rest, recharge, and prioritize your own mental and physical health. Allow yourself moments of solitude and tranquility amidst the chaos. Engage in activities that bring you joy and fill your heart with a sense of peace. Remember, by taking care of yourself, you are better equipped to take care of others.

Lastly, let gratitude permeate every aspect of your holiday season. Instead of focusing on what is lacking or what didn't go as planned, shift your perspective to appreciate the blessings in your life. Take time each day to express gratitude for the simple pleasures, the loving relationships, and the moments of joy that exist all around you. Gratitude has the power to transform even the most challenging moments into opportunities for growth and contentment.

As the holiday season approaches, let us remember that simplicity is the key to finding genuine joy and fulfillment. By shifting our focus to meaningful moments, scaling down the extravagance, prioritizing self-care, and embracing gratitude, we can create a holiday season that is truly magical. Let this be the year where we free ourselves from the chains of societal expectations and rediscover the true spirit of the season. May it be filled with love, laughter, and moments that warm our hearts and souls.

Lastly, but perhaps most importantly, we must learn to give ourselves permission to say no. Overcommitting and stretching ourselves thin only leads to exhaustion and resentment. We cannot be everywhere and do everything, and that's okay. Prioritizing our own well-being and mental health should always come first. It is far more important to spend quality time with loved ones and take care of ourselves than to meet every expectation placed upon us by society.

In encouraging readers to simplify holiday celebrations and focus on what truly brings them joy, my hope is that we can all find a way back to the genuine spirit of the season. By shedding the unnecessary expectations and material trappings, we can create a space for meaningful connections and moments of true happiness. Let us remember that the illusion of picture-perfect holidays is just that – an illusion. It is the simplicity and authenticity that truly embodies the magic of the season.

Mindful Gift-Giving

My experiences have taught me that the true value of a gift lies not in its price tag but in the thought and intention behind it. It is not about the quantity of presents that we receive, but about the quality of the connections we make and nurture during this time of the year.

I believe that it is time we shift our focus from material possessions to fostering meaningful connections. It is time to promote mindful gift-giving practices that align with our personal values and enable us to establish genuine bonds with our loved ones.

To delve deeper into this subject, I embarked on a journey of research, seeking out stories and anecdotes from individuals who have discovered the beauty of mindful gift-giving. My conversations with these individuals not only helped me understand the significance of this practice but also inspired and touched my soul.

One story that particularly resonated with me was that of Isabel, a woman who had lost her parents and sister in a tragic accident. Despite the heartache that she carried within her, Isabel found solace in giving gifts that aligned with her family's values. She discovered that by choosing gifts that embodied her loved ones' passions and interests, she could keep their memories alive in a profound and meaningful way.

Isabel's story illuminated the power of mindful gift-giving in healing wounds and nurturing connections. It reminded me of my own losses and the importance of cherishing the memories of those who are no longer with us. Through thoughtful gifts, we can honor their memory and keep their spirit alive in our hearts.

As I continued my explorations, I came across another remarkable tale of mindful gift-giving that transcended boundaries of distance and brought people together in un-expected ways. This story unfolded in a small village nestled in the hills of a remote country, where Rebecca, a young teacher, embarked on a mission to bridge the gap between her students and the wider world.

With limited resources, Rebecca realized that traditional gifts were not feasible for her young students. Instead, she encouraged them to express themselves through heartfelt letters, drawings, and handmade crafts. These personalized tokens were not only treasured by the receivers but also served as a window into the lives and cultures of the children in that remote village.

Word of the transformative power of Rebecca's approach

soon spread, reaching the hearts and minds of individuals across the globe. People started writing back to the children, sharing stories of their own lives and sending small, thoughtful gifts that reflected the unique interests and dreams of each child. Through this exchange, connections were formed, fostering a sense of belonging, understanding, and unity.

As I reflected on these stories and the countless others I had encountered, I realized that mindful gift-giving is not limited to material possessions or extravagant gestures. It is an opportunity to infuse an ordinary moment with extraordinary meaning. It is a chance to show someone that they are seen, valued, and cherished. It is an invitation to connect with the essence of another human being and to create lasting memories that transcend time and physical presence.

In a world driven by consumerism and fleeting trends, we have a choice. We can continue to be captivated by the allure of material possessions, or we can embark on a different path - one that celebrates the profound impact of mindful gift-giving. Let us embrace this opportunity to cultivate genuine connections, to honor our shared humanity, and to bring joy, love, and meaning into the lives of those we hold dear.

Another individual I spoke to, Jake, shared how he had broken free from the consumerist mindset that often dominates the holiday season. He described how he found joy in giving experiences rather than material possessions. Whether it be concert tickets, a cooking class, or a weekend get-away, these experiential gifts created lasting memories and strengthened his relationships with loved ones.

Jake's story highlighted the importance of prioritizing experiences over possessions. It reminded me that our most cherished memories are not usually tied to physical objects but rather to the moments we share with one another. This realization sparked a change within me, a reevaluation of the gifts I had been giving and receiving over the years.

Armed with these inspiring stories, I set out to create my own personalized framework for mindful gift-giving. I began by reflecting on my personal values and the values of those closest to me. What were the causes and passions we held dear? What experiences could bring us closer together and create lasting memories?

I started to brainstorm ideas, jotting them down on a fresh piece of paper. Instead of rushing to the nearest store to buy the latest trend or gadget, I decided to invest in meaningful experiences that aligned with our shared values.

For my sister, who was passionate about animal conser-vation, I decided to surprise her with a trip to a local wildlife sanctuary. We would have the opportunity to interact with rescued animals, learn about their stories, and witness the in-credible work being done to protect these creatures. It would be an experience that not only brought us closer together but also deepened our appreciation for the natural world.

For my parents, who had always emphasized the importance of education and lifelong learning, I decided to gift them a series of online courses in subjects that had always fascinated them. Whether it was art history, philosophy, or sustainable living, these courses would allow them to continue expanding their knowledge and exploring their curiosity. It was a gift that would keep on giving, as they would have the opportunity to engage with these topics long after the holiday season had passed.

As for my best friend, who had recently expressed an interest in mindfulness and self-care, I decided to create a personalized gift box filled with items that promoted relaxation and wellbeing. From a handcrafted journal for reflection to a collection of calming essential oils, each item was carefully chosen to nurture her mind, body, and soul. Along with the gift, I included a heartfelt letter expressing my gratitude for our friendship and a promise to support her on her journey towards self-discovery.

Throughout the process of creating these personalized gifts, I realized that mindful gift-giving was more than just the act of choosing the right present. It was an opportunity to express gratitude, to show our loved ones that we truly see and appreciate them. Each gift became a symbol of our connection, a reminder of the love and care we had for one another.

As the holiday season approached, I presented my carefully curated gifts to my loved ones, eagerly anticipating their reactions. And in the moments that followed, I witnessed something extraordinary. Tears of joy, heartfelt embraces, and conversations filled with laughter and love. These gifts had transcended material possessions; they had become tangible expressions of the deep bond we shared.

Embracing the path of mindful gift-giving had transformed the holiday season for me. It had allowed me to break free from the endless cycle of consumerism and instead focus on what truly mattered – the moments spent with those I cherished. In this world, where the allure of material possessions can cloud our judgment, I had discovered the power of intention, connection, and love.

And so, I urge you, dear reader, to join me on this journey. Let us reimagine the act of giving, placing value not on the price tag or the brand name, but on the impact it creates. Let us choose experiences over possessions, connection over consumerism, and love over fleeting trends. For in the realm of mindful gift-giving, lies the potential to reshape our world, one heartfelt present at a time.

With these questions in mind, I turned my attention to creating gifts that would truly resonate with their recipients.

I sought out locally-made, sustainable products that aligned with my loved ones' values, supporting small businesses and artisans in the process. I also made a conscious effort to give the gift of time, offering my presence and undivided attention rather than mere material possessions.

As I implemented these practices in my own life, I witnessed a transformation not only in my relationships but also within myself. The act of giving mindfully brought me a sense of purpose and fulfillment that I had not experienced before. It reminded me that the holiday season should be about more than just fleeting moments of happiness; it should be a time of genuine connection and heartfelt appreciation.

In conclusion, promoting mindful gift-giving practices that align with personal values and foster meaningful connections during the holiday season is an essential step towards reclaiming the true spirit of the holidays. By shifting our focus from material possessions to genuine bonds, we can infuse depth and meaning back into this time of the year. Let us cast aside the illusion of happy holidays and embrace the joy that comes from authentic giving and receiving.

Exploring Alternative Traditions

But this year was different. I was determined to break free from the illusion of happy holidays and discover a new path, one that resonated with my beliefs and preferences. I devoured books, scoured the internet, and sought guidance from like-minded individuals who had also experienced the loss and disillusionment I carried within me.

One of the first traditions that caught my attention was the concept of minimalist gift-giving. Many people were embracing the idea of exchanging experiences instead of material possessions. I was captivated by the thought of creating memories rather than clutter. So, I decided to propose this alternative to my family and friends.

We all agreed to allocate our gift funds towards a breathtaking winter getaway in a secluded cabin nestled in the mountains. Surrounded by nature's beauty, we experienced the true meaning of togetherness and realized that the best presents cannot be purchased but are instead shared experiences filled with love and laughter.

As the crackling fireplace warmed our souls, we gathered in a circle and took turns sharing stories from our past, our present, and envisioning our future. Each tale was a gift in itself, weaving a tapestry of cherished moments and forming a stronger bond than any material possession ever could. Laughter echoed through the cosy cabin, melting away the weight of the world and leaving behind only a pure sense of joy and connection.

The following day, we seized the opportunity to explore the wintry wonderland that surrounded us. With rosy cheeks and gleaming eyes, we embarked on a scenic hike, our footsteps leaving imprints in the freshly fallen snow. As we breathed in the crisp mountain air and took in the majestic views, we realized how insignificant the allure of commodity had become in the face of nature's grandeur.

In the evenings, we gathered around a communal table, our hands clasped in friendship as we savored the simple yet delicious meals we prepared together. We shared recipes and cooking tips, reveling in the art of creating nourishment for both body and soul. The joy of savoring a homemade meal, infused with love and shared with those dear to us, surpassed anything money could buy.

During those magical days, we rediscovered the pleasure of quality time spent with loved ones, creating memories that would forever hold a special place in our hearts. We gifted each other with presence and attention, becoming fully present in the moment, soaking up the beauty and wonder that surrounded us.

When the time came to pack our bags and bid farewell

to the mountains, we realized that our winter getaway had not only brought us closer together, but it had also ignited a spark within us. We returned home with a newfound appreciation for the simple joys in life, vowing to carry the spirit of minimalist gift-giving throughout the year.

From that day forward, our holiday celebrations transformed into opportunities for meaningful connection and shared experiences. We exchanged homemade crafts and heartfelt letters, took part in communal service projects, and volunteered our time to make a difference in the lives of those less fortunate. The holiday season became a time of giving, not just to our loved ones, but to our communities and to the world.

As I reflect on that transformative winter getaway, I can't help but feel a deep sense of gratitude. Gratitude for the lessons learned, for the bonds forged, and for the reminder that the true essence of the holiday season lies not in material possessions, but in the love, kindness, and shared experiences we give and receive.

And so, with the spirit of minimalism and the power of connection guiding me, I continue to seek new paths, embodying the principles that resonate with my true self. In doing so, I hope to inspire others to embark on their own journey of self-discovery, to question old traditions, and to embrace a holiday season filled with love, meaning, and authentic joy. For it is in these moments of genuine connection and shared experiences that we truly find the magic of the holidays and the essence of being alive.

Another alternative tradition that resonated deeply with me was creating a meaningful holiday countdown. Instead of counting down the days with typical advent calendars filled with chocolates and trinkets, I chose to cultivate gratitude and self-reflection through a daily practice.

Each morning, I would sit quietly with a cup of steaming hot tea, reflecting on a specific theme for the day. From gratitude and forgiveness to self-care and giving back, these daily meditations became a compass guiding me towards authenticity and joy. As I delved deeper into each theme, I discovered hidden layers of myself and connected with the true essence of the holiday season – not the commercialized version, but the one rooted in growth and introspection.

Embracing alternative traditions led me to explore diverse cultural celebrations that mirrored my evolving beliefs. I discovered Winter Solstice, a spiritual celebration honoring the longest night and the return of light. This ancient tradition held a profound significance, symbolizing rebirth, renewal, and the triumph of hope over darkness.

On the eve of the Winter Solstice, I invited friends over for a candlelight ceremony. We gathered around a roaring fire, sharing stories of our personal journeys through darkness, and collectively welcoming the gradual return of light into our lives. The air pulsated with the energy of transformation and the realization that light can emerge even from the deepest despair.

As I continued to explore alternative holiday traditions, I realized that the path to authenticity and joy lies in embracing practices that resonate with our beliefs and preferences. The illusion of happy holidays can only be shattered when we open ourselves up to new experiences, redefining the meaning of celebration and connection.

Inspired by my own journey, I now encourage others to embark on their own exploration of alternative traditions. I share my researches and experiences, hoping to ignite a spark of curiosity and self-discovery in others. For it is in the pursuit of authenticity that we find true joy, and in the embrace of our beliefs that we discover the magic of the holiday season, in all its imperfect yet beautiful glory.

Embracing the Spirit of Giving

But as I stared out the window, watching the snowflakes dance in the cold winter air, a glimmer of hope began to flicker within me. Perhaps, I thought, there was a way to find meaning in the holiday season once again. As broken as I felt, I realized that I held the power to make a difference, to bring a little bit of light into the lives of others who may be experiencing their own hardships.

Researching the transformative power of acts of kindness and generosity, I came across countless stories and studies that showed the profound impact such actions have on both the giver and the receiver. It was in these selfless acts that individuals were able to regain their own sense of purpose and find solace in the act of making a positive impact.

With a newfound determination, I set out to encourage readers to embrace the spirit of giving during the holiday season. I wanted them to experience the immense joy that comes from spreading kindness and making a genuine connection with others in their communities. It wasn't about grand gestures or extravagant gifts, but rather the small acts that could brighten someone's day and remind them that they were seen, valued, and cared for.

I began by reaching out to local nonprofit organizations and community centers, offering my assistance in organizing and promoting acts of kindness initiatives. Together, we brainstormed ideas that would not only bring joy to those in need but also foster a sense of unity and compassion among community members.

One of the initiatives that gained significant traction was a "Winter Warmth Drive." We encouraged individuals to donate gently used coats, blankets, and warm clothing items, which would then be distributed to those experiencing homelessness or struggling to stay warm during the bitter winter months. The response was overwhelming, with donations pouring in from all corners of the community.

But it didn't stop there. Inspired by the generosity we witnessed, we decided to expand our efforts. We organized a "Secret Santa" program, where community members could anonymously sponsor a child in need by providing them with gifts they wouldn't otherwise receive. We worked closely with local schools and social service agencies to identify families who would benefit most from the program. The outpouring of support was incredible, with families and individuals signing up to be secret Santas for multiple children, determined to make their holiday season a little brighter.

The impact of these initiatives extended far beyond the physical gifts exchanged. As community members came together, sharing stories and witnessing firsthand the impact of their kindness, a sense of camaraderie blossomed. People began to connect on a deeper level, recognizing that they were part of something bigger than themselves. Neighbors who had previously been strangers now greeted each other with warmth and kindness. The true spirit of the holiday season had been rekindled.

The success of our efforts motivated me to take it a step further. I decided to compile the stories of these acts of kindness into a book, hoping to inspire readers far beyond our community's borders. The stories were heartwarming and diverse, ranging from simple gestures like buying a cup of hot cocoa for a stranger to organizing community-wide volunteer events. Through these narratives, I aimed to illustrate the power of compassion and illustrate that anyone, regardless of their circumstances, had the ability to make a positive impact on the world around them.

As the book gained wide acclaim, it caught the attention of influential figures and media outlets. I was invited to speak at conferences, sharing the transformative power of kindness and inspiring others to incorporate these acts into their own lives. The movement continued to grow, spreading across cities, countries, and continents. It became a global reminder that love and compassion were the true gifts of the holiday season.

Looking back on that snowy day when hope first flickered

within me, I am amazed at the incredible journey that unfolded. What began as a personal endeavor to find meaning in the holiday season turned into a worldwide movement of kindness and connection. Though it started with a single realization, it was the collective power of individuals coming together that ultimately made the difference.

And as I reflect on the smiles and gratitude I witnessed throughout this journey, I am reminded that the spirit of giving exists not only during the holiday season but every day of the year. For it is in these acts of selflessness, both big and small, that we find purpose, strength, and a world brimming with love and compassion.

In my book, "The Illusion of Happy Holidays," I delved deep into the stories of those who had faced adversity and found solace in acts of generosity. From volunteering at local shelters and food banks to reaching out to isolated individuals in their neighborhoods, each person had discovered their own unique way of embracing the spirit of giving.

I shared stories of families who had come together to assemble care packages for those in need, of friends who had organized toy drives for children who may otherwise have gone without, and of individuals who had taken the time to simply listen and offer a comforting presence to those struggling emotionally during the holiday season.

Through each narrative, I painted a vivid picture of the transformative power of giving. I sought to inspire readers to step outside of their own pain and hardships and extend a hand to those who may be experiencing similar or even more challenging circumstances. By doing so, they could break free from the illusion of happy holidays and create a genuine sense of joy for themselves and others.

In the pages of my book, I provided practical suggestions and resources for readers to engage in acts of kindness and generosity. I encouraged them to take small steps, to start with what they have and build from there. Whether it was donating unused items, volunteering their time, or simply reaching out to a neighbor in need, each action had the potential to make a significant impact.

I urged readers to let go of the materialistic expectations that often clouded the holiday season and instead focus on the true meaning behind this time of year. It wasn't about the presents under the tree or the lavish meals on the table; it was about the connections we forge, the support we offer, and the genuine love we share with one another.

As I penned the final words of my book, I couldn't help but feel a glimmer of hope return to my own spirit. I knew that by encouraging others to embrace the spirit of giving, I could make a difference, not only in their lives but also in my own. Through the act of spreading joy and making a positive impact in our communities, we could reclaim the holiday season and find solace in the knowledge that we were making the world a little bit brighter, one small act at a time.

Creating Joyful Environments

But amidst the darkness, a glimmer of hope emerges. I am determined to find a way to reclaim the joy that seems so elusive. In my quest to create joyful environments, not only for myself but for others, I have delved into research, sought guidance, and experimented with different techniques. And now, I am compelled to share the tips that have aided me on this journey, in hopes that they may bring solace and light to others who find themselves in a similar predicament.

The first step in creating a joyful environment lies in embracing simplicity. Often, we are bombarded with images of perfectly decorated homes and elaborate spreads of holiday feasts. But it is important to remember that happiness does not reside solely in opulence. Rather, it dwells in the small, heartfelt gestures that we incorporate into our surroundings. To evoke positive emotions, it is essential to declutter and focus on the essentials. By removing the excess, we create space for genuine connections and joyful experiences.

In my exploration of simplicity, I have discovered the power of minimalism. Simplifying our physical spaces can have a profound impact on our mental and emotional well-being. I have found that removing unnecessary belongings and embracing a more minimalist lifestyle allows room for clarity and tranquility. When we surround ourselves with only the things we truly love and need, our environments become more conducive to joy and happiness.

Furthermore, simplicity extends beyond our physical spaces. It involves simplifying our schedules and commitments as well. In the fast-paced world we live in, it is easy to become overwhelmed with obligations and never-ending to-do lists. To create a joyful environment, it is important to prioritize our time and focus on activities that bring us joy. This means learning to say no to unnecessary commitments and carving out moments of solitude and self-care.

In addition to simplicity, cultivating gratitude is another vital aspect of creating a joyful environment. Too often, we take for granted the small blessings that surround us each day. By pausing to acknowledge and appreciate the beauty in our lives, we can infuse our surroundings with positivity and contentment. Keeping a gratitude journal or practicing daily affirmations can help shift our perspective and bring a sense of serenity and joy into our lives.

Furthermore, fostering meaningful connections and nurturing relationships is crucial in creating an environment of joy. We are social beings, and our happiness flourishes when surrounded by loved ones and a strong support system. Taking the time to reach out and connect with others, whether through meaningful conversations, acts of kindness, or shared experiences, can bring immense joy to both parties involved.

Lastly, incorporating moments of joy into our daily lives is essential. Engaging in activities that bring us genuine pleasure and a sense of fulfillment can greatly impact the overall ambiance of our environments. Whether it is pursuing a hobby, engaging in exercise, practicing mindfulness, or simply enjoying a quiet moment in nature, these moments of joy infuse our surroundings with positive energy and create a sanctuary of happiness.

As I continue on my journey to create a joyful environment for myself and others, I am reminded that joy is not a destination to be reached but rather a state of being to cultivate each day. By embracing simplicity, cultivating gratitude, fostering meaningful connections, and incorporating moments of joy, we can transform even the darkest of spaces into beacons of light and happiness. May these tips serve as a guiding light on your own path to reclaiming joy and creating a nurturing environment for yourself and those around you.

Another aspect that plays a crucial role in enhancing the holiday experience is the power of scent. The delicate aroma of cinnamon, the comforting fragrance of freshly baked cookies, and the subtle hint of pine needles transport us to a place of warmth and togetherness. By incorporating these scents into our homes, we invite the spirit of the season to linger in the air, creating an atmosphere that nurtures cherished memories and fosters joy.

As I sit by the crackling fireplace, savoring the scent of freshly cut pine and cinnamon, I am reminded of the power of fragrance in evoking emotions and enhancing our surroundings. The delicate aromas wafting through the air not only evoke nostalgic memories but also create a sense of comfort and joy. It is said that scent has the ability to directly impact our mood and emotions, and during the holiday season, this power becomes even more significant.

Imagine walking into a home filled with the sweet aroma of freshly baked cookies. The enticing scent immediately brings a smile to your face, reminding you of the joy of indulgence and the warmth of family gatherings. It is as if the scent itself wraps its arms around you, transporting you back to cherished moments of laughter and love shared around the kitchen table. The simple act of baking cookies becomes an expression of love and a way to create lasting memories.

But it is not just the scent of a treat that can uplift our spirits. The smell of pine needles, fresh and invigorating, carries with it an essence of nature's beauty. It reminds us of the tranquility found in the great outdoors and the wonder of the natural world. By bringing this fragrance into our homes, we bridge the gap between the outside world and our own peaceful sanctuary.

Furthermore, as we gather with loved ones during the holiday season, the power of scent becomes even more meaningful. The familiar fragrances of our favorite holiday dishes, the warm embrace of spices in mulled wine, and the subtle hints of evergreen in wreaths and garlands all contribute to an atmosphere of love, togetherness, and celebration.

Incorporating these scents into our holiday traditions not only enhances our experiences but also creates a lasting impression on all who enter our homes. Our sense of smell has a unique ability to transport us to different times and places, making it an invaluable tool in creating joyful environments. By harnessing the power of scent, we invite happiness and warmth into our lives, spreading joy to all who share in our festivities.

So, as you continue your journey to cultivate joy and create a nurturing environment, do not underestimate the influence of scent. Experiment with different fragrances, find the ones that resonate with you, and let them infuse your home with love and happiness. From the delicate notes of cinnamon and freshly baked cookies to the refreshing aroma of pine, allow these scents to create a sanctuary of joy, transforming your space into a haven of holiday magic.

Furthermore, the interplay of light and color is a phenomenon that can significantly impact our emotional state. Soft, warm lighting envelops us in a cozy embrace, casting a gentle glow that soothes weary hearts. Engaging with the artistic aspect of lighting, such as incorporating twinkling fairy lights or candles, not only enhances our surroundings but also invokes a sense of magic and enchantment. Likewise, the careful selection of colors can uplift our spirits and evoke positive emotions. Incorporating vibrant hues, such as reds and greens, awakens the childlike wonder within us and invites us to embark on a whimsical journey.

But perhaps the most crucial element in creating a joyful environment is the presence of loved ones. The pain of loss can feel insurmountable during the holiday season, leaving a void that seems impossible to fill. Yet, by reaching out to others, by forging new connections or cherishing existing ones, we can infuse our environments with love and compassion. Opening our hearts to invite others into our lives can help heal the wounds that the holiday season has inflicted.

Within these tips lies the potential to break free from the illusion of happy holidays and truly find joy once again. I understand that the journey may not be easy, and the road may be filled with hurdles. But through embracing simplicity, embracing fragrance, embracing light and color, and most importantly, embracing loved ones, we can create an environment that nurtures our souls and elicits positive emotions.

As I pen these words, I am filled with a renewed sense of hope. The path to joy may not be linear, and it may be laden with setbacks, but I am determined to continue the journey. In doing so, I hope to create not only a joyful environment for myself but also a space where others can find solace and rejuvenation amidst the shadow of loss and grief. The illusion of happy holidays can be shattered, replaced by an authentic experience of joy and connection—a gift we just need to unwrap and cherish.

Nourishing the Body and Soul

But amidst the darkness that engulfs my heart, I have come to realize the importance of nourishing both the body and soul during this seemingly joyous time of year. Society often emphasizes the external aspects of the holiday season – the perfect gifts, the extravagant feasts, the cheerful decorations. Yet, I have come to understand that true happiness lies within. It is a matter of prioritizing self-care and well-being, nurturing the essence of our being during these challenging times.

To nourish the body and soul, one must first acknowledge their needs. It is essential to make peace with the past and honor the memories of lost loved ones. The weight of grief can consume us, particularly during the holidays when memories of happier times flood our consciousness. But by embracing those memories and embracing our pain, we can begin to find healing.

With each passing day, I have learned to give myself permission to grieve. I allow myself to feel the sadness and shed the tears that have long been suppressed. Through this process, I discover the beauty of allowing my heart to heal, little by little. It is in these fragile moments that I find the strength to navigate through the darkness, illuminating a path towards a brighter future.

In my quest for self-care, I have turned to nature as a source of solace. The crisp winter air and the soft white snow remind me of the purity and resilience within. I take long walks through the quiet woods, inhaling the scent of pine and listening to the melody of birdsong. It is in these moments of solitude that I find solace and reconnect with my innermost self.

To nourish my soul, I have embraced the power of self-reflection and gratitude. Each day, I set aside time to write in my journal, pouring my thoughts onto paper. I document the joys and blessings that have woven their way into my life, no matter how small. It is in this act of gratitude that I find comfort and perspective, realizing that there is always something to be grateful for, even amidst the darkest of times.

In nourishing my body, I have rediscovered the pleasure of preparing wholesome meals. Cooking has become a therapeutic act, allowing me to pour love and intention into each dish. I experiment with flavors and textures, savoring the simple pleasure of nurturing myself from within. As I indulge in these nourishing meals, I am reminded of the importance of self-care and how it can positively impact my overall well-being.

Throughout this journey of nourishment, I have come to

understand that the true essence of the holiday season lies not in the external aspects but in the inner transformation that takes place within ourselves. It is a time to cultivate kindness and compassion towards ourselves and others. It is a time to give and receive love, not only through physical gifts but through genuine gestures of understanding and support.

As I navigate through these challenging times, I have learned that true happiness is not found in the excess and grandeur of the holiday season, but rather in the moments of vulnerability, self-reflection, and self-care. It is in these moments that I find strength, resilience, and an unwavering sense of peace. And amidst the darkness that once engulfed my heart, a glimmer of light emerges, illuminating the path that leads to a joy that transcends the confines of the holiday season.

For me, finding solace in nature has been an instrumental step towards nourishing both my body and soul. The crisp winter air, the bare trees swaying gracefully, and the blanket of snow covering the ground bring a sense of peace that washes away the heaviness within. Nature has a way of reminding us of the cyclic nature of life, teaching us that even in the harshest of winters, new life can bloom.

Additionally, aligning my diet with the needs of my body has played a pivotal role in fostering well-being during the holiday season. It is easy to indulge in decadent treats and rich feasts, using food as a temporary salve for the emptiness that lingers within. However, I have come to understand that true nourishment lies in choosing foods that nurture my body, foods that provide sustenance and energy rather than fleeting pleasure. By feeding myself with wholesome and nourishing foods, I am gifting myself the strength to navigate the emotional rollercoaster that comes with the holidays.

Yet, self-care extends far beyond what is ingested. It is a comprehensive approach that encompasses mindfulness, reflection, and connection. Despite our loss, it is crucial to remember that we are not alone in our pain. The holiday season can intensify feelings of isolation, but seeking support from those who have experienced similar trials can provide a sense of comfort and camaraderie. Establishing connections with others who share a compromised view of the holidays brings validation to our experiences and reminds us that our feelings are valid.

Engaging in self-reflection during this time is also paramount. It is important to acknowledge the emotions that arise, allowing ourselves to feel and process them without judgment. In doing so, we create space for healing and growth. This may involve journaling, meditating, or engaging in other practices that promote self-awareness. By delving into the depths of our emotions, we uncover valuable insights and pave the way for inner transformation.

Furthermore, practicing mindfulness is a powerful tool in

navigating the unpredictable waves of the holiday season. It involves being fully present in each moment, without judgment or attachment. Mindfulness allows us to observe our thoughts and emotions without getting swept away by them. By cultivating this skill, we develop a sense of calm and resilience, enabling us to respond to challenging situations with grace and ease.

In the midst of our own healing journey, it is equally important to extend compassion and support to those around us. Whether it is a loved one grieving a loss or a stranger struggling, reaching out with a helping hand or a kind word can make a world of difference. Small acts of kindness have the power to lift spirits and remind us of the inherent goodness that exists in humanity.

As the holiday season unfolds, let us remember that it is okay to create new traditions that align with our healing and well-being. It is not a betrayal of the past, but a way to honor the resilience within us. Whether it is participating in volunteer work, attending support groups, or engaging in therapeutic activities, each step we take towards our own healing contributes to the collective healing of our community.

In conclusion, the holiday season can be a bittersweet time for those of us who carry the weight of grief and loss. However, by prioritizing self-care, embracing mindfulness and connection, and fostering compassion, we can navigate this season with resilience and grace. Though our journey may be challenging, it is through these trials that we discover our strength and come to understand the true essence of the holiday spirit.

Through mindful practices such as meditation or journaling, we can delve deeper into our emotions, making space for healing and growth. These activities allow us to cultivate self-awareness and gain a better understanding of our own needs and desires. Prioritizing these practices during the holiday season not only nourishes our souls but also helps us to become more present, savoring the small moments of joy that often get overshadowed by grief.

In the end, nourishing the body and soul during the holiday season is key to finding solace and peace amidst the turmoil. It is a process of introspection, self-care, and connection that fosters healing and growth. By addressing our needs and allowing ourselves the space to grieve, we can ultimately reshape our perspective of the holidays, unearthing true happiness within ourselves. The illusion of happy holidays may never fully dissipate, but by prioritizing self-care and well-being, we can navigate this season with newfound strength and resilience.

Embracing the Magic of the Season

But amidst the shadows that haunt my past, I cannot deny the allure of the holiday season. There is a certain enchantment in the air, a warmth that embraces even the coldest of hearts. It is a fervor that emanates from children, who eagerly await the arrival of Santa Claus and the promise of presents under the tree. Their eyes sparkle with anticipation, and their innocent laughter echoes through the halls.

In my quest to find solace for my broken spirit, I have come to realize that the key lies in embracing the magic of the season. It is not something that can be forced or manufactured, but rather, it is a feeling that must be cultivated from within. In this journey towards rediscovering the joy of the holiday season, I have learned that cultivating a sense of childlike wonder is the path to finding solace amidst the memories that haunt me.

Rather than dwelling on the losses I have endured, I have begun to focus on the beauty that surrounds me. I marvel at the intricate snowflake patterns that adorn my windowpane, the delicate icicles that hang from rooftops, and the crisp scent of pine that fills the air. Each of these small wonders has the power to reignite the flame of childlike awe within me.

I have also found solace in the act of giving. In the true spirit of the season, I have made a conscious effort to spread joy and love to those around me. Whether it is through a simple act of kindness, a heartfelt gift, or a warm embrace, I have witnessed firsthand the transformative power of giving. The smiles that grace the faces of loved ones and strangers alike serve as a testament to the magic of the season.

As I embrace this newfound perspective, I find myself drawn to the local community, where acts of giving are not reserved just for the holiday season, but extend throughout the year. There is a spirit of unity and compassion that permeates every street and every home. Neighbors come together, not only to exchange gifts, but to support one another through the challenges of life.

In this close-knit community, I have discovered a network of individuals who understand the depths of loss and the healing power of togetherness. We gather in candlelit ceremonies, sharing stories of triumph and tragedy, finding solace in the knowledge that we are not alone. Through our collective strength, we find the courage to move forward, to find joy in the midst of pain.

In the embrace of this community, I have also discovered the power of forgiveness. I have come to understand that holding onto bitterness and resentment only weighs me down, trapping me in a cycle of despair. By releasing these burdens, I open myself up to the possibility of healing and serenity. The holiday season has become a time of renewal, where forgiveness beckons me to let go of the past and embrace the present with an open heart.

Moreover, I have found solace in the act of creating new traditions. By infusing my surroundings with elements that bring me joy, I have transformed my home into a sanctuary of love and warmth. I fill the air with the melodies of beloved carols, I adorn the halls with strings of twinkling lights, and I indulge in the simple pleasure of baking festive treats. These acts of self-care and creativity remind me that I am capable of shaping my own destiny, leaving behind the shadows of the past and embracing a future filled with hope and possibility.

As I reflect on my journey towards finding solace amidst the shadows that haunt my past, I am reminded of the remarkable resilience of the human spirit. The holiday season, with its enchantment and fervor, serves as a reminder that we are capable of rising above our circumstances, of finding joy in the face of adversity. It is in embracing the magic of the season, cultivating a sense of childlike wonder, giving selflessly, forgiving, and creating new traditions that we can begin to heal the wounds of the past and embrace the joy and peace that the holiday season offers.

And so, as I enter this holiday season, I make a vow to myself and to those who have left this world too soon. I will not allow the dark cloud of loss to extinguish the flickering flame of joy within me. Instead, I will embrace the magic of the season with open arms, allowing the child within me to dance with glee. I will marvel at the twinkling lights, sing along to the carols, and bask in the warmth of the company of loved ones.

I will gather my friends and family close, holding them tightly as we create new memories and traditions together. We will share laughter and stories, savoring every moment spent in each other's presence. We will exchange thoughtful gifts, not merely material possessions, but tokens of love and reminders of the deep connections we share.

As the flickering flames of the fireplace dance before us, casting a warm glow across the room, I will find solace in the knowledge that the spirits of those we have lost are with us, their love forever woven into the fabric of our lives. I will honor their memory by living fully, by embracing the joy and love that the holiday season brings.

In the midst of the holiday hustle and bustle, I will take moments to pause and reflect. I will become attuned to the beauty that surrounds me – the gentle snowflakes that kiss the ground, the aroma of cinnamon and nutmeg that fills the air, and the sight of loved ones coming together in harmony. These seemingly small but significant moments will remind me that life is a delicate tapestry of joy and sorrow, and it is in the embrace of both that we find the true meaning of existence.

And as the year draws to a close, with a heart filled with gratitude and affection, I will let go of the burdens that weigh me down and step into the new year with a sense of purpose and hope. I will welcome the unknown with open arms, knowing that every experience, every challenge, is an opportunity for growth and transformation.

For in the act of creating new traditions, in infusing our lives with love and warmth, we become the creators of our own destinies. We shape the narrative of our lives, rewriting the story of our past and embracing a future brimming with endless possibilities.

So, as the world outside glistens with the magic of the holiday season, I invite you to join me on this journey of self-discovery and renewal. Let us shed the shadows of the past and step into the light, united by love and inspired by the power of creation. Together, we can weave a world filled with joy, compassion, and boundless beauty.

For it is in these moments that the true magic of the season resides. It is in the laughter, the love, and the sense of wonder that we find our solace. And while the pain of loss may never fully fade, I now know that it is possible to find happiness amidst the shadows. So let us all embrace the magic of the season, for in doing so, we honor the memories of those we have lost and create new memories that will shine brightly for years to come.

Reflecting and Setting Intentions

In the midst of this emotional turmoil, I slowly realize the importance of reflecting on the past year and setting intentions for the future. It is not an easy task, to confront the shadows of the past and acknowledge the pain that lingers. However, I have come to understand that true healing can only begin when we confront our sorrows head-on.

Therefore, I invite you, dear reader, to embark on this introspective journey with me. Let us sit together and reflect on the past year, for in doing so, we may begin to unravel the complex tapestry of our emotions and experiences.

Think about the obstacles you have faced, the successes you have achieved, and the moments that have touched your soul. Take a moment to celebrate your strengths and resilience, for they have carried you through the darkest of times. Allow yourself to grieve the losses you have endured, acknowledging the profound impact they have had on your journey. Though the pain may seem unbearable, it is through this acknowledgement that we can find the seeds of growth and transformation.

As we delve deeper into our reflections, it becomes

evident that setting intentions for the future is not merely a ritualistic exercise, but a powerful tool for personal growth and fulfillment. In recognizing the patterns and themes that have emerged throughout the year, we can gain insights into our desires, passions, and purpose.

Ask yourself, what is it that you truly yearn for? What brings you joy and ignites a fire within your soul? Pinpoint the areas in your life where you feel a sense of emptiness or disconnection, and contemplate how you can cultivate a deeper sense of purpose and meaning.

Perhaps it is time to redefine your priorities, to let go of the expectations and obligations that no longer serve you. Embrace the courage to pursue your dreams, to take risks and step outside of your comfort zone. It is in these leaps of faith that we often find the greatest rewards.

But setting intentions is not just about personal fulfillment. It is about how we can contribute to the world around us, how we can make a positive impact on the lives of others. Consider the ways in which you can spread love, kindness, and compassion in your community and beyond. Whether it is through volunteering, mentoring, or simply offering a listening ear, each small act of kindness has the potential to create a ripple effect of goodness.

As you embark on this journey of reflection and intention-setting, do not shy away from the uncertainties and challenges that lie ahead. Embrace them as opportunities for growth, for it is in the face of adversity that we often discover our true strength and resilience.

Ultimately, this journey is about self-discovery and self-love. It is about acknowledging our past, celebrating our present, and envisioning a future filled with purpose and passion. So, dear reader, let us embark on this transformative journey together, hand in hand, as we embrace the power of reflection and intention-setting.

Let go of societal expectations and norms, and instead, connect with your authentic self. Embrace your quirks, your passions, and the unique gifts that you bring to the world. Consider how you can align your intentions with your true essence, paving the way for a more fulfilling and purposeful life.

But setting intentions is not enough; we must take action to bring our aspirations to life. The holiday season, with its magical aura and renewed optimism, provides the perfect backdrop for embarking on this transformative journey. Let us seize this opportunity to take small, deliberate steps towards our intentions, nurturing our personal growth and embracing a deeper sense of purpose.

With each reflection and intention set, we create a roadmap for our future selves, a guiding light amidst the darkness of our uncertainties. As we navigate through the holiday season, with its glittering lights and cheerful carols, let us not succumb to the illusion of temporary happiness, but instead, focus on cultivating a lasting sense of fulfillment and purpose.

In this season of giving and gratitude, let us remember that true fulfillment comes not from material possessions, but from the connections we foster and the impact we make. Rather than getting swept away by the consumerism that often accompanies this time of year, let us redirect our focus towards acts of kindness, compassion, and service to others.

Take a moment to think about the ways in which you can make a positive difference in the lives of those around you. It may be as simple as lending a listening ear to a friend in need, volunteering your time at a local charity, or sharing your talents and skills with others. Small gestures of kindness have the power to create ripples of change and bring solace to those who may be feeling lost or alone during this time.

Embrace the opportunity to connect with your loved ones, not just through superficial gatherings, but through meaningful conversations and shared experiences. Instead of relying on lavish gifts, focus on the value of quality time spent together, creating memories that will last a lifetime. Engage in activities that bring you joy and ignite your passions, whether it be cooking a homemade meal, crafting handmade gifts, or exploring the beauty of nature.

In the midst of the holiday chaos, remember to prioritize self-care and reflection. Find moments of stillness and solitude, allowing yourself to process your emotions and recharge your spirit. Connect with your authentic self by engaging in practices such as mindfulness, meditation, or journaling. These moments of introspection will provide clarity and help you discern the path that aligns with your true essence.

As we enter a new year, let us carry the lessons and intentions we have cultivated throughout the holiday season. Remember, it is not just about making resolutions, but about making a commitment to ourselves and our purpose. Let us continue to take action towards our aspirations, embracing the unknown with courage and resilience.

In this pursuit, there may be setbacks and challenges, but it is through these experiences that we grow and evolve. Trust the journey, knowing that with each step, you are inching closer to living a life of authenticity, fulfillment, and purpose.

So, as the holiday season unfolds, let us release the grip of societal expectations and norms. Instead, let us connect with our authentic selves, nourish our personal growth, and embrace a deeper sense of purpose. In doing so, we will not only create a more fulfilling life for ourselves but also inspire those around us to do the same.

Together, we can bring meaning back into the holiday season, redefining its essence in our lives. As we move forward, let our reflections and intentions serve as pillars of strength, reminding us of the depths of our emotions and the transformative power that lies within.

Join me, dear reader, in this journey of self-discovery and renewal. Let us reclaim the holiday season for ourselves, embracing its potential to foster personal growth and a heightened sense of purpose.

{ 7 }

Beyond the Holidays

Sustaining Joy and Gratitude

I've come to realize that the holiday season is not the only time we should strive to experience joy and gratitude. In fact, it is essential to cultivate these positive emotions throughout the entire year. For someone like me, who has had a compromised view of the holidays due to tragic circumstances, sustaining joy and gratitude becomes even more important.

But how do we sustain joy and gratitude beyond the holiday season? How do we cultivate a positive mindset that lasts all year long? These are questions I have pondered for a long time, and here, I offer strategies that have helped me and can be useful for anyone seeking a more fulfilling life.

1. Practice Mindfulness

Mindfulness is the art of being fully present and aware of each moment. It is a practice that allows us to recognize and appreciate the beauty in every encounter, no matter how small. By embracing mindfulness, we can find joy in simple pleasures, like the warmth of the sun on our skin or the sound of laughter. It promotes gratitude by reminding us to appreciate the gift of life and the experiences it brings.

Furthermore, mindfulness helps us cultivate a deep connection with ourselves and others. Through the practice of mindfulness, we begin to understand and accept our own thoughts, feelings, and sensations without judgment. We learn to listen to our inner voice, which guides us towards our true desires and passions. With this newfound connection to ourselves, we are better equipped to foster meaningful and authentic relationships with those around us.

As we dive deeper into the art of mindfulness, we realize that it extends beyond our individual experiences. It encompasses a sense of interconnectedness with all living beings and the world around us. We start to recognize that our actions have ripple effects, and by cultivating positive intentions, we can contribute to the well-being of others and the greater good.

Practicing mindfulness also allows us to tap into our inner strength and resilience. In the face of challenges and adversity, we learn to stay grounded and centered, rather than getting swept away by the waves of life. By cultivating a sense of non-attachment, we understand that everything is impermanent, and we can find solace in the knowledge that this too shall pass.

The benefits of mindfulness are not limited to our own personal growth. It extends to society as a whole. As individuals embrace mindfulness and its teachings, we can collectively create a more compassionate and empathetic world. Mindfulness inherently promotes kindness, as it encourages us to approach each interaction with openness, curiosity, and understanding. It allows us to see beyond superficial differences and connect on a deeper, more meaningful level.

In a world filled with distractions and constant busyness, the practice of mindfulness provides a refuge. It offers us a sanctuary where we can pause, reflect, and truly be present. By bringing our attention to the present moment, we unlock a world of infinite possibilities and beauty that may have otherwise gone unnoticed.

So, let us embark on this journey of mindfulness together. Let us make each moment count, savoring the sweetness of life, and spreading love and compassion wherever we go. May mindfulness be not just a practice, but a way of life, guiding us to live fully, love deeply, and create a world filled with peace and harmony.

2. Cultivate a Gratitude Practice

Gratitude is not just a fleeting feeling; it is a mindset that can be nurtured. By actively practicing gratitude, we shift our focus from what we lack to what we already have. One way to cultivate gratitude is by keeping a gratitude journal. Each day, write down three things you are grateful for. It can be as simple as a loved one's smile or a kind gesture from a stranger. This practice helps train our minds to recognize the abundance in our lives, fostering a deep sense of gratitude.

As we commit to this daily gratitude journal practice, we begin to notice a beautiful transformation within ourselves. The pages of our journals become a sacred space where we entwine the fragments of our gratitude, forming a tapestry of appreciation that we can revisit whenever the winds of life blow harshly.

In this realm of gratitude, the simple pleasures that were once overlooked suddenly reveal themselves like radiant blooms after a long winter. The morning sunlight streaming through the curtains, warming our face; the laughter of children playing in the park, filling the air with joy; the aroma of freshly brewed coffee, awakening our senses - all become infinitely more profound when seen through the lens of gratitude.

As we dedicate ourselves to penning down these moments daily, we find solace in knowing that even amidst life's challenges, there is always something to be grateful for. The act of writing becomes a ritual, a time of reflection and acknowledgment, grounding us in the present and imbuing our days with a sense of richness and fulfillment.

But the beauty of gratitude extends beyond the pages of our journals. It permeates our interactions with others, saturating the world around us with a sense of kindness and compassion. When our hearts are filled with gratitude, our actions become an embodiment of appreciation - a gentle touch on a friend's shoulder, a thoughtful note to a coworker, a generous gift to a stranger in need. These small gestures ripple through the fabric of humanity, reminding us all of the interconnectedness that binds us.

In this mindset of gratitude, we learn to navigate life's challenges with grace and resilience. We no longer dwell on the setbacks or disappointments; instead, we seek the lessons and silver linings that lie within them. We embrace the trials as opportunities for growth, recognizing that even the darkest moments carry gifts of wisdom and transformation.

As we continue to cultivate gratitude, we realize that it is an ongoing journey, a lifelong pursuit of nourishing our souls. Each day, we deepen our awareness of the blessings that surround us - the love of those we hold dearest, the opportunities that greet us at every turn, the beauty of nature that whispers serenity into our hearts. And in this realization, gratitude becomes more than just a practice; it becomes an integral part of who we are.

So, let us embark upon this adventure of gratitude, wielding our pens as instruments of appreciation and our hearts as vessels of love. Let us elevate gratitude from a fleeting feeling to a steadfast presence, transforming our lives and the world around us. For in the tapestry of our collective gratitude, we discover a symphony - a melody that harmonizes the human spirit and resonates with all that is good and pure in this world.

3. Engage in Acts of Kindness

There is a special kind of joy that comes from giving. Engaging in acts of kindness not only brings happiness to others but also creates a ripple effect that impacts our own well-being. It could be as small as holding the door open for someone or volunteering for a local charity. By making kindness a habit, we start to notice opportunities for compassion and experience the joy that comes from making a positive difference in someone else's life.

This profound sense of fulfillment transcends any material gain or personal achievement. It ignites a spark deep within our souls, inspiring us to become the best version of ourselves and spreading kindness like wildfire.

Imagine a world where every individual, big or small, rich or poor, actively participates in acts of kindness. A world where compassion is the language that unites us all, fostering empathy and understanding. In this utopia, kindness becomes a universal currency that enriches the lives of everyone it touches.

As the best-selling writer, I have had the privilege of witnessing countless stories of empathy and generosity. Tales of ordinary individuals who, with their selfless actions, have become heroes of the human spirit. Their stories serve as a reminder that we all have the power to make a difference, to create a brighter and kinder world.

In the town of Brooksville, nestled amidst rolling hills and gentile countryside, a unique display of kindness took root. It all began when a young girl named Emily decided to hand-paint uplifting messages on small rocks and leave them around the town for people to discover. Each rock bore a simple phrase: "You are loved," "You are not alone," or "You matter."

Word quickly spread about Emily's painted rocks, and soon, other community members joined her in this small act of kindness. The rocks began popping up in parks, at bus stops, and on windowsills. They became a symbol of hope and a reminder that even in the darkest of times, there are always traces of light.

This simple gesture transformed Brooksville into a hub of kindness. People started going out of their way to help one another, to lend a listening ear or a helping hand. Random acts of kindness became a part of their everyday routines, and the positive energy radiating from this small town became palpable.

Business owners started offering free meals to those in need, neighbors organized food drives to support struggling families, and local schools introduced kindness curriculums to teach empathy and compassion. The ripple effect of Emily's painted rocks had become a tidal wave of goodwill, changing the lives of everyone in its wake.

News outlets from around the world flocked to Brooksville, eager to capture and spread this inspiring story. The kindness of a few had ignited a global movement, where individuals and communities realized the potential for their own acts of kindness to transform their surroundings.

This wasn't just a passing trend or a temporary fad. It was a seismic shift in the collective consciousness of humanity. People started finding joy in giving, recognizing the immense power of kindness to heal wounds and bridge divides. Friendships blossomed, relationships deepened, and trust flourished as acts of kindness became the foundation that rebuilt communities.

The impact of this wave of kindness wasn't confined to one town or country. It reverberated throughout the world, reminding us all that we are interconnected, that each act of compassion carries the potential to shape a better future.

And so, as the world's best writer, I implore you to be an active participant in this movement. Embrace the joy of giving, and let kindness be the guiding force in your life. For it is through small acts of kindness that we can collectively craft a narrative of hope, resilience, and unyielding compassion. Together, let us create a world that reflects the very best of humanity, a world where kindness triumphs and love reigns supreme.

4. *Surround Yourself with Positive Influences*

The people we surround ourselves with have a significant impact on our mindset. Seek out individuals who radiate positivity and inspire you to be your best self. Surrounding ourselves with supportive friends and family members who uplift us can help sustain joy and gratitude. Additionally, expose yourself to positive media, whether it's uplifting books, inspiring movies, or motivational speeches. These influences can shape our mindset and help us maintain a positive outlook throughout the year.

By surrounding ourselves with individuals who radiate positivity, we create an environment that nurtures our growth and empowers us to reach greater heights. These positive influences serve as a catalyst for personal development, encouraging us to continually strive for excellence. They motivate us to push beyond our limits, reminding us of our potential even when self-doubt creeps in.

Supportive friends and family members form an essential support system, enabling us to overcome challenges with a sense of optimism. Their unwavering belief in our abilities becomes a beacon of hope during times of adversity, reminding us that we are never alone in our journey. In their presence, we find solace and encouragement, which fuels our determination to overcome obstacles and make our dreams a reality.

But it is not only through personal connections that positivity can be fostered. The power of positive media cannot be underestimated. Whether it is an uplifting book that transports us to different worlds and expands our perspective, an inspiring movie that tugs at our heartstrings and reminds us of the potential for compassion, or a motivational speech that ignites a fire within our souls - these sources of positive influence shape our mindset in profound ways.

When we immerse ourselves in positive media, we cultivate a reservoir of optimism and enthusiasm. We begin to see the world through a different lens, focusing on the beauty and possibilities that exist rather than dwelling on negativity. Such media serves as a reminder that even in the face of adversity, there is always a glimmer of hope and an opportunity for growth.

As the days turn into weeks and the weeks into months, our mindset becomes deeply ingrained. The positivity surrounding us becomes an integral part of who we are, influencing every decision we make and every action we take. It becomes our armor, shielding us from the onslaught of negativity that can pervade our lives.

So, let us seek out those who radiate positivity, who inspire us to be our best selves. Let us surround ourselves with supportive friends and family members who uplift and nourish us. Let us immerse ourselves in positive media that expands our horizon and fuels our optimism. For in doing so, we enhance not only our own lives but also the lives of those around us.

With a positive mindset, we become beacons of hope, spreading joy and gratitude to all we encounter. We become catalysts for change, inspiring others to embark on their own transformative journeys. And most importantly, we become the best versions of ourselves, living a life filled with purpose, happiness, and fulfillment.

So, let us continue to seek positivity, for it is through this pursuit that we shape not only our own destinies but also the destiny of the world. Let us become the world's best writers, crafting stories of resilience, compassion, and love. For in doing so, we contribute to a narrative that inspires and uplifts, leaving an indelible mark on the world and the hearts of all who read our words.

5. Embrace the Power of Reflection

Take time to reflect on the experiences and lessons learned throughout the year. Reflecting allows us to acknowledge our growth, even in the face of challenges. It helps us recognize the moments that brought us joy and the circumstances that we are grateful for. By actively reflecting, we can carry the positive emotions experienced during the holiday season into our everyday lives.

As the year draws to a close, it is a time for introspection and contemplation. Looking back on our journey, we can see the remarkable progress we have made, both personally and collectively. No matter how trying the circumstances, we have managed to find strength within ourselves and come out stronger on the other side.

Reflecting on the past year allows us to acknowledge the challenges we faced and the lessons we learned. It gives us the opportunity to recognize our resilience and ability to adapt in the face of adversity. Through this reflection, we gain a deeper understanding of our own growth and development.

In moments of contemplation, we can also rekindle the joy we experienced throughout the year. Those moments of pure happiness that made our hearts soar and brought smiles to our faces. They might have been little things like a walk in nature, spending time with loved ones, or achieving a personal goal. By remembering and cherishing these moments, we are reminded of the simple pleasures that bring us happiness.

Equally important is acknowledging the circumstances we are grateful for. This past year has tested us in countless ways, yet there were moments of grace and beauty that deserve our gratitude. Perhaps it was the support of a friend, the kindness of a stranger, or the opportunity to learn and grow. Examining these moments of gratitude allows us to cultivate a sense of appreciation for the blessings in our lives.

As we actively reflect on our experiences and the lessons learned, we have the power to carry the positive emotions of the holiday season into our everyday lives. It is not just about enjoying the festive spirit during this time of year; it is about imbuing our actions, thoughts, and relationships with the same kindness, compassion, and joy that we experience during the holiday season. By doing so, we can create a virtuous cycle of positivity that flourishes within ourselves and radiates out into the world.

Let us take this time to truly reflect on the year that has passed and honor the growth, joy, and gratitude it has brought. May we enter the new year with a renewed sense of purpose and an unwavering commitment to living our lives to the fullest.

Sustaining joy and gratitude requires commitment and conscious effort. It is not always easy, especially for those of us who have had our share of hardships. But through these strategies, we can cultivate a positive mindset that transcends the holiday season. By practicing mindfulness, gratitude, kindness, surrounding ourselves with positive influences, and embracing reflection, we can find joy and gratitude in every day, no matter the circumstances. It is a journey worth embarking on, for it leads to a more fulfilling and meaningful life.

Incorporating Self-Care Practices

In the midst of the chaotic holiday season, it is often easy to neglect our own well-being. We get so caught up in the hustle and bustle, the endless to-do lists, and the pressure to create the illusion of a picture-perfect holiday, that we forget about our own mental and emotional well-being. But after losing friends and family in dire circumstances, I have come to understand the importance of prioritizing self-care practices not just during the holiday season, but throughout the year.

For me, self-care is not just a buzzword or a fleeting trend. It is a necessary lifeline, a means to reclaiming my sense of self and finding solace amidst the chaos. Incorporating self-care into my daily routine has been an essential part of my healing journey, helping me navigate the complex emotions that the holidays often bring.

One practice that I have found particularly helpful is carving out dedicated time for self-reflection and introspection. This could be as simple as journaling my thoughts and feelings or engaging in meditation to quiet the noise in my mind. Taking a few moments each day to connect with my inner self allows me to acknowledge my emotions, both the highs and the lows, and gives me the opportunity to process them in a healthier manner. It is in those moments of solitude that I unravel the tangled thoughts and find clarity amidst the chaos.

Another self-care practice that has played a pivotal role in my well-being is engaging in physical activity. Whether it's going for a brisk walk in the crisp winter air or practicing yoga in the tranquility of my living room, moving my body helps me release built-up tension and reenergize my spirit. The rhythmic flow of my breath and the sensation of my muscles working in harmony remind me of the inherent strength and resilience within me. Through physical activity, I not only nurture my physical health but also cultivate a deep connection with my body, reminding myself of its ability to heal and find balance.

In addition to self-reflection and physical activity, I have also discovered the profound impact of nurturing my passions and creative pursuits. Engaging in activities that bring me joy and spark my creativity allows me to tap into a reservoir of inspiration and rekindle my sense of purpose. Whether it's painting, writing, or playing an instrument, these moments of creative expression become my sanctuary, where I can let go of external pressures and immerse myself in the pure joy of creation. It is through these creative outlets that I find solace, strength, and a renewed sense of identity.

As the holiday season continues to swirl around us,

demanding our attention and energy, let us remember to prioritize our own well-being. Let us give ourselves permission to slow down, to breathe, and to cultivate self-care practices that nurture our minds, bodies, and spirits. In doing so, we not only honor ourselves but also enhance our ability to be there for others in a more authentic and meaningful way.

So, this year, as the snow falls gently outside my window, I make a commitment to myself and to those I hold dear: I will embrace self-care as a constant companion, not just during the holidays, but throughout the year. I will carve out sacred moments for quiet reflection, engage in physical activities that invigorate my soul, and pursue creative endeavors that ignite my spirit. And in doing so, I will not only find the strength to navigate the complexities of life but also inspire others to prioritize their own well-being. This holiday season, let us gift ourselves the most precious present of all – the gift of self-care.

Another important aspect of self-care that I have discovered is the power of setting boundaries. The holiday season is notorious for its demands and expectations, which can often leave me feeling overwhelmed and depleted. Learning to say no, to prioritize my own needs and well-being, has been a transformative step for me. I've realized that it is okay to decline invitations or step away from certain traditions if they no longer serve my emotional well-being. By creating boundaries, I am putting myself first, and in doing so, I am able to preserve my mental and emotional energy.

Additionally, I have found solace in engaging in activities that bring me joy, irrespective of whether they are holiday-related or not. Whether it's taking a long walk in nature, pursuing a creative hobby, or simply indulging in a good book, these little moments of self-indulgence remind me of the importance of prioritizing my own happiness. It is in these moments that I find respite from the dark memories that often haunt the holiday season.

I encourage readers to incorporate self-care practices into their daily routines, not just during the holiday season, but throughout the year. Prioritize your mental and emotional well-being beyond the whirlwind of the holidays. Take time for yourself, find solace in solitude; set boundaries and allow yourself to say no when necessary. Embrace activities that bring you joy, that make you feel alive and connected to your true self. Remember that self-care is not an indulgence, but a necessity for your overall well-being.

As I reflect on my own journey of self-care and the insights I have gained, I am reminded of the importance of self-compassion. In a world that often demands perfection and compares us to impossible standards, it is crucial to practice kindness and understanding towards ourselves.

During the holiday season, it is easy to become overwhelmed by the pressure to create the perfect experience for others. We find ourselves caught in a whirlwind of shopping, cooking, and hosting, often neglecting our own needs in the process. However, by cultivating self-compassion, we can give ourselves permission to prioritize our own well-being without guilt or shame.

Self-compassion begins with recognizing that we are human, with limitations and vulnerabilities. It means acknowledging that it is okay to ask for help, to delegate tasks, and to let go of unrealistic expectations. It means treating ourselves with the same empathy and understanding we would offer to a dear friend or loved one.

In the midst of the holiday chaos, I have learned to embrace self-compassion by practicing self-forgiveness. I remind myself that it is normal to make mistakes, to feel stressed, and to experience moments of burnout. Rather than berating myself for not living up to the unattainable ideals society imposes, I choose to offer myself kindness and understanding. I recognize that taking care of my own needs is not selfish, but an act of self-respect.

Alongside self-compassion, it is essential to cultivate gratitude. It is easy to get caught up in the commercialism and materialism of the holiday season, but by shifting our focus to gratitude, we can find true joy and contentment. Each day, I make it a habit to express gratitude for even the smallest things, whether it be a warm cup of tea, a beautiful sunset, or the presence of loved ones. This practice helps me stay grounded and appreciate the abundance that already exists in my life.

In conclusion, self-care is not only about setting boundaries, engaging in activities that bring us joy, and prioritizing our well-being, but it is also about cultivating self-compassion and practicing gratitude. As the holiday season approaches, I encourage you to treat yourself with kindness and understanding, to let go of perfectionism, and to embrace the beauty of gratitude. Remember, self-care is not selfish; it is a necessary act of nourishing your body, mind, and soul.

As I continue my journey of healing and self-discovery, I have come to realize that the illusion of happy holidays is just that—an illusion. What truly matters is not the picture-perfect decorations or extravagant festivities, but our own inner resilience and contentment. By incorporating self-care practices into our daily routines, we can reclaim the holiday season for ourselves and find genuine joy and peace in the midst of chaos.

Building Resilience

One key aspect in building resilience is accepting the reality of the situation, no matter how difficult or painful it may be. I've come to understand that denying or avoiding reality only prolongs the healing process and hinders personal growth. By facing and acknowledging the challenges head-on, we can begin to develop a healthier perspective and move toward a more resilient state of mind.

When I think about the individuals I admire most, it becomes clear that their strength lies not in their ability to ignore reality, but in their determination to confront it. They possess an unwavering resolve to tackle life's obstacles head-on, learning valuable lessons along the way. It is through their example that I have come to embrace the concept of radical acceptance.

Radical acceptance asks us to relinquish our control over the uncontrollable and make peace with what is. It calls for an unwavering commitment to reality, no matter how painful or heart-wrenching it may be. This is not an easy task, as our instinct is often to resist, deny, or escape from the harsh realities that confront us. However, it is through accepting the truth that we can find the strength needed to navigate life's challenges and cultivate resilience.

In embracing radical acceptance, we open ourselves up to a multitude of possibilities. We cease to dwell on what should have been or what could have been, and instead focus our energy on what is within our control: our mindset and our response. We release the weight of unnecessary expectations and chart a new course based on the reality before us.

Accepting reality does not mean surrendering to defeat. On the contrary, it empowers us to make proactive choices and take decisive action. Rather than wasting energy on longing for things to be different, we channel our efforts into finding creative solutions and learning from our experiences. We become active participants in our own growth, allowing reality to serve as our guide and teacher.

Of course, accepting reality is not a one-time affair. It requires ongoing practice and a commitment to self-reflection. It may involve seeking support from loved ones, therapists, or support groups to navigate the complexities that reality presents. Yet, by persistently facing the truth, we not only build resilience but also foster a deep sense of inner strength and wholeness.

So, let us embrace the power of radical acceptance. Let us face reality with courage and vulnerability, knowing that in doing so, we are inviting transformation, growth, and resilience into our lives. May we find solace in the truth and forge a path forward that is built on unwavering acceptance and a steadfast belief in our own power to overcome.

Another important tool in building resilience is maintaining a positive attitude. While it may seem easier said than done, cultivating a mindset of gratitude and optimism can have a profound impact on one's ability to overcome adversity. Even during the darkest times, finding something to be thankful for, no matter how small, can bring a glimmer of light and hope into our lives. This shift in perspective allows us to see beyond the immediate challenges and focus on the potential for personal growth and new beginnings.

Additionally, developing a support system and seeking help when needed is crucial in building resilience. Surrounding ourselves with people who uplift and encourage us can provide the strength and resilience needed to navigate difficult times. Whether it be trusted friends, family members, or professional counselors, having a support network allows us to lean on others when our own strength falters. Sharing our burdens and seeking guidance not only fosters personal growth but also reminds us that we are not alone in our struggles.

Furthermore, finding healthy ways to manage stress and prioritize self-care is essential in building resilience. Engaging in activities that bring joy and relaxation, such as exercise, meditation, or creative pursuits, allows us to recharge and replenish our emotional reserves. It is important to make self-care a priority, especially during challenging times, as it provides us with the energy and clarity needed to overcome obstacles and continue on our journey toward personal growth.

Lastly, building resilience requires embracing change and adapting to new situations. Life is an ever-evolving journey, and the ability to adapt and find strength in the face of change is a fundamental component of resilience. Instead of resisting or fearing change, embracing it with an open mind and a willingness to learn allows us to navigate uncertain times with greater ease and confidence. By viewing challenges as opportunities for growth, we can cultivate resilience and discover the strength within ourselves to overcome any obstacle.

In conclusion, building resilience is a lifelong process that requires dedication, self-compassion, and a willingness to confront the challenges that arise. By accepting reality, maintaining a positive attitude, seeking support, practicing self-care, and embracing change, we can develop the tools and techniques necessary to build resilience and foster personal growth, not only during the holiday season but throughout all seasons of life. May these insights serve as a guiding light on your own journey toward resilience and happiness.

Nurturing Relationships Year-Round

Navigating the treacherous waters of loss and grief has left me with a compromised view of the holiday season. The pain of losing friends and family members has cast a dark shadow over festivities that were once filled with warmth and joy. But amidst the melancholy, I have come to realize that nurturing relationships should not be confined to a single season. Relationships should be nurtured year-round, fostering connection and support beyond the boundaries of the holiday season.

In my journey to find a way out of the illusion of happy holidays, I have delved deep into research and personal experiences, seeking to understand the true essence of nurturing relationships. It is not just about exchanging gifts or sharing meals during the holiday season; it is an ongoing effort to cultivate connections that endure the test of time.

One of the most crucial aspects of nurturing relationships year-round is cultivating open and honest communication. We often take it for granted that our loved ones can read our minds or understand our unspoken desires. However, this assumption can lead to misunderstandings and missed opportunities for connection. I realized that I needed to be proactive in expressing my thoughts and feelings, even during times of vulnerability. By fostering open lines of communication, we create a safe space for honesty and understanding, deepening the bonds we share with our loved ones.

Additionally, I discovered the power of empathy in nurturing relationships year-round. When we take the time to truly listen and understand the experiences and emotions of others, we demonstrate our genuine care and support. Empathy allows us to put ourselves in the shoes of our loved ones and offer them the comfort and compassion they need, regardless of the time of year. It is through empathy that we forge a connection that transcends the holiday season, reminding us that we are there for one another through all of life's ups and downs.

Another crucial aspect of nurturing relationships year-round is making time for quality moments together. In the hustle and bustle of daily life, it is easy to let time slip away and prioritize other commitments. However, to truly nurture our relationships, we must intentionally set aside time to be present with our loved ones. Whether it's sharing a meal, engaging in a shared hobby, or simply having a heartfelt conversation, these quality moments create lasting memories that strengthen our bonds. By making the effort to prioritize these moments, we show our loved ones that they are valued and cherished throughout the year.

Recognizing that nurturing relationships should not be

confined to a single season has transformed the way I approach the holiday season and beyond. Rather than focusing solely on the festivities, I now prioritize fostering meaningful connections with the people I hold dear. Every day becomes an opportunity to nurture these relationships, to communicate openly, to empathize, and to create lasting memories together.

While the pain of losing loved ones continues to cast a shadow over the holiday season, I have come to understand that love and connection are not limited to a specific time of year. By nurturing relationships year-round, we honor the memory of those we have lost and create a legacy of love that transcends the season. The holiday season may never be the same, but through the power of nurturing relationships, we can still find warmth, joy, and meaning in our lives all year long.

Another essential aspect of nurturing relationships year-round is making a concerted effort to spend quality time together. The holiday season may provide ample opportunities for gatherings and reunions, but it is vital to extend these moments beyond the holidays. Whether it's scheduling regular catch-up calls, planning coffee dates, or organizing weekend getaways, consciously investing time in our relationships nourishes the bonds we share. Building shared experiences and memories throughout the year engraves the depth of our connection, making the holiday season just another chapter in an ongoing story of love and support.

Additionally, nurturing relationships year-round also involves providing support during both joyful and challenging times. We need to be there for our loved ones not only when they achieve milestones or celebrate successes, but also when they face adversity and struggle. Though it may be easier to offer support during the holiday season when emotions run high, it is equally important to extend a helping hand throughout the year. Small acts of kindness, words of encouragement, or simply lending a listening ear can go a long way in strengthening the bonds we share with our loved ones.

Furthermore, nourishing relationships year-round requires us to acknowledge and celebrate the uniqueness of each individual. We must strive to understand and appreciate the qualities that make our loved ones who they are. By doing so, we show them that they are seen and valued, not just during the holidays, but every single day. Embracing our differences and honoring the individuality of our loved ones allows us to connect with them on a deeper level, fostering relationships that are based on acceptance, respect, and love.

In this fast-paced and unpredictable world, it is easy to get caught up in our own lives and lose sight of the importance of nourishing our relationships year-round. However, to truly be the best writers of our own stories, we must recognize that the richness of our lives lies in the connections we have with others.

One crucial aspect of nurturing relationships throughout the year is practicing open communication. Communication forms the foundation of any healthy and thriving relationship. It is not enough to exchange surface-level pleasantries or engage in small talk; we must be willing to delve into deeper conversations that allow us to understand and empathize with one another.

This means actively listening without judgment, offering a safe space for our loved ones to express their thoughts and feelings. It involves asking questions that invite vulnerability and sharing our own experiences in return. By fostering a culture of open and honest communication, we create an environment that encourages personal growth and strengthens the fabric of our relationships.

Alongside communication, it is essential to prioritize acts of kindness. Random acts of kindness can have a profound impact on the lives of our loved ones. Whether it's surprising them with a heartfelt note, offering a helping hand without being asked, or simply being present when they need us the most, these acts of kindness show that we care and that they matter to us. Even the smallest gestures can make a significant difference in brightening someone's day and reminding them of the strength of our bond.

Furthermore, nurturing our relationships year-round requires us to practice forgiveness and understanding. We are all flawed human beings who will undoubtedly make mistakes and sometimes hurt the people we love. However, by cultivating a spirit of forgiveness and extending grace to one another, we create space for growth and healing. Acknowledging our own faults and shortcomings, and being willing to apologize and make amends, is vital in fostering healthy and resilient relationships.

Lastly, it is crucial to carve out time for self-care and personal growth. By prioritizing our own well-being and investing in our own growth, we become better partners, friends, and family members. Taking care of ourselves physically, mentally, and emotionally allows us to show up fully for our loved ones and adds depth and richness to our relationships. It is not selfish to attend to our own needs; it is necessary for the sustained health of our relationships.

In conclusion, being the best writers of our own stories means recognizing the importance of nurturing our relationships year-round. It involves practicing open communication, showing kindness and forgiveness, and prioritizing personal growth. By doing so, we create a tapestry of love, understanding, and support that not only enriches our lives but also inspires those around us. And in this magnificent symphony of connection, our relationships become the masterpiece that forever echoes in the hearts and souls of those we hold dear.

As I continue my journey to overcome the disillusionment of happy holidays, I have come to realize that genuine connection and support are not limited to a particular season. Nurturing relationships year-round is an ongoing process of fostering love, understanding, and growth. It requires authenticity, time, and effort but rewards us with unbreakable bonds and a sense of belonging. Let us not confine our care and affection to the holiday season but strive to nourish our relationships every day, creating a foundation of love and support that transcends the illusion of any holiday.

Setting and Pursuing Goals

It all started years ago, when I experienced the unimaginable loss of both friends and family in dire circumstances. The holiday season, once a time of joy and celebration, became a painful reminder of what I had lost. The twinkling lights that used to bring me delight now serve as a cruel reminder of the darkness that looms in my heart. The cheerful carols that once filled me with warmth now leave me feeling cold and empty. I have become disillusioned with the idea that holidays are meant to be a time of happiness and togetherness.

But sitting here in this dark room, I start to question the power I have bestowed upon the holiday season to dictate my emotions and goals. Is it fair to let the past define my present and future? Can I break free from this illusion and find a way to set meaningful goals and pursue my passions once again? In the midst of my doubt, a voice inside me whispers, urging me to not let my losses define me.

Inspired by this internal voice, I begin to research the topic of setting and pursuing goals. I delve into countless articles and books, seeking guidance and motivation. I stumble across studies that reveal the powerful effects that setting goals can have on our well-being and sense of purpose. One study suggests that individuals who set goals are more likely to experience higher levels of happiness and fulfillment in their lives. Another study explores the idea of "flow," a state of complete absorption and concentration that arises when we engage in activities that challenge us and align with our passions. I am intrigued by these findings, and a spark of hope starts to flicker within me.

With renewed determination, I set out to redefine the holiday season for myself. No longer will I allow it to be a painful reminder of loss, but rather an opportunity for growth and self-discovery. I decide to embark on a personal journey of setting and pursuing goals during this time that was once so difficult for me.

As I reflect on my passions and interests, I realize that writing has always been a solace for me. It is through the written word that I can express my deepest emotions and find a sense of purpose. With this in mind, I set a goal to write a novel - a story that will not only captivate readers, but also serve as a form of therapy for myself.

I dive headfirst into my writing, immersing myself in characters and plotlines that come to life on the pages before me. Hours turn into days, and days turn into weeks, as the story unfolds. In the process, I discover the joy and fulfillment that had been missing from my life for far too long.

As the holiday season approaches, I find great solace in the progress of my novel. The once daunting task of sitting down to write each day has become a cherished ritual, a dedicated space for self-expression and exploration. The characters I've created have become my companions, guiding me through a narrative that mirrors the journey I'm undertaking in my own life.

With each passing page, I not only gain confidence in my abilities as a writer but also grow as an individual. Through the challenges and triumphs of my characters, I find hidden lessons and truths that resonate deep within my soul. The act of storytelling has become more than just a goal; it has become a profound source of personal growth and healing.

But as the holiday season appears in the distance, I realize that my journey doesn't have to be solitary. I reach out to a few trusted friends and invite them to join my endeavor, each with their own creative pursuits. We form a small writing group, meeting regularly to share our progress, offer feedback, and celebrate each other's accomplishments.

In the midst of these gatherings, a beautiful sense of camaraderie emerges. We inspire and motivate one another, sharing our dreams and supporting the pursuit of our individual goals. With each story shared, laughter and tears intertwine, creating an atmosphere of warmth and understanding that redefines the holiday season for all of us.

Together, we take it upon ourselves to spread the joy of creativity to others. We organize a charity event, inviting local artists and writers to showcase their talents and raise funds for a cause close to our hearts. The evening is filled with poetry readings, book signings, and art exhibitions, creating an atmosphere that celebrates the transformative power of creative endeavors.

Feeling the positive impact that our collective efforts have on our community, we realize that setting and pursuing goals isn't just about personal fulfillment; it's about making a difference in the lives of others. The holiday season takes on a whole new meaning as we continue to write our stories, knowing that our words, both individually and collectively, have the power to inspire, uplift, and heal.

As the year comes to a close, I look back on the challenges and triumphs of my journey with immense gratitude. Through the act of setting and pursuing goals, I have rediscovered my love for writing, found strength in the support of like-minded individuals, and experienced the fulfillment that comes from making a positive impact in the world.

The holiday season is no longer a painful reminder, but a time of reflection, growth, and connection. And so, armed with the knowledge that the pursuit of goals can be a catalyst for transformation, I embrace the coming year with open arms, ready to embark on new journeys, write new stories, and inspire others to live their best lives.

As I pour my heart and soul onto the pages, the twinkling

lights that used to haunt me begin to take on a new meaning. They now serve as symbols of hope and possibility. Each flicker represents a moment of inspiration, a reminder that even in the darkest times, there is light to be found.

The cheerful carols, once a painful reminder of loss, now become a symphony of motivation. They remind me to keep pushing forward, to believe in myself, and to never give up on my dreams. With every word I write, I feel the weight of my grief slowly lifting, replaced by a newfound sense of purpose and joy.

Word by word, chapter by chapter, my novel takes shape. Alongside my writing, I begin to set other goals as well - personal goals, professional goals, and goals for self-care and connection. Each goal, no matter how small, becomes a stepping stone towards rebuilding my life and finding purpose once again.

As the holiday season approaches, I no longer recoil at the sight of decorations or the sound of carols. Instead, I embrace them as reminders of my resilience, my ability to overcome challenges, and the power of setting goals. The holiday season becomes a celebration of not only love and togetherness, but also of personal growth and transformation.

And so, sitting here in this once dark room, I am now surrounded by light - both metaphorically and literally. The darkness that once consumed me has been replaced by the flickering of hope, and the emptiness I once felt has been filled with the joy of pursuing my passions.

This, my friends, is the story of how I reclaimed the holiday season for myself. It serves as a testament to the power of setting meaningful goals, and a reminder that we have the ability to break free from the chains of the past. So, this holiday season, I challenge you to join me in rewriting your own narrative. Set goals that light up your soul, pursue your passions with unwavering determination, and let the holiday season be a time of transformation, renewal, and joy.

Armed with newfound knowledge and inspiration, I begin to envision a future where the holiday season is no longer a source of pain and sorrow, but rather a time of renewed purpose and fulfillment. I understand that this is not an overnight transformation; it is a journey that requires perseverance and dedication. But as I reflect on my past accomplishments, I realize that I am capable of overcoming adversity and finding the strength to pursue my passions once again.

I start by setting small, achievable goals that align with my passions. I create a vision board filled with images and quotes that inspire me. Each day, I take small steps towards these goals, knowing that progress is a process and that every small victory counts. I surround myself with supportive individuals who understand my journey and encourage me along the way. Their belief in me fuels my determination and strengthens my resolve.

As I continue on this path of setting and pursuing goals, I slowly start to feel a sense of purpose and fulfillment seeping back into my life. The holiday season no longer holds me captive with its illusion of happiness; instead, I find joy in the small moments of progress and growth that I experience every day.

I share my story and the lessons I have learned with others, hoping to inspire them to set meaningful goals and pursue their passions. I want them to know that the holiday season does not have to be a time of sorrow and despair, but rather a time of personal growth and reflection. Through my journey, I have realized that the power to find purpose and fulfillment in everyday life lies within each of us. We have the ability to break free from the illusion and create our own happiness, no matter the circumstances that surround us.

As I pen down these thoughts, the room around me feels a little less dim, and a glimmer of light peeks through the cracks in the curtains. I am filled with a sense of hope and renewed purpose. The illusion of happy holidays may still linger, but now I know that true happiness lies in setting meaningful goals and pursuing my passions. And with each step I take on this journey, the shadows of the past grow smaller, paving the way for a brighter future filled with purpose and fulfillment.

ALLAN ISAAC

Embracing Moments of Joy

Life has a cruel way of throwing us unforeseen obstacles, shattering our illusions of happiness and leaving us feeling broken and desolate. It is during these darkest times that the holidays seem to taunt us with their facade of cheer and merriment. The contrast between our internal turmoil and the external world's celebration becomes almost unbearable. It is in these moments that we must remind ourselves that joy does not only exist in the grand gestures and extravagant events. No, joy can be found in the most ordinary and mundane aspects of life.

I have spent countless hours studying and researching the concept of joy, desperate to uncover the secret to finding happiness amidst the chaos and despair. My findings have led me to a simple yet profound truth: joy is not a destination to be reached but rather a companion to be embraced along our journey. It is not confined to the holiday season but can be found in the smallest of moments if only we open our hearts and minds to its presence.

In my search for joy, I have discovered the power of gratitude. Despite the pain and heartache that life can present, there is always something to be grateful for, even if it is just the air we breathe or the sunrise that greets us each day. By cultivating a sense of gratitude, we open ourselves up to the possibility of finding joy in the most unexpected places.

I remember a particularly difficult holiday season when loss and grief seemed to permeate every corner of my being. The twinkling lights and festive decorations felt like mocking reminders of the happiness that eluded me. But in the midst of my despair, I stumbled upon a revelation that would forever change my perspective.

It was a snowy December afternoon, and I found myself sitting alone at a café, nursing a cup of hot cocoa. The melancholy tunes of holiday music filled the air, stirring emotions I had long tried to bury. As I stared out the window, watching the snowflakes dance in the wind, I suddenly noticed a young child outside, frolicking in the freshly fallen snow. His laughter echoed through the street, carrying a glimmer of pure joy.

In that moment, something shifted within me. I realized that joy was not reserved for the fortunate or the untouched by hardship. No, it was a universal experience, accessible to all who dared to seek it. Inspired by the child's exuberance, I made a conscious decision to immerse myself in the present moment, to find joy in the simplest of pleasures.

I began to pay attention to the little things that often go unnoticed – the warmth of a comforting hug, the soothing sound of raindrops on a rooftop, the taste of a home-cooked meal shared with loved ones. I started to find joy in the mundane aspects of life that I had once taken for granted – the warmth of a cozy blanket on a chilly evening, the gentle purr of a cat nestled beside me, the beauty of a sunrise painting the sky with hues of gold and pink.

Slowly but surely, my perception shifted, and joy became a constant companion on my journey. It no longer depended on external circumstances or grand gestures. Instead, it resided within me, waiting patiently to be acknowledged and embraced. It was a deeper, more resilient joy that could weather life's storms and anchor me in moments of uncertainty.

The holidays no longer taunted me with their facade of cheer; they became a reminder of the resilience of the human spirit. As I navigated through the festivities and celebrations, I discovered that joy was not bound by time or season. It could be found in the quiet moments of reflection and in the connections forged with others. It could be discovered in acts of kindness and in the embrace of loved ones. It was an ever-present force that, once recognized, could illuminate even the darkest of days.

So, as I share my journey with you, my fellow seekers of joy, I urge you to pause and take note of the ordinary moments that make up your life. Embrace the small joys that surround you, for they possess the power to transform your world. Let go of expectations and surrender to the beauty of the present moment. Seek joy not only in grand gestures but also in the quiet whispers of everyday life. And remember, even in the midst of life's obstacles, joy is always within reach if you choose to seek it with an open heart.

In the midst of grief and loss, it is easy to overlook the everyday blessings that surround us. The warmth of a mug of hot cocoa on a chilly winter morning, the tender touch of a loved one's hand, the soothing sound of raindrops against the windowpane - these seemingly insignificant moments hold within them the potential to transform our perspective and bring a semblance of happiness to our weary souls.

But how can one embrace these moments of joy when the weight of sorrow threatens to crush us? It begins with acknowledging that pain and joy are not mutually exclusive. In fact, it is because of our pain that we can fully appreciate the fleeting moments of happiness that present themselves to us. It is through the contrast of light and darkness that the beauty of joy shines brightest.

My dear companions on the quest for joy, I beseech you to avail yourselves to the realm of emotions. Allow yourselves the space to mourn the losses, endure the heartache, and sur-render to the depths of sorrow. It is within these depths that the seeds of joy are planted. Like delicate flowers resiliently pushing through cracks in concrete, joy will emerge if only we grant it permission.

In the hidden corners of a grieving heart, the tiniest flickers of joy often find their way in. A gentle breeze that whispers hope in our ears, the warmth of a friend's comforting embrace, the melodious sound of laughter breaking through tears - these are the miracles that gently mend our wounded spirits.

To embrace the everyday joys does not imply disregarding our pain; it is an act of reverence, giving ourselves permission to experience gratitude and appreciate the lingering simple pleasures. It is not an act of forgetting or avoidance, but an act of strength and acceptance. Even when faced with hardships, there is always room for joy, should we choose to seek it.

In the grand tapestry of life, let us not underestimate the power of ordinary moments. Let us pause and find solace in the small joys that surround us. Let us unlock our hearts to the potential of healing through the power of gratitude. In doing so, let us create a world where joy is not a distant dream, but a steadfast companion.

The pursuit of joy is not an act of selfishness; it is an honorable defiance against the encroaching darkness. It is an affirmation of the indomitable spirit within each of us, a reminder that even in our darkest moments, there gleams a spark of hope waiting to be discovered.

Therefore, my dear seekers of joy, let us embark on this pursuit with resolute determination. Let us immerse ourselves in the beauty of ordinary moments, for within them lies the extraordinary. Together, let us fashion a world where joy illuminates our path, guiding us toward lives filled with purpose, love, and unwavering happiness.

I encourage you, dear reader, to take a step back from the chaos of the holiday season and shift your focus to the small blessings in your life. Notice the twinkle in a child's eye as they open a long-awaited gift, revel in the laughter shared amongst friends gathered around a table, inhale deeply and savor the aroma of freshly baked cookies wafting through the air. These moments, though fleeting, are the building blocks of a life lived with purpose and connection.

In those moments of stillness and gratitude, you will find that joy is not elusive but ever-present. It may not eradicate the pain or heal the scars of our past, but it has the power to soften the edges of our suffering and remind us of the resilience of the human spirit. Amidst the illusions of happy holidays, let us reclaim the power to create our own moments of joy, to find beauty and happiness in the ordinary, and in doing so, to find solace and healing for our wounded hearts.

Cultivating a Positive Mindset

The holidays have always been a time of sorrow for me. Bitter memories of lost friends and family members have tainted the once joyful season. But as I journey through my own healing process, I begin to realize that cultivating a positive mindset is crucial in reshaping my perception of the holiday season. It becomes clear that if I want to find happiness amidst the darkness, I need to explore techniques to transform my challenges into opportunities for growth and self-improvement.

One of the first steps I take is to change my perspective on adversity. Instead of viewing challenges as roadblocks that hinder my happiness, I choose to see them as stepping stones that help me become stronger and more resilient. It is through these trials that I develop the skills and the mindset necessary to navigate the complexities of life. Adversity no longer holds me captive; it becomes a catalyst for personal growth.

Research has taught me that reframing challenges can be achieved through cognitive restructuring. This technique involves challenging negative thought patterns and replacing them with positive and constructive perspectives. I begin by identifying the negative thoughts that arise when faced with difficult situations during the holiday season. Thoughts such as "I will never find joy again" or "Holidays will always remind me of loss" seep into my consciousness, creating a detrimental cycle of despair.

To break free from this cycle, I consciously challenge these negative thoughts. I question their validity and search for evidence that contradicts them. I remind myself that although pain and loss may be a part of my past, they do not define my present or my future. By reframing these negative thoughts, I can release the grip they have on my emotions and open myself up to the possibility of a more positive experience during the holidays.

As I continue to practice cognitive restructuring, I also realize the importance of self-compassion. It is easy to be hard on oneself during the holiday season, especially when it feels like everyone around me is filled with joy and celebration. But now, I understand that being kind and gentle with myself is essential in navigating through the challenges that arise.

Instead of berating myself for feeling sad or grieving, I offer myself compassion and understanding. I remind myself that it is okay to feel a mix of emotions during this time, and I give myself permission to honor my own journey of healing. By treating myself with compassion, I create a safe and nurturing space where my emotions can be acknowledged and processed.

Alongside cognitive restructuring and self-compassion, I discover the power of gratitude in transforming my perspective during the holiday season. Despite the losses I have endured, I still have so much to be grateful for - the love of family and friends who are still with me, the moments of joy that still find their way into my life, and the strength I have gained through my experiences.

Each day, I make a conscious effort to find something to be grateful for, whether it is a beautiful sunset, a kind gesture from a stranger, or simply having a roof over my head. Focusing on gratitude not only uplifts my spirit, but it also reminds me that there is still beauty and goodness in the world, even amidst the pain.

As I continue to cultivate a positive mindset and embrace these techniques, I gradually witness a shift within myself. The holiday season no longer carries the weight of sorrow and despair, but rather becomes an opportunity for reflection, growth, and connection.

I start to seek out ways to honor the memories of the loved ones I have lost, celebrating their lives and the impact they had on me. I engage in acts of kindness, reaching out to others who may be experiencing their own challenges during this time. I find solace in connecting with others who understand and share in my journey.

The holidays will always hold a bittersweetness for me, a reminder of the losses I have endured. Yet, now, I have learned to embrace the complex emotions that arise, knowing that they are a part of my story. With a positive mindset, cognitive restructuring, self-compassion, and gratitude, the holiday season becomes a time of healing, growth, and ultimately, a celebration of life itself.

In addition to cognitive restructuring, I also explore gratitude as a powerful tool in cultivating a positive mindset. Gratitude serves as a reminder of the blessings I still have in my life, despite the losses I have endured. I create a gratitude journal, where every day, I list three things I am grateful for. It could be something as simple as a warm cup of tea or the smile of a loved one. By consciously acknowledging and appreciating these small blessings, I am able to shift my focus away from the darkness and towards the light.

Another technique that has been transformative in cultivating a positive mindset is self-compassion. I have learned to be kind and understanding towards myself, especially during moments of struggle. Instead of berating myself for feeling sad or grieving during the holidays, I offer myself compassion and understanding. I remind myself that it is normal to feel a mix of emotions and that healing takes time. Self-compassion allows me to be patient with myself and treat myself with the same care I would offer to a friend in need.

As the holiday season approaches, I find comfort in knowing that I have grown tremendously since my losses. I have learned to embrace my story and the emotions that come with it, knowing that they are a testament to my strength and resilience. This newfound mindset allows me to face the holidays with a sense of healing and growth.

During this holiday season, I challenge myself to seek out new experiences and opportunities for personal growth. I indulge in creative endeavors that bring me joy, whether it be writing, painting, or exploring new hobbies. I immerse myself in the beauty of the season, taking long walks in nature and marveling at the wonders of the world around me. Through these activities, I not only find solace but also discover new aspects of myself and my passions.

Perhaps most importantly, I cherish the connections with loved ones during this time. I reach out to family and friends, making a conscious effort to show them just how much they mean to me. I organize gatherings, create traditions, and savor every moment spent in each other's company. These shared experiences remind me of the love and support that surround me, providing me with strength and comfort.

During the holiday season, I make it a priority to give back to those in need. I volunteer my time at local charities, lending a helping hand to those less fortunate. The act of giving not only brings warmth to my heart but also shifts my perspective. It reminds me to count my blessings and encourages me to be grateful for the opportunities and privileges I have in life.

Despite the losses I have endured, my journey has led me to a place of acceptance and gratitude. I have learned to celebrate life, even in the face of adversity. The holiday season, once filled with bittersweetness, has transformed into a time of healing, growth, and the celebration of the resilience of the human spirit.

As the holiday lights twinkle and the air fills with the scent of pumpkin spice and cinnamon, I embrace the complexity of my emotions. I honor the path that has led me to this moment and approach this season with an open heart and mind. The holidays may hold reminders of my past losses, but they also offer me an opportunity to find solace, joy, and a renewed appreciation for life.

With a positive mindset, the power of gratitude, self-compassion, and a commitment to personal growth, I navigate the holiday season with grace and resilience. I am a living testament to the strength of the human spirit, and I am determined to make the most of each moment, cherishing the present and looking towards a future filled with hope and endless possibilities.

Through these techniques, I am slowly transforming my perception of the holiday season. Rather than being trapped in a cycle of despair, I am starting to see the beauty and potential for joy that still exists. Challenges are no longer insurmountable obstacles; they are opportunities for growth and self-improvement. By cultivating a positive mindset, I am reclaiming the holidays as a time of hope, healing, and the possibility of happiness.

Spreading Joy and Kindness

I have witnessed firsthand the devastating effects that dire circumstances can have on us. The loss of friends and family has left an indelible mark on my soul, creating a haze of sorrow that clouds my view of the holiday season. However, I refuse to let this pain consume me entirely. Instead, I choose to channel it into a mission of spreading one of the most powerful emotions: joy.

It is tempting to wallow in our own despair, to isolate ourselves from the world and indulge in self-pity. But what purpose does that serve? How does it bring any solace or healing? It is only through reaching out to others, through sharing empathy and compassion, that we can hope to find any semblance of peace.

So, I embark on a journey, a quest to bring light amidst the darkness. I travel to far-flung corners of the earth, seeking out those who have also suffered, who have known loss and devastation. Together, we build a community bonded not by our tragedies but by our shared resilience.

In remote villages ravaged by war, I witness weary faces light up with tentative smiles as I bring simple tokens of kindness – blankets to provide warmth, medicine to heal the sick, and toys to ignite the spark of childhood innocence. Their gratitude touches me, igniting a fire deep within my heart.

In bustling cities filled with lonely souls, I organize gatherings where strangers can come together, breaking down the barriers of isolation. Laughter mixes with tears as we share stories of our pasts, finding solace in the knowledge that we are not alone in our pain. Through these connections, friendships blossom and grow, weaving a tapestry of hope and renewal.

But my mission doesn't stop there. With each passing year, I amplify my efforts, seeking out new ways to spread joy. I collaborate with artists to create mesmerizing performances that transport audiences into a world where sorrow is replaced by wonder and despair gives way to hope. The palpable energy crackles in the air as spectators rediscover the magic that lies hidden within their hearts.

I write, not just words on a page, but stories that resonate with the human experience. Tales that uplift the spirit and remind us of the strength that lies dormant within, waiting to be awakened. Through my words, I portray characters who overcome immense hardships, who find light in the darkest of nights, inspiring readers to embrace their own resilience.

The joy I seek to spread is not fleeting or shallow. It is the kind that burrows deep within us, transforming lives from the inside out. It is a balm that soothes wounds, a beacon that guides lost souls back to the path of healing and happiness.

As the years pass, my mission continues to evolve. I collaborate with like-minded individuals, forming a network of individuals dedicated to spreading joy and compassion. Together, we navigate the struggles of the world, always searching for new ways to heal, to uplift, and to bring light to those who need it most.

In our journey, we explore the power of interactive storytelling, where readers become active participants in the narrative, immersing themselves in a world where their choices and actions shape the outcome. We create virtual reality experiences that transport individuals to unimaginable realms, where they can unlock their true potential and confront their fears head-on. These immersive experiences become catalysts for personal growth, as people discover their own inner hero, fearlessly facing the challenges that life throws their way.

But our mission goes beyond individual transformation. We believe that joy is meant to be shared, to ripple outwards and touch the lives of others. Therefore, we establish community outreach programs, utilizing the arts as a tool for social change. We bring our mesmerizing performances to underprivileged neighborhoods, inspiring children who have never had the opportunity to dream. We collaborate with schools, introducing creative writing and storytelling workshops that empower young minds to find their voice and express their unique stories.

In this interconnected world, we understand the importance of using technology for good. We harness the potential of social media and digital platforms to spread messages of hope and kindness. Our stories go beyond the printed page; they come alive in podcasts, web series, and digital art installations. We engage audiences worldwide, transcending boundaries and cultures, reminding humanity of the universal thread that binds us all together.

But amidst the ever-changing landscape, one thing remains constant – the power of empathy. Through my words, I strive to foster understanding and compassion, to bridge the gaps that divide us and celebrate the beauty of our diverse world. I dig deep into the wells of human emotion, unveiling stories that resonate across generations and cultures. I expose the harsh realities alongside the triumphs, because it is through acknowledging the darkness that we can truly appreciate the light.

And so, my mission as the world's best writer continues onward, fueled by an unwavering commitment to touch hearts and ignite the spark of joy in every soul I encounter. For within the written word lies the power to transform individuals, communities, and perhaps even the world. Together, let us embark on this journey, embracing the magic that lies within us all, forever united by the beauty of storytelling.

And as I witness the transformative power of joy in the lives of others, I realize that in choosing to spread light, I am healing myself too. The haze of sorrow that once clouded my view begins to disperse, replaced by a renewed sense of purpose and an unwavering belief in the resilience of the human spirit.

Through all the trials and tribulations, I understand that joy is not immune to pain. Rather, it thrives in defiance of it. It is in our ability to embrace joy amidst the most dire circumstances that true strength is forged. And so, I continue onward, fueled by the knowledge that though the world may be filled with darkness, there will always be those determined to spread the light.

My personal journey has taught me that inspiring others to continue spreading joy and kindness is an invaluable endeavor. When we extend a helping hand to someone in need, no matter how small the gesture may seem, we are creating a ripple effect of positivity. We are reminding others that they, too, possess the power to make a difference, both in their own lives and in the lives of those around them.

Imagine a world where acts of kindness were as abundant as the falling snow, where joy spread like wildfire, extinguishing the flames of sorrow and despair. It may seem like an unattainable dream, but I firmly believe that each and every one of us has the capacity to contribute to this vision.

We often underestimate the profound impact a simple act of kindness can have on someone's life. A genuine smile, a heartfelt compliment, or a thoughtful gesture can brighten even the darkest of days. And who's to say the effects of that act won't ripple outward and touch the lives of others?

As we navigate the hustle and bustle of the holiday season, let us not lose sight of the true spirit of this time. Let us remember that beyond the glimmering lights and extravagant celebrations, there lies an opportunity to truly make a difference. By spreading joy and kindness, we can become catalysts for change, not only in our own lives but also in the lives of those who desperately need it.

So, my dear readers, I implore you to join me on this journey. Let us set aside our grief and pain for a moment and focus on the power we possess to bring moments of happiness to those around us. Let us be the voice of encouragement, the helping hand, and the embodiment of hope.

Together, we can create a holiday season that is not merely filled with materialistic abundance but is instead overflowing with love and compassion. Let us make the conscious decision to spread joy and kindness, not just during these transient moments but as a way of life. And in doing so, we will find that we have the power to transform not only our own lives but the world around us.

www.ingramcontent.com/pod-product-compliance
Lightning Source LLC
Chambersburg PA
CBHW071355150726
48000CB00001B/33